D0364544

West Bengal Family Structures: 1946–1966

BY THE SAME AUTHOR

The Rise and Fall of the East India Company
The Sociologist and Social Change in India Today

Data Inventory in Social Sciences–India
Six Villages of Bengal
The Dynamics of a Rural Society
The Problem of Uganda
The Physical Characteristics of the Ancient Inhabitants of Jebel Moya, Sudan
Famine and Rehabilitation of Bengal
Social Indicators
Family and Planning in India

West Bengal Family Structures : 1946-1966

An Example of Viability of Joint Family

RAMKRISHNA MUKHERJEE

First Published 1977 by

THE MACMILLAN COMPANY OF INDIA LIMITED

Delhi Bombay Calcutta Madras

Associated companies throughout the world

SBN : 33390 131 2

The publication of this book has been financially supported by the Indian Council of Social Science Research. Responsibility for the facts and interpretations presented here, however, is that of the author alone, and not of the Indian Council of Social Science Research.

Published by S G Wasani
for the Macmillan Company of India Limited
and printed at Prabhat Press, Meerut.

TO
MY MOTHER
Sati Rani Devi

Contents

Acknowledgements

This is a study in collaboration, as all macro-studies involving large-scale field survey and secondary analysis of the data collected from other such surveys are likely to be. Suraj Bandyopadhyay has been a collaborator for all stages of this study, from its inception to the final write-up. Prafulla Chakrabarti, who joined this venture as a field investigator in 1960, became indispensable since then—especially in regard to the primary and secondary analysis of the data the study contains and their computerisation. Without the sustained assistance of these two colleagues, I could not have completed, this voluminous assignment.

My thanks are also due to the other scientific workers and all the secretarial workers of the Sociological Research Unit of the Indian Statistical Institute. They have willingly done their chore in the context of this study, whenever called upon to do so. Special mention should be made in this respect of K. Chattopadhyay, B. Ray, T. N. Ghosh, M. Chattopadhyay, P. N. Mohalanobish, A. K. Basu, N. C. Das, and A. Chatterjee.

Advice and assistance sought for this study from other workers of the Indian Statistical Institute were readily given. The following names are particularly noteworthy in that context: Professors C.R. Rao, B. P. Adhikari, J. Roy, M. N. Murti, and P. Chatterjee of the Field Branch, and S. Das Gupta of R.T.S.

Calcutta
July 1976

RAMKRISHNA MUKHERJEE

Acknowledgements

This is a study in collaboration, as all macro-studies involving large-scale field survey and secondary analysis of the data collected from other such surveys are likely to be. Sutapa Bandyopadhyay has been a collaborator for all stages of this study, from its inception to the final write-up. Pradip Chakravarti, who joined this venture as a field investigator in 1966, became indispensable since then—especially in regard to the primary and secondary analysis of the data the study contains and their computerisation. Without the sustained assistance of these two colleagues, I could not have completed this voluminous assignment.

My thanks are also due to the other scientific workers and all the secretarial workers of the Sociological Research Unit of the Indian Statistical Institute. They have willingly done their share in the context of this study, whenever called upon to do so. Special mention should be made in this respect of K. Chattopadhyay, B. Ray, T. N. Ghosh, M. Chattopadhyay, P. N. Mahalanobish, A. K. Basu, N. C. Das and A. Chatterjee.

Advice and assistance sought for this study from other workers of the Indian Statistical Institute were readily given. The following names are particularly noteworthy in that context: Professors C.R. Rao, B. P. Adhikari, I. Roy, M. N. Murti and P. Chatterjee of the Field Branch, and S. Das Gupta of R.T.S.

Calcutta
July 1978

RAMKRISHNA MUKHERJEE

ERRATA

Page 43	Footnote 7 line 2	For 23–34 Read 21–24
Page 80	Table 2.17 column 1 main item 7	For Religious groupings Read Religious grouping
Page 90	Table 2.21 column 2 heading	For *Catagory* Read *Category*
Page 92	Table 2.23 second sub-heading	For *parental sibling* Read *parental, sibling*
Page 92	Table 2.23 column 4 row 1	For (218) Read (219)
Page 130	Line 22	For 'heads's' Read 'head's'
Page 130	Line 23	For Sibiling (s) Read Sibling (s)
Page 135	Table 3.19 heading second line	For of the 'Head' as Specified Read of the 'Head' (as Specified
Page 149	Table 3.29 heading first line	For *Estimated Percentage of Total* Read *Estimated Percentage to Total*

Page 151	Table 3.30 column 4 rows 16, 17, 18	For subsidary Read subsidiary
Page 156	Last line	For indic Read indicates
Page 157	Last line	For join Read joint
Page 158	Line 14	For 'cutting off Read 'cutting off'
Page 161	Table 3.33 column 2 row 18 item 18	For Urhan Read Urban
Page 162	Line 19	For conterpart Read counterpart
Page 171	Line 35	For sons' sons' sons', Read 'sons' sons' sons'.
Page 222	Line 15	For thesa mpled Read the sampled
Page 231	Line 12	For tabl Read table
Page 231	Line 13	For sa Read so
Page 246	Line 5	For secietal Read societal
Page 248	Table 7.3 column 4 row 1	For 26 63 Read 26.63

Page 250	Table 7.7 column 2 row 8	For 0 00 Read 0.00
Page 251	Table 7.9 column 8 row 5	For 19 58 Read 19.58
Page 255	Table 7.17 heading second line	For (Rural Only) Read (Rural only)
Schedule 1.0	Block 3 Table 10 column 1	For (10,0) Read (10.0)
	Block 3 Table 10 column 11	For (When $i \geqslant 0$, Read [(When $i \geqslant 0$.

Introduction

This volume is the outcome of a research project undertaken by the author under the auspices of the Research Programmes Committee, Planning Commission, Government of India. The research project was entitled 'Changes in Family Structures—Urban/Rural—in West Bengal'. Details of its history, design of study, field-work, reliability and precision of the data collected, etc., are given in Part 2 of this volume. Here we are concerned with the principal points in the conceptual framework of the study, its scope and limitation.

The first term of reference to the project was to evolve a scheme of classification of family structures. This we shall not discuss in this volume since it has called for a separate monograph in which the efficiency of the 'population' approach to classification has been discussed as against the commonly adopted 'typological' approach, and a model for the classification of family structures has been developed according to the former approach. A concise version of the concepts and methods involved in thus classifying family structures has been published [Mukherjee, 1972]. The present study is based on this model and, in a sense, demonstrates its utility or failure.

Apart from the above explanation, we should note that the title of the research project involves us, prima facie, with an explanation of what we mean by: (i) family, (ii) structure, and (iii) changes therein. As to the first of these three, any discussion on the definition of the 'family' and the consequent identification of family-units may appear as a pedantic exercise. But subtle and occasionally major variations are detected in their aspects. As we found in course of this study, to one person the term family may mean only himself or herself and his/her consort; to another, his/her parents and siblings (and not the consort); to a third, his/her consort and children (and not the parents and siblings); and to others, a bigger kin group of a specific coverage for reasons peculiar to themselves.

Besides those variations which are intrinsic to the mental make-up of different persons, variations may be noticed in defining the family as a *locally functioning* societal unit. The time factor is involved in specifying the attribute of coresidence for family members, namely, for how long. If the attribute of commensality is taken into account (independently of, or concurrently with, the attribute of coresidence), the time factor as well as the issue of the number of meals consumed collectively by the members of the group becomes relevant. Similar qualifications will be appropriate in respect of any other attribute chosen to distinguish family-units as locally functioning entities.

The family could also be defined in a longitudinal perspective. To some, such a definition is essential to the appreciation of this social institution [Fortes, 1949: 64]. The argument is that as a societal unit the family is always in the process of revising and replacing its members through, say, births, deaths, or migration reasons. So, it has been argued, to examine this societal entity at a point of time would be partial; it may give an incomplete and erroneous picture of what it represents in the society in question. On this count, however, another set of attributes may be required to identify family-units. Some characteristics, relevant to the previously mentioned definition of the family, may now be regarded as random variations due to (1) birth or death in a 'family', (2) economic or other motivations of persons to enter or leave the 'family', and so on. The definition of the family in terms of its *development cycle* demands, therefore, a different formulation of the characteristics of family organization and the introduction of attributes relevant to denote these characteristics.

For example, if the family is defined in terms of the 'growth cycle of (the effective minimal) lineage' [ibid.: 63], a set of attributes will be required to identify the effective minimal lineage and to measure its range of variation as, say, $l_1, l_3, \ldots, l_n$. Another set of attributes will be required to denote the temporal dimension of the growth cycle of the effective minimal lineage as, say, $t_1, t_2, \ldots, t_r$; so that the most frequent occurrence of l_i over the entire time-period, as inferred probabilistically, may be regarded to represent the 'family' in the given society. Alternatively, a constellation of, say, (l_i, l_j, l_k) may be inferred probabilistically in order to represent the intrinsic development cycle of the family in terms of its definition in the longitudinal perspective.

Further illustrations can be given to substantiate the fact that there cannot be a universally accepted definition of the 'family' and, consequently, a uniform manner of identification of family-units. That, however, may not be necessary. What is required, instead, is to state the definition, or definitions of the family that we have adopted for this study and why we have adopted them. This will be understood from a description of how the family-units were identified for the main sample of data collected for this study in 1960–61.

We shall describe in Part 2 how the households were selected to represent the West Bengal society. These households referred to mutually distinguished, coresident and commensal groups of people who usually lived together and ate from the same kitchen; so that the locally functioning family-units identified in this way will represent stable societal entities.

Next it was ascertained who, among the members of each sampled household was unanimously accepted as its 'head', and this person was asked to state who his 'family members' were. Against each person, thus enumerated, was recorded his or her relationship with the 'head' in kinship terms[1] or otherwise, in case that person did not draw any kinship relation with the head but the latter considered him as a 'family member'. Also, whether or not he or she is a constituent of the 'head's' household was noted. Thereafter the 'head' of the household was asked whether there were other persons in his or her household who had not been enumerated as 'family members'; and, if so, what their relationships were (kinship or otherwise), with him or her (*vide*, Block 9 of Schedule 1.0 in the Appendix to Chapter 6 in Part 2).

Six sets of persons were thus enumerated with reference to the 'head' of each of the sampled households:

(1) Those who are regarded by the 'head' as 'family members', are related to him or her by kinship, and are members of his/her household.

(2) Those who are *not* regarded by the 'head' as 'family members' *but* are related to him or her by kinship, and are members of his/her household.

[1]Unless otherwise stated, we have meant by the word 'kinship' the relationships of both kinship and affinity; that is, by blood, marriage, or adoption.

(3) Those who are regarded by the 'head' as 'family members', are related to him or her by kinship, *but* are *not* members of his/her household.

(4) Those who are *not* regarded by the 'head' as 'family members' and are *not* related to him or her by kinship, *but* are members of his/her household.

(5) Those who are regarded by the 'head' as 'family members' *but* are *not* related to him or her by kinship, and are members of his/her household.

(6) Those who are regarded by the 'head' as 'family members' *but* are *not* related to him or her by kinship, and are *not* members of his/her household.

Sets 1 and 2, taken together, will represent a family-unit in terms of forming a *coresident and commensal kingroup*. As referring to the physical integration of a number of individuals within a familial coverage, this unit implies the operation of the privileges and obligations (as well as of rights and duties) of the family members in an intimate, sustained, and regular manner.

Sets 1 and 2 may also comprise only one person, namely, the 'head' of the household. For example, an unmarried or ever-married man may form a household all by himself, or may have a cook and a servant in the household. This person, then, will have a specific position in the schema of family structures as a 'non-familial unit', namely, a corollary to a family-unit.[2]

[2]The concept of 'non-familial unit' does not imply that the individuals under reference may not have any privileges and obligations (or rights and duties) in reference to the family as a social institution. Many of them are likely to have left their 'family' elsewhere and maintain the familial integration in ways other than forming a domestic group. This will be substantiated from this study. It is useful, however, to identify these persons as 'non-familial units' and examine them (if necessary) in light of their specific characteristics of familial integration. Because, for whatever reason it may be, the fact that these persons cannot function in families forming locally functioning units (or they do not consider themselves to belong to any 'family') points to an important aspect of family organization in the society as a whole.

The non-familial units, thus, claim a significant share of the relevant background to appreciate the constellation of family structures in West Bengal society; and so it was decided that the *units* to be taken into account for this study will comprise both non-familial units and family-units.

Sets 1 and 3, taken together, will distinguish kingroups as family-units in terms of the mental make-up of the 'heads' of the locally functioning family-units. Their orientation towards family organization in society will not be of casual relevance to the operation of the family as a social institution. Instead, the family organization they live in by forming the locally functioning units, and the family structure they have in mind, should provide us with a cue to examine the dynamics of the family in West Bengal society. The cue would be the more noticeable if the former is just a single person, that is, a 'non-familial unit', and the latter is a family-unit either nuclear or extended.

Sets 4 and 5, taken together, will represent those persons who belong to the household but have no kinship relation with its 'head'. For example, there may be a number of servants living with a family-unit (and eating from the same kitchen) who do not draw any kinship relation with the 'head' of the household. Among themselves, these persons may be unrelated or form one or more coresident and commensal kingroups, while the remaining ones may be unrelated by kinship terms. For instance, two servants may be related as husband and wife; a few others may be related as sibling, cousins, and/or parents-children; and the others may be unrelated persons.

From the above, it can be ascertained whether a household is composed of two or more coresident and commensal kingroups, of one or more coresident and commensal kingroups and one or more 'non-familial units', or only of one coresident and commensal kingroup. In the last case, no one of the household will be represented under the sets 4 and 5.

Evidently, these possibilities should be taken into account for a precise and comprehensive identification of the locally functioning family-units (and 'non-familial units') in West Bengal society. Therefore, Schedule 1.1 (reproduced in the Appendix to Chapter 6 in Part 2) was used when required in addition to Schedule 1.0 for the head of the same household. A representative sample of family-units and non-familial units was, thus, obtained for West Bengal in reference to the family organization the people were found to live in. Moreover, since similar data were collected in Block 9 of Schedule 1.1 as described for the same block in Schedule 1.0, the coverage of the family structures the people have in mind in West Bengal society was also made precise and comprehensive by combining the corresponding sets 1 and 3.

In reference to each of the Schedules 1.0 and 1.1, the sets 5 and 6 taken together referred to the inclusion of those persons in the 'family' of the 'heads' of the coresident and commensal kingroups (and unrelated persons) who are not related to them by kinship terms. It is not customary in sociological studies to regard them as 'family members'. For the family is defined, almost invariably, as comprising a number of persons related to one another by blood, marriage, or adoption. Even so, it was regarded useful to take account of also this dimension of subjective interpretation of 'what is a family' so as to appreciate its dynamics in society.[3]

Thus, a wide latitude has been given to define the 'family' (and identify the family-units and the 'non-familial units' correspondingly) in West Bengal society, so that, even from the structural aspect alone, we may have a fuller view of this social institution than is usually obtained. It may appear, however, that the longitudinal perspective in characterizing family structures has not been taken into account, but that conclusion will not be justified. The design of the study was a *replicated* cross-sectional coverage of the society in order to ascertain the prevalent characteristics of family structures in the time-dimension. We shall examine for this purpose the representative samples of locally functioning family-units and 'non-familial units' in 1946–47, 1950, 1956, 1960–61, and 1965–66.

We may now pass on to what we mean by 'structure' and, more specifically, 'family structure'.

II

'Structure' has been defined as the 'static' aspect of the descriptive

[3]Cases of inclusion of 'non-kins' as family members were, however, only 3 out of 4,119 family-units brought under examination during the 1960-61 sample survey:

(1) The head of a Brahmin family insisted upon declaring his religious preceptor's wife (also a Brahmin) as a member of the family.

(2) The head of a Kayastha family considered a Rajput boy as a member of the family since he is with them from his childhood.

(3) The head of another Brahmin family regarded the resident private tutor for the children (also a Brahmin) as a family member.

mode of treatment of a system'; so that, from the structural point of view, 'a system is composed of *units*, of sub-systems which potentially exist independently, and their structural interrelations' [Parsons, 1954: 214]. We shall now examine whether these characteristics are present in our concept of 'family structure' and what are their significance to our study.

We may begin with the formulation that the descriptive mode of treament of any societal system refers to 'any arrangement of persons in institutionalized relationships', and that 'the components of social structures are human beings, and a structure is an arrangement of persons in relationships institutionally defined and regulated' [Radcliffe-Brown, 1950: 43, 82]. The institutionalized relationships stand, prima facie, for the customary and/or the legally assumed dyadic relations of specific privileges and obligations, and of the corresponding rights and duties. For the family system, therefore, these relationships will refer to the arrangement of persons in terms of their bonds of kinship and affinity since the mode of social interaction among the members of a family is expected to be governed by them. Obviously, therefore, the characteristics of kinship and affinal relations expressed by the 'family members' will represent one aspect of family structures.

The relationships of kinship and affinity, however, are not to be considered in terms of the kinship system *per se*. In the present context, we cannot lump together all those persons who are genealogically related in any way. Since these relationships must refer to the family system, they must operate within the bounds of specific conditions and stipulations for holding a number of persons together as 'family members' under mutually distinguished family-units, although the constituents of these family-units may be related genealogically. The identification of relevant kingroups as family-units will, therefore, represent another aspect of family structures. This we have already taken note of while explaining what we mean by 'family'.

Finally, in order to place the family-units under one or another structural category within the family system, the characteristics of the kinship and affinal relations they contain may not be given equal importance. The occurrence of one particular characteristic of kinship and affinal relations (or one particular set of characteristics) may be regarded as of cardinal importance to define a family structure category; and, in that context, the occurrence of corresponding or allied characteristics may be considered as of ancillary or incidental relevance only. For example, the 'extended family' category may be defined to contain one or more lineal and/or affinal relations, with or without the concurrent presence of the conjugal, parental, and sibling relations. These considerations of selection and judgement will represent the third aspect of family structures.

The above definition and characterization of family structures may be disputed. It may be argued that by taking note of only the 'institutionalized' relationships we shall fail to consider all the nuances and ramifications of structural variations within and between family-units. It may also be pointed out that by allowing the sampled 'heads' of family-units (and the non-familial units) to consider even those persons as their 'family members' who are not related to them by kinship terms, we have already forfeited the use of a circumscribed description of family structures and become involved in an exhaustive schema of family structure classification. These contentions, however, will not be appropriate if we keep room for such eventualities in the successive stages of classification and analysis of family structures.

For example, one can suggest that the coverage of dyadic relations in family organization should extend beyond customary assumptions and legal jurisdiction so long as they are still institutionally defined and regulated. As we found during our study, it may not be impossible to find a situation in India wherein a person insists on regarding his old servant or family tutor or preceptor's wife as a 'family member'. This kind of insistence, therefore, may be acceptable provided the assumed relative is found to be designated with a specific kinship term, more like, 'elder brother' for the old servant, 'uncle' for the family tutor, 'mother' for the preceptor's wife, and the appellation is found to be 'egocentric' and not 'sociocentric' [Service, 1960: 752–54]. For, in this case, there remains the scope that the assumed relative becomes subject to similar (if not the same) customary rules and regulations of privileges and obligations (and of rights and duties) as would have been applied to him or her if he or she had drawn that kinship relation directly and unconditionally.

There can also be suggestions to override altogether the institutional control from the dyadic relationships, although one may argue that it is *sui generis* to the study of a social institution—the family or any other. The relevance of all these suggestions, however, follows from the feasibility of their application. We had, therefore, made provision to account for such possibilities, and found that familial relationships other than those of kinship and affinity (directly established) are virtually non-existent even in the mental make-up of the people. However, cases of this nature, have been taken care of. Our concept of family structure, therefore, may not be regarded as inappropriate; at any rate, for the primary course of their classification and analysis, which is the objective of the present study.

Proceeding further, we find in reference to the 'structural point of view' of the family system that the three aspects of family structures we have described will represent three distinct fields of variation, behaving as three sub-systems which 'potentially exist independently':

(1) The demarcation of the kingroups into family-units can be (and has been) made in more than one way, irrespective of what the composition of these kingroups is, and how the characteristics of such composition are taken into account for the formulation of structural categories.

(2) The composition of the kingroups will be in terms of all possible variations in the kinship and affinal relations they contain, irrespective of how these kingroups are identified as family-units and how these family-units are taken into account for the formulation of family structure categories.

(3) The formulation of the family structure categories can be made in any possible manner irrespective of the details of how a particular set of family-units has been identified and/or what are the details of kinship and affinal relations with which the family-units are concerned.

We find, moreover, that the nature of variation exhibited by these three fields will refer to three mutually distinct but allied terms of reference to the classification and analysis of family structures:

(1) The field of variation dealing with the identification of mutually distinguished kingroups as family-units will refer to the *unit* of classification and analysis, as exhibiting the unit-characteristics of family structures.

(2) That dealing with the composition of family-units in terms of the relations of kinship and affinity they contain, respectively,

will refer to the *content* of classification and analysis, as exhibiting the *content*-characteristics of family structures.

(3) That dealing with the formulation of structural categories will refer to the *object* of classification and analysis, as exhibiting the sociological meaning attributed to a structural entity.

Thus, each of these three fields of variation being a depository of variable characteristics of a particular kind, the classification and analysis of family structures in their respective accounts should promote our understanding of the family system in West Bengal society. We may now explain this.

If we wish to examine the inter-connection among the family and other societal systems, we shall need a classification and analysis of family structures according to the different manner of identification of kingroups as family-units. Otherwise, our knowledge on this aspect of family structures will remain unorganized and circumscribed to one social scientist or another; it will not be systematized for further and continual accumulation of information. In this context, therefore, we have taken note of the interrelations between the family system and the economic system (as well as of the demographic system) by identifying the locally functioning family-units (and non-familial units) in reference to the coresident and commensal grouping of 'household'. We have also taken note of the interrelation between the family system and the kinship system *per se* (as well as of the inter-personal system of the people) by identifying family-units (and non-familial units) in terms of whom the sampled individuals regard as their 'family members'. So that, further explorations in this field of variation may be made in the future.

If we wish to examine the family system *per se*, we should classify and analyze family structures according to their varying content characteristics; for, in terms of the 'organized, purposeful system of human effort and achievement' depicted by the family as a social institution [Malinowski, 1944: 51], the different kinds and degrees of kinship and affinal relations contained in the respective family-units must imply specifically different functions therein. The implication may vary from one society to another, or in the same society in the time perspective, but for a society at a given time the distinctive occurrence of certain family structures to denote some particular content characteristics must indicate how to proceed with the 'functional' analysis of the institution under reference.

Regarding the characteristics of family structures as the objects of classification and analysis, the distinctive occurrence of certain structural categories (constructed and taken note of in any manner whatsoever) should be of specific significance to the understanding and interpretation of the family system. For, on the one hand, the structure of a system 'ensures that nothing of vital importance is inadvertently overlooked', and it thus 'minimizes the danger, so serious to common-sense thinking, of filling gaps by resort to uncriticized residual categories' [Parsons, 1954: 217]. On the other, such distinctive occurrence of structural entities will be *expected* in a society rather than their random occurrence (that is, as denoting any content characteristic at random) being the hypothetical standpoint. Otherwise: 'It is hard to believe that social scientists could have worked out many generalizations about the behaviour of men in groups, if there had been no persistencies in this behaviour' [Homans, 1950: 311]. Therefore, the relevant course of such persistent behaviour in any society at a given point of time will be suggested, at the first instance, by the characteristically selected occurrence of structural categories.

Finally, while giving equal importance to the three fields of variation as three distinct terms of reference to the classification and analysis of family structures, our concept of family structure will represent the family system as not only composed of variable sets of 'units' and of 'sub-systems which potentially exist independently' but also of the 'structural interrelations' among these sub-systems. For the study cannot but take a deliberate note of the three fields of variation jointly and, thus, set the scene for the appraisal of the dynamics of the family system in the society at large. This should be evident from the foregoing discussion, and will also be elucidated in Part 1 of this study. For, to quote Radcliffe-Brown in this context: 'The continuity of structure is maintained by the process of social life, which consists of the activities and interactions of the individual human beings and of the organized groups into which they are united' [Radcliffe-Brown, 1959: 180].

This, therefore, is what we mean by 'structure' and, more specifically, 'family structure', and how we wish to take note of the nature and the scope of variation of its field severally as well as jointly.

III

The objective of this study was not only to classify and analyze family structures. It had the ultimate aim of noting 'changes' therein. An explanation is thus called for on what we mean by 'change' in the given context.

Apparently, that explanation is unnecessary, as it was in the case of defining the 'family'. It is not uncommon to find that *any* alteration in a time-series of the objects under reference is regarded as change. That way, however, change loses its meaning as an *analytical concept*, and thus its primary usefulness to social studies. It substantiates the obvious fact that the objects are in a state of *dynamic equilibrium*, where alterations must be effected in some way or other since the state of *static equilibrium* is impossible for a live system. Moreover, viewed in this manner, 'change' fails to take note of those situations where it can justifiably be inferred in reference to variations in the place and/or objects of change, without taking a time-series into account. The necessity of examining changes in family structures from these aspects will be discussed in due course. For the present, we should state that an explanation of what we mean by 'change' in family structures is surely necessary.

Only in the last analysis, when a phenomenon has undergone *total transformation*, can change be established as a *social fact*. For example, the social structure of India, as based on the four *varnas*, was replaced at one stage of her history by a matrix of an increasingly large number of *jatis* [Oldenberg, 1897: 267–90]. Or, to cite an example in reference to the contemporary situation and with respect to family structures in India, the 1955 Act to prohibit polygyny among the Hindus has effected a change in family structures relating to the forms of marriage their constituents can undergo. Short of such total transformation, we cannot *deduce* change automatically and invariably. For example, if the phenomenon of polygynous marriage had not been prohibited by law, we could not have established, *ipso facto*, that the low incidence of polygynous families in the society points to 'change'. There could be other inferences; such as, the low incidence has always been the case or it is a transitory phenomenon over the time period $(t_1 \ldots t_n)$ since the longer range of $(t_1 \ldots t_i \ldots t_n \ldots t_r)$ records the persistence of the phenomenon *sine die*.

Change *per se*, thus, falls under the purview of historical analysis, as concomitant to an *accomplished fact*. It loses its usefulness to contemporary studies where we are concerned with change *as a process*. What we may deduce for contemporary studies are the characteristics of *variations* recorded in cross-sectional and/or temporal studies. These variations may be interpreted as 'change', as 'fluctuations' around a central tendency, or as *sui generis* to the operation of the system (such as the family system under reference). Chagne to us, thus, becomes a *matter of inference* and not a *matter of deduction*.

To be precise and objective, therefore, any inference on change in family structures should be based on the application of inductive reasoning and the logic of probability, with specific reference to the *place, time* and *object* of change: the three dimensions of variation which must be taken into account to draw a logical inference on any phenomenon, as has been stressed in Indian philosophy under the phrase '*sthān, kāla, pātra*'. Otherwise, either in the diachronic or in the synchronic aspect, our evaluation and measurement of change in family structures may be fallacious, inadequate, or inconsequential [Mukherjee, 1968].

In respect of each of these three dimensions of variation, we have to conceive of a *direction of change* and a *static point* to represent the base of any course of change, so that the variations observed in the given context can be inferred as change or otherwise. However, both the direction and the static point (which would be the point of departure to infer change) are matters of assumption. The appreciation of change itself, thus, becomes a variable phenomenon. It can be specified only against the assumptions made, and its validity will rest upon the intrinsic merit of the assumptions. Let us illustrate these reservations with reference to the place, time, and objects of changes in family structures.

To take up, first, the 'object' as the dimension of variation, it may be assumed that as representing the 'traditional norm' for the West Bengal society, the patrilineal-patrilocal joint family structure represents the static point (that is, the point of departure to infer change). It may also be assumed that the direction of change from this point is towards the nuclearization of family structures. Or, the other way round, the existence of 'non-familial units' in West Bengal society may be assumed to record change if the family as a societal unit represents the point of departure and the atomization of family structures indicates the direction of change.

With reference to 'place' as the dimension of variation, it may be assumed that the constellation of family structures in the rural sector of West Bengal represents the static point and the direction of change is indicated by the rural-urban differentiation in this context. Or, more specifically, the point of departure may be represented by the predominant family structure among the agriculturists (located in the rural sector of the society) and the direction of change may be towards the predominant family structure among the the industrial workers (located in the city sector of the society). The non-agriculturists in the rural areas, the townfolk, and the remaining city dwellers will, then, map out the course of change

With reference to 'time' as the dimension of variation, a number of comparable cross-sectional studies, undertaken at different points in time, may form a time-series. The static point, then, will be represented by the study located at the lowest point in the time-series, and the direction of change will be represented by the successive studies in the time-series. Thus, the year 1950, at the onset of the Five Year Plan programmes for India's development, may represent the base year, and any difference noticed in the configuration of family structures in West Bengal at the end of the first, second, and the third Five Year Plan periods may indicate a process of change in family structures in the society.

'Time' is also the built-in dimension of variation in a longitudinal study, as 'place' is in a cross-sectional study. And, either way, more than one of the three dimensions of variation may be brought to account, at a time, to represent the point of departure and the direction of change. The characteristics of the *patrilineal-patrilocal joint family* structure in the *rural areas* of West Bengal may represent the point of departure and the direction of change may refer to the 'differences' from this pattern in rural and urban areas. Or, the constellation of family structures in the *rural area* of West Bengal in *1950* may represent the starting point, and the direction of change may refer to the 'differences' in the rural and urban areas in 1956 and 1961. Or the predominant charactristics of the *patrilineal-patrilocal joint family* structure for the whole of West Bengal society in *1950* may represent the starting point, and the direction of change may refer to the 'differences' in 1956 and 1961. Or, the characteristics of the *patrilineal-patrilocal joint family* structures in *rural areas* of West Bengal in *1950* may represent the base, and the direction of change may refer to the 'differences' in rural and urban areas as well as in 1956 and 1961.

Also, as two at the time or all at a time, the three dimensions of variation may be brought to account in any other manner to represent the point of departure and the direction of change. Such as, it may be assumed that the structural configuration of the family in the mental make-up of the people represents the initial point; for they may have to live under different familial organizations due to what will now be regarded as extraneous circumstances. On this count, the direction and the course of change will be indicated by any variation found between what one supposes his or her family structure to be, and what the actual structure is, that he or she lives under.

Thus, many *a priori* derived static points (or points of departure) and directions of change may be brought to account, each having a specific relevance to the objective of a study. Consequently, there cannot be an *invariable* approach to the analysis of change and, therefore, while the research project was entitled 'Changes in Family Structures in West Bengal', what has been specifically analyzed and presented in this volume may be labelled as an examination of the *patterns of variation in family structures in West Bengal* in various space and time perspectives. Any inference on change may be drawn by those interested, as they decide what should be the static point and the direction of change.

IV

The revision of the scope of this study does not absolve us from undertaking responsibilities in relation to the professed aim of the research project. Indeed, the responsibility now devolved upon us is greater than before. Whether or not we draw any inference from the data and the analysis presented in this volume, we shall have to have some critical thresholds in view when choosing factors to represent patterns of variation in family structures, and we shall also have to bear in mind the consequent directions of change. Otherwise how will one be able to infer change from the data and the analyses supplied?

Theoretically, the argument is irrelevant. On that count, all possible factors to denote patterns of variation in family structures should be taken into account in the light of our current knowlege. In practice, however, it would be impossible to consider all of them for a single study. A selection has to be made, therefore, from the theoretically possible lot on the basis of our *a priori* knowledge on their relative importance to the subject under reference and we should explain the *rationale* behind the course of selection.

Thus, in reference to the 'object' as the dimension of variation to infer change in family structures, we can take into account all possible variations in those three aspects of the constitution of family structures which we have brought forward earlier for their characterization. We have, however, defined the 'family' in some particular ways only. We shall also take note of the content of the family-units and the formulation of structural categories in some particular manners only.

After examining, briefly, the formation of family-units by different forms of union between their constituent males and females, we shall examine their kinship composition in terms of the presence or absence of the main categories of intra-family relations labelled: (i) *conjugal*, between husband and wife; (ii) *parental-filial* (in short, *parental*), between father and/or mother, on the one hand, and son and/or daughter, on the other; (iii) *sibling*, between brothers and/or sisters; (iv) *lineal*, between those related by common descent from the same ancestor as traced through males and/or females, excluding those related by parental or sibling relations; and (v) *affinal*, between those related through the spouse of one or both of them, or through the spouse of their consanguineous relatives.

For those family-units which are involved with lineal and/or affinal relation(s), we shall focus our attention on the patrilineal pattern of these relations, and we shall categorize any other pattern as 'non-patrilineal'. That way, of course, we could lose some information on other possible patterns of intra-family relations. However, those family-units in West Bengal, which are involved with lineal and/or affinal relations, were found to subscribe predominantly to the patrilineal pattern; and there was none which conformed to other known pattern formations (for example, matrilineal, matripatrilocal, avunculocal, and natolocal—the institution of *taravad* among the traditional Nayars of South India) which have been discussed elsewhere in the context of presenting a tentative model for the classification of family structures in the dimension of their kinship composition [Mukherjee, 1962: 361–97]. In place of the apprehended loss, the present course of analysis will give us a fuller view of the pattern of variations in intra-family relations. This will be seen from Chapter 1 which deals with the above and allied courses of *variations* in family structures in West Bengal.

In Chapter 2 we shall discuss the *interrelations* between family structures and other facets of the social structure of West Bengal. This chapter thus refers, essentially, to the space perspective of change; that is, to 'place' as the dimension of variation to infer change in family structures. We have selected, for this purpose, certain forms of *social stratification*, out of all those possible, in consideration of their importance to West Bengal society.

We have considered the religion-wise stratification as Hindu, Muslim, and 'other' communities, and the caste-wise stratification of the Hindus and the Muslims as 'high', 'middle', or 'low' in accordance with the traditionally ordained social segregation among the Hindu castes and the differentially enjoyed social prestige among the Muslim sects.[4] Such involuntary groupings of the

[4]Among the Hindus of West Bengal, the Brahmin, Vaidya, and Kayastha castes are regarded to represent the top of the social hierarchy. Those from whom an orthodox Brahmin may accept water (i.e., the 'pure castes') are regarded to represent the middle stratum. And those from whom the orthodox Brahmin will not accept water (i.e., the 'impure castes') are regarded to represent the bottom of the social hierarchy. Accordingly, the family-units (and the non-familial units) belonging to the respective sets of Hindu castes were categorized as 'high', 'middle', and 'low'. (For details see the Appendix to Chapter 6 in Part 2.)

The Muslims of West Bengal do not subscribe to social segregation on a traditional basis as the Hindus. Nonetheless, among themselves they consider the 'functional' groups like the *jolahas* (weavers), *dhunia* (cotton carders), *nikaris* (fishermen), *khulus* (oilpressers), *kalal* (liquor distillers and sellers), as the inferior-most in status. The 'non-functional' Muslims, therefore, do not practise connubium (and, in certain cases, also commensality) with these people. Accordingly, they have been regarded to belong to the lowest stratum of the social hierarchy. Also, among the 'non-functional' Muslims, those who designate themselves as Moguls, Pathans, Khans, Saiyyads, etc., are regarded to belong to the top of the social hierarchy; and the rest in the middle stratum.

However, since this form of categorization of the Muslims is not traditionally ordained, the 'heads' of the Muslim family-units (and the non-familial units) were asked to affiliate themselves to one of these three grades. Our

people are claimed, on the basis of objective findings, to have profound bearings upon the social life of Bengal. It would be desirable, therefore, to investigate whether this form of social stratification is associated with any particular pattern of variation in family structures.

We have also taken into account the ecological stratification of West Bengal since it is regarded to account for the historically engineered social ecology of the State. For instance, the 'arid plain' area represents, largely, the *Radh Desh* where the Bengalees have been claimed in historical literature to behave somewhat differently from their compatriots living in *Samatata*, the 'riverine plain' [Ray, 1949: 82–156]. It would be desirable to ascertain whether this form of stratification is associated with any particular pattern of variation in family structures.

We have considered the rural-urban distinction of West Bengal society, as also its further segmentation into city-town-urban-rural zones. It is often asserted that the urban development and the process of urbanization of our society are having a decisive effect on the structural articulation of family-units. In terms of the above form of stratification, therefore, one should be able to examine whether the pattern of variation in the configuration of family structures is amenable to the concept of rural-urban dichotomy or rural-urban continuum, or of neither; and, thus, whether or not it indicates a process of change [Mukherjee, 1965: Chapter 2]. We have also taken into account the age of the 'head' of the family as another demographic variable, with some interesting results recorded in Chapter 2.

We have examined the economic stratification of West Bengal society in terms of its three social connotations: (1) the sectors of the national economy from which the non-familial units and family-units earn their livelihood, in the main; (2) the occupations which, solely or principally, provide incomes for these units; and (3) the relations of production they have thus entered into in the society as a whole. The reason behind our selection of these three economic attributes is that interrelations between them and

field investigators explained to them the principle of grading, but not the categorization we had envisaged accordingly. And we found from the field data that our course of categorization was not contrary to what they professed themselves.

various configurations of family structures are often brought up to hypothesize 'change' [ibid.: Chapters 2 and 3].

We have considered further the maximum educational attainments of the members of the family-units, and of the non-familial units, as outlining another form of social stratification; for the differential cultural impulses felt by the units, on this basis, are often subsumed to register distinctive 'value considerations' on their structural articulation. Moreover, we have stratified the family-units (and non-familial units) in terms of legal rights of their constituents over dwellings as well as other forms of real estate and properties. Such characteristics may produce specific motivation for the maintenance of a particular configuration of family structures. For example, a 'patrilineal' joint family may be maintained because the 'brothers' (with their wives and children) are co-parceners of the ancestral house. Alternatively, a 'patrilineal and non-patrilineal' joint family may be maintained because the 'brothers' as well as the 'evermarried sisters' (with their consorts and children) are so privileged.

In this manner, we have considered in Chapter 2 various forms of social stratification in light of their specific and relative importance to the configuration of family structures in West Bengal society. These sharply distinguished forms of social stratification, therefore, may show whether one, or more than one, pattern of variation exists in the constellation of family structures in West Bengal in terms of its territorial, ecological, social, economic, cultural, and other factors of differentiation. A point of departure can be located, thereafter, and a direction of change can be assumed, in respect of each one of these forms of social stratification so as to fulfil the objective of ascertaining changes in family structures in West Bengal.

Ultimately, however, it should be ascertained whether specific structural configurations of the family-units (and non-familial units) are associated with particularly comprehensive characterization of the people in terms of the societal attributes considered so far severally. This may provide us with the clue to any systematization of the variations noted among family structure categories in the space perspective. Also the static point or the point of departure may, then, be located in reference to the *ensemble* of the important facets of the social groups. The structural categories taken into account to represent different forms of social stratification may, therefore, be combined to characterize a social group, say s_r, by the attributes $(a_i b_j c_k d_l e_m \ldots .)$ in reference to the matrix of social stratification. A set of social groups, say $(s_1, \ldots, s_t)$, may be identified in this way, and whether a particular family structure category, say F_x, is exclusively (or predominantly) associated with social group s_1, F_y with s_2, and so on, may be ascertained next. The joint consideration of the 'object' and the 'place' as two dimensions of variation to infer change may thus be made comprehensive in order to depict the social reality. This has been attempted at the end of Chapter 2.

In Chapter 3, we shall examine the *trend* of variations in family structures which have already been brought to sharper focus in Chapter 2 than in Chapter 1. To the 'object' and the 'place' as the dimensions of variation to infer change in family structures, we shall now add the dimension of 'time'. For this purpose, we shall now consider five landmarks in the time-dimension in order to ascertain any trend of variation in the association between family structures and other facets of social structures in West Bengal. These are the situations in West Bengal from 1946–47 through 1965–66 at every five years' interval. The rural data have been analyzed for all the five time-periods covered. Since around 1955 the urban sector attracted the attention of social planners, we have covered the urban data for the latter three time-periods only. There is also the point that urban data for periods earlier than 1956 are scarcely available.

The year 1946–47 has been regarded as the 'base period' because it combines three distinct strains in the social current which eventually emerged in West Bengal: (1) the position immediately after rehabilitation from the shock of the Second World War and the great famine and epidemics of 1943–44, (2) the situation just before the partition of Bengal, and (3) the 'kaliedoscopic arrangement of West Bengal society after the influx of the refugees from East Pakistan. The next four periods are also of crucial importance to West Bengal society: at the onset of the Five Year Plans (1951), and at the completion of the first, second, and the third plans (1956, 1960–61, and 1965–66, respectively). The trend to be examined on the basis of these five time-periods (or only the last three of them, where unavoidable) should, therefore, be of significant relevance to the revised objective of the present study.

Moreover, on the basis of the data specifically collected for this study in 1960–61, we shall examine in Chapter 3 the trend of variation in family structures in a quasi-temporal perspective, that is, in terms of who constitute the coresident and commensal kingroups in the society and whom the 'heads' of these family-units (and non-familial units) consider as their 'family members'. This is because a time lag may be assumed between what one thinks and what one is forced to do, or does voluntarily, as has been pointed out earlier. Additionally, an examination of the constituents of the kingroups, who while acclaimed as family members did not belong to the coresident and commensal units, will throw significant light on the functioning of the family as a social institution in West Bengal society. Information regarding those members of the locally functioning family-units who were not considered as 'family members' by the 'heads' of such units would be equally relevant. Therefore, this course of analysis will be employed in Chapter 3 in order to substantiate and amplify the results obtained from the analysis of the trend of variation in respect of the five (or three) time-periods specified above.

V

The scope of the present study may now be outlined as follows:

(1) The relative incidence of different categories of family structures in West Bengal society (Chapter 1) will give us an answer to the question 'what' in respect of the phenomenon under reference. That is, what are the different kinds of structural arrangement we find for the 'family' in West Bengal?

(2) The association of these family structure categories with particular societal strata and their composite characterization (Chapter 2) will tend to supply an answer to the question 'how' in respect of the phenomenon under reference. That is, whether one or more distinct characteristics of family structure can be detected in reference to various other structural configurations of the West Bengal society.

(3) The relationship, if any, over time between distinct family structure categories and the 'social groups' represented by a multiple of social characteristics (Chapter 3) will orient us towards

the answer to the question 'why' in respect of the phenomenon under reference. That is, whether one can hypothesize, at this stage of our knowledge on family structures in West Bengal, regarding specific *social groups* functioning as the *media* for the emergence (or persistence) of distinct configurations of the institutionalized relationships depicted by the social institution of 'family'.

A further examination of the dynamics of the social institution under reference may thus proceed objectively in light of the findings contained in Part 1 of this volume.

One point requires mention in this context. The aim of our study could not be met by one, or a few, 'micro' investigations. It had to be a large-scale undertaking since an extensive and representative coverage of relevant information is denied to: (a) any manner of examination of one or a few purposively selected small areas, or (b) an impressionistic appraisal of the desired information. The need for such an undertaking was felt by Parsons when he wanted to examine the 'kinship system of the contemporary United States', and he noted [Parsons, 1954: 177]:

> ... on the sociological side, family studies have overwhelmingly been oriented to problems of individual adjustment rather than comparative structural perspective; while from the anthropological side, a barrier has grown out of the fact that a major structural aspect of a large-scale society cannot be observed in a single program of field research. To a considerable extent the material must come from the kind of common sense and general experience which have been widely held to be of dubious scientific standing.

This statement, we believe, is also appropriate to West Bengal society. Our present endeavour is to initiate attempts in this respect.

Any attempt of this kind must take recourse to the interview method of surveys, based on the principle of random sampling. This is no novelty to social research in India. But sample surveys have their inherent limitations. It is necessary, therefore, to state the scope and limitation of the surveys taken for the present study, and how these surveys have been integrated to meet our objective. It is also necessary to explain the order of reliability and precision of the data collected from these surveys. On the one hand, we cannot ignore the immense potentiality of sample surveys to provide us with extensive and representative coverage of the fields of variation under reference, and with precise and comprehensive collection of the desired information, given the limitations imposed by time, money and manpower. On the other, we cannot be unmindful of the fact that random sample surveys are sometimes regarded as the panacea for all problems relating to the above requirements, without a critical evaluation of their scope and limitation.

The task to be undertaken, however, may not interest all readers, as it must be of a technical nature. We have, therefore, discussed the questions relating to the design, data, and analysis for this study in Part 2 of this volume. In course of this discussion also we shall try to avoid technicalities insofar as that is possible. We should point out, pursuantly, that any study which is based on one or a series of sample surveys will have to depend upon limited coverage of the fields of variation, although these fields should be conceived, theoretically, as infinite but enumerable [Mukherjee, 1968], and in practice also they are immensely large even for such a small society as that of West Bengal. Hence, although the design of the surveys, the reliability of the data collected, and other prerequisites to any course of analysis may be attended to satisfactorily, the classification of different kinds of social stratification and the range of categorization of family structures give rise to at least three basic questions:

(1) How many structural categories for each of these forms of social stratification may be brought under consideration in view of the fact that large numbers of such categories can be evolved for the West Bengal society while the sample on which the study is based is not likely to reflect all of them properly or adequately?

(2) How many catogories of family structures can be brought under examination for the above reason, while in terms of variation in institutionalized relationships within respective family-units an immensely large number of such categories can be evolved?

(3) How many structural categories, formed in relation to

(1) and (2) considered together, can thus be examined; and how the average characteristics of these categories can be duly represented?

To answer these questions, we cannot rely on our esoteric judgement. On the other hand, the technical arguments on the basis of which objective answers have been given to them, will be unsuitable to this study which is not an exercise in methodology. Therefore, we have only touched upon these questions in Part 2; and in those places in Part 1 where we felt that mention must be made of their relevance, we have indicated it in footnotes. We have, however, borne them in mind, and have formulated the categories of classification and analysis accordingly.

Moreover, these categories have been so formulated that they are mutually distinct and analogous. If we represent them schematically as $(c_1 \ldots c_n)$, then, any one, as c_i, say, can be further categorized into mutually distinct and analogous entities as, say, $(c_{i_1}, c_{i_2}, \ldots, c_{im})$. Equally, any two or more of them can be collated to form composite categories as, say, $(c_{2-3}, c_{5-7}$, etc.). We may also make use of both the alternatives while retaining some of the categories considered for this study as, say, $(c_1, c_{2-3}, c_4, c_{5-7}, c_8, \ldots, c_{i_1}, c_{i_2}, c_{i_3}, \ldots, c_n)$. All these manoeuvres will be uniformly applicable to the classification and analysis of family structures. This study, therefore, may be regarded as a part of a more exhaustive or intensive study which can be undertaken in future. Accordingly, its basic data have been stored in the Sociological Research Unit of the Indian Statistical Institute, Calcutta, and what they refer to will be obtained from the facsimile of the field schedules reproduced in Part 2.

One may point out, however, in reference to the immediate scope of this study, that the deductions drawn in this volume, and the inferences which may be drawn on their basis, are incomplete. To answer this point, we should like to state: (1) we have endeavoured to draw the deductions objectively and precisely in order that valid inferences can be drawn on their basis; (2) all scientific discussions are as incomplete as the present one; and (3) like others, the scope of this study will be to add something to our previous state of knowledge on the subject matter, and not to make it complete or irrefutable.

PART ONE

Deduction and Inference

CHAPTER ONE

Variations

Virtually all the families surveyed in West Bengal during the period 1960–61, identified as coresident and commensal kingroups, are formed by monogamous first marriage of men and women. Rarely do the men form families by monogamous remarriage while families formed by monogamous remarriage of women, polygynous marriage or unsanctified union between sexes (only 4 out of 4,119 family-units in 1960–61 sample) are practically absent from the society. Step-relationship was present in only 38 of the 4,119 family-units: the most frequently in the polygynous families (19 out of 25), and in equal proportion but infrequently in the families formed by remarriage of men only (11 out of 173) or remarriage of women (3 out of 42).

TABLE 1.1

Forms of Marriage in the Family	*Sample*	*Estimated Percentage* (± *s. e.*)
(1)	(2)	(3)
Monogamous first marriage of men and women	3852	94.58±2.21
Monogamous remarriage of men, first marriage of women	173	3.53±1.62
Monogamous remarriage of women, first marriage or remarriage of men	42	0.88±0.61
Polygynous marriage or unsanctified union between sexes, with or without monogamous marriage in the family	29	0.63±0.09
Nevermarried persons only in the family (e. g., unmarried brothers only)	23	0.38±0.17
Total	4119	100.00

N.B.: The reference period of this and all the subsequent tables is 1960–61 unless otherwise mentioned.

Interestingly, in 5 out of 23 families formed by nevermarried persons only, the family members drew step-relationships among some of them.

Obviously, further search for variations in family structures cannot be made exclusively with reference to the formation of family-units from a stable union between sexes. We should, therefore, examine other aspects of family organization in West Bengal and, in this context, the kinship composition of family-units draws our attention because variations can then be examined with reference to all our units of observation and analysis, namely the non-familial units and family-units; that is, from no kinship relation in a unit to its composition by all possible distinctions in the kinship relations present. We may first examine the relationship between the forms of marriage in the families and their kinship composition as represented by:

TABLE 1.2[1]

Forms of Marriage in the Family	*Sample*	*Estimated Percentage to Total (±s.e.)*		
		Nuclear Structure	*Extended Structure*	*Total*
(1)	(2)	(3)	(4)	(5)
Monogamous first marriage of men and women	3852	61.90± 3.11	38.10± 3.11	100.00
Monogamous marriage of men and/or women	215	59.09± 5.79	40.91± 5.79	100.00
Polygynous marriage or unsanctified union between sexes, with or without monogamous marriage in family	29	87.12± 9.24	12.88± 9.24	100.00
Nevermarried persons only in the family	23	77.20±14.83	22.80±14.83	100.00

[1]A polygynous family of 'parents and children' has been categorized as nuclear by giving emphasis to the conjugal, parental, and sibling relations therein. It could be categorized differently because the relationship among co-wives may be denoted as 'affinal'. This relationship, however, is *sui generis* to a polygynous marriage, and so it is already indicated with the characterization of the family as 'polygynous'. On the other hand, the distinction drawn between one set of polygynous consorts (and/or their children) and the inclusion of any other relationship in such a family gives us additional information regarding variations in family structures.

(i) the nuclear structure containing conjugal, parental, and/or sibling relation only, and (ii) the extended structure containing lineal and/or affinal relation, with or without the concurrent presence of the conjugal, parental and sibling relations.

Since the nuclear structure holds the majority of families under all forms of marriage, it will obviously strike the dominant note in West Bengal society. It is of interest to find, however, that the non-familial units, which as a corollary to the coresident and commensal kingroups refer to persons living without any kin or affine, comprise an appreciable share of the total number of units for our observation and analysis.

TABLE 1.3

Coresident and Commensal Kingroup	*Sample*	*Estimated Percentage* (±*s.e.*)
(1)	(2)	(3)
Non-familial unit	815	13.44±1.93
Nuclear family	2622	53.66±3.60
Extended family	1497	32.90±2.28
Total	4934	100.00

If we, therefore, examine the non-familial units against the background of family organization of West Bengal society, we find that 70.82 (±4.28) per cent of them are men, 29.18 (±4.28) per cent are women. The marital status of the men and women non-familial units are different. Most of the men are unmarried *or* married but living away from their wives. The women are

TABLE 1.4

Marital Status of Non-familial Units	*Sample*		*Estimated Percentage* (±*s.e.*)	
	Men	*Women*	*Men*	*Women*
(1)	(2)	(3)	(4)	(5)
Unmarried	260	13	39.09±4.29	10.21±8.69
Married but living away from consort	339	2	46.96±4.80	0.14±0.10
Widowed, divorced, legally separated	63	138	13.95±2.55	89.65±8.66
Total	662	153	100.00	100.00

mostly widows. Divorced and legally separated male non-familial units were only 3 and 1, respectively, out of 662 in the 1960–61 sample; the female non-familial units were correspondingly 1 and 1 in the sample of 153.

These characteristics of the non-familial units conform to a pattern in reference to the family organization of West Bengal society if we examine: (1) their familial integration, and (2) the reason for their living without any kin or affine. Most of the men have a 'family' elsewhere; the women do not. When the non-familial units were asked to specify their 'family members' before stating the composition of their coresident and commensal units, 57.60 (±5.33) per cent of the men indicated that they had a 'family' elsewhere. The corresponding percentage for the female non-familial units is only 6.86 (±2.50).

The men live alone mainly to earn a livelihood; the women, because they have nowhere to go.

TABLE 1.5

Cause for Living without Kin or Affine	*Sample*		*Estimated Percentage (±s.e.)*	
	Men	*Women*	*Men*	*Women*
(1)	(2)	(3)	(4)	(5)
To earn a livelihood	466	24	63.47±5.03	10.00± 5.31
Nowhere to go	177	115	36.16±4.99	79.43±12.47
Any other reason	19	14	0.37±0.25	10.57± 7.44
Total	662	153	100.00	100.00

It was also found that most of the male non-familial units who have their 'family' elsewhere stay alone for 'work and earnings', whereas most of those who have no 'family' elsewhere stay alone since they have 'nowhere to go'. The distinction is irrelevant to the female non-familial units because most of them have been atomized possibly to the point of no return with reference to the familial organization of society.

The women, however, constitute a small share of all non-familial units in the society. The bulk of the men, on the other hand, represents a vital adjunct to family organization as earners

TABLE 1.6

Cause for Living without Kin or Affine of Male Non-familial Units	*Sample of Those Who Report on their 'Family' Elsewhere to be*		*Estimated Percentage (±s.e.) of Those Who Report on their 'Family' Elsewhere to be*	
	Present	*Absent*	*Present*	*Absent*
(1)	(2)	(3)	(4)	(5)
To earn a livelihood	385	81	93.60±2.86	22.53±6.57
Nowhere to go	20	157	6.05±2.84	77.08±6.51
Any other reason	16	3	0.35±0.26	0.39±0.48
Total	421	241	100.00	100.00

for their respective 'families'. Under a favourable economic situation, therefore, they may become affiliated to either a nuclear or an extended family structure, as we shall examine further in a following chapter. For the present, we may note that the pattern of variation among the non-familial units provides us with a significant background to variations in family structures in West Bengal, and prompts us to examine their primary categorization as nuclear or extended.

II

Definitions differ regarding the nuclear structure. To some, the simultaneous existence of the conjugal and the parental-filial relation in the structure is of decisive importance; to some others, the two relations are of equal and independent relevance [Murdock et al., 1950: 86; Ogburn and Nimkoff, 1953: 459]. These variations, however, may be of distinct sociological relevance, as it is with the presence or absence of the sibling relation in the nuclear structure. A couple may set up a 'family', but have no children; or it may have only one child. Those families also may occur in a society in which one or both the parents are absent. Thus, while the nuclear structure generally conveys to us the presence of conjugal, parental, and sibling relations in a family-unit, variations are possible with respect to the presence or absence of any one or any two of these relations.

Often there is another limitation to our understanding of the nuclear structure. It refers to the presence of parent(s) and/or *unmarried* child(ren) in a family, since the presence of evermarried 'children' in a nuclear structure is regarded to affect the logical formulation of extended structures of particular patterns of lineal and affinal relations. For example, under the patrilineal pattern, the evermarried women should not belong to their family of orientation; under the matrilineal pattern, the same restriction is imposed on the evermarried men; and so on for other consistent patterns of lineal and affinal relations in a set of extended families. The primary distinction between the extended and the nuclear structure, however, is in terms of the presence or absence of lineal and/or affinal relations. The distinction between unmarried or evermarried 'children' or 'siblings' in a nuclear structure attains a secondary importance in that context. Otherwise ambiguity arises from the presence of evermarried 'child', 'children', or 'siblings' in a family, without consort(s). For they will not draw lineal or affinal relation with any other family member.

On the other hand, in those societies where the extended family structures are found in appreciable numbers, the nuances of family organization in the nuclear structures may be lost if the distinction between the unmarried and evermarried 'children'/'siblings' is disregarded. The presence of such 'children'/'siblings' in these families who are widowed, separated or divorced from their consorts may not mean a reversal to *status quo ante*. Moreover, if in that society the majority of the extended families are likely to conform to a particular pattern of their lineal and affinal relations, then the aforesaid distinction gains in importance. For, by law or custom, various forms of discrimination are possible in that society between all, or specified kinds of, unmarried and evermarried 'children'/'siblings' with respect to the inheritance of family property, succession to sacred or secular office in the family, etc.; as for example, among the unmarried and evermarried 'daughters'/'sisters' in a patrilineally oriented society.

Therefore, given the definition of nuclear family as comprising a set of parent(s) and/or child(ren), the presence or absence of evermarried 'children'/'siblings' in them points to a course of variation to be examined. For West Bengal society, however, the course of variation is hardly of any relevance because only

3.69 per cent of the nuclear structures were estimated to contain evermarried 'child', 'children', or 'siblings' in 1960–61.[2]

The majority of nuclear families in West Bengal contain all the three possible kinship relations: conjugal, parental and sibling. Those which definitely register a partial disintegration of the nuclear structure, by containing parental and/or sibling relations only because of the absence of one or both 'parents', are rare in occurrence. Not so rare are those nuclear families which contain the conjugal and parental relations, or only the conjugal relation. They represent a structure which contains only one child to the parents, or which is not fully emerged yet with progeny in the family, or which is partially disintegrated by the progeny leaving the family.

All the variants of nuclear structure are, thus, seen in West Bengal. The full-fledged configuration of parents and child/children, however, is the dominant phenomenon in the society, comprising three-fourths of the total nuclear families. Of the others, it is of interest to notice that although the partially disintegrated configurations of parent and child/children occur infrequently, they are more as mother and child/children than as father and child/children. This is possibly due to the fact that, relatively speaking, more families are formed by monogamous remarriage of men than of women (as recorded in Table 1.1). The appreciable number of male non-familial units who have

[2]For purposes of future reference, the presence of evermarried 'children'/'siblings' in the nuclear families of West Bengal has been recorded as follows:

TABLE 1.F.1

Presence of Evermarried 'Children' or 'Siblings' in Nuclear Family-units		*Sample*	*Estimated Percentage (±s.e.)*
(1)		(2)	(3)
Sibling family:	brother(s) only	37	28.22±10.30
	sister(s) only	3	2.47± 1.67
	brother(s) and sister(s)	1	0.80± 0.79
Parent-child family:	son(s) only	38	40.79±13.12
	daughter(s) only	25	27.72±10.68
	son(s) and daughter(s)	—	—
Total		104	100.00

TABLE 1.7

Kinship Relations	*Variants of Nuclear Structure*	*Sample*	*Estimated Percentage* (±*s.e.*)
(1)	(2)	(3)	(4)
Conjugal, parental, sibling	Parents-children	1466	54.69±1.00
Conjugal, parental	Parents-child	442	18.24±0.87
Conjugal	Husband-wife	327	13.00±0.75
Parental, sibling	Father-children	49	1.76±0.25
	Mother-children	132	4.51±0.53
Parental	Father-child	51	2.07±0.26
	Mother-child	96	4.10±0.73
Sibling	Brother(s)/Sister(s)	59	1.63±0.48
Total		2622	100.00

a 'family' elsewhere may also be a contributory factor to this course of variation.

The authority in these families is vested, predominantly, in the 'husband-father', who is obviously a 'husband' only in the conjugal structure and a 'father' (as also a 'husband' when the consort is present) in the parental structure. 'Wife-mother' as the 'head' of the family, correspondingly, is a rare phenomenon, as it is for the 'son' to assume authority over the family. 'Daughter'

TABLE 1.8

'Head' of Nuclear Families		*Sample*	*Estimated Percentage* (±*s.e.*)
(1)		(2)	(3)
Conjugal structure	Husband	326	12.91±0.78
	Wife	1	0.09±0.09
Parental structure	Father	2008	77.22±1.40
	Mother	106	3.71±0.53
	Son	118	4.25±1.03
	Daughter	4	0.19±0.14
Sibling structure	Brother	59	1.63±0.49
	Sister	—	—
Total		2622	100.00

as the 'head' of the family occurs hardly at all, while 'brother' is obliged to assume that role in a sibling family due to the absence of 'parents' and the subservient role accorded to the 'sister'.

The obligation to provide for the family members is usually that of the 'head'. A departure from this rule is noticeable only in the case of the mother as the 'head'. The suggestion is, therefore, that authority is vested on a 'child' only when he or she is also the provider for the family, but the converse is not always true. An 'earning' child does not, *ipso facto*, become the 'head' of the family.

TABLE 1.9

'Head' of Nuclear Family	*Sample*	*Estimated Percentage (±s.e.) to Total Families, According as the Main or Only Provider for the Family is its*		
		'Head'	*Any Other Family Member*	*Total*
(1)	(2)	(3)	(4)	(5)
Father	2334	98.37±0.51	1.63±0.51	100.00
Mother	107	75.47±8.82	24.53±8.82	100.00
Son, daughter, brother	181	91.39±3.41	8.61±3.41	100.00
Total	2622	97.08±0.83	2.92±0.83	100.00

The nuclear family of West Bengal is, thus, seen to be a family of procreation, in which the male progenitor has the privilege to run the family and the obligation to provide for the family members. Variations from this arrangement occur infrequently; and, if they occur at all, they refer to the female progenitor assuming the role of her consort. To the 'children', this is almost invariably the family to grow up in their unmarried state.

What happens, then, when the 'children' marry? Do the 'daughters' move out of the family in conformity with the patrilineal pattern of family organization in the society? In that case, where do they move into—a nuclear or an extended family? Correspondingly, do the 'sons' set up their respective families of procreation? Or, do they transform the nuclear family of their 'parents' into an extended family by making it their family of orientation and procreation? Any attempt to answer these questions requires, prima facie, an examination of the characteristics of the extended family structures in West Bengal society.

III

The scope of variation in the extended family structures is infinite, theoretically, because the lineal and/or affinal relations they contain may represent kinship-wise integration of the family members over a virtually unlimited sphere. If, however, there is a pattern in the occurrence of these two relations in a set of family-units, the sphere of variation becomes limited. We hypothesized, therefore, that the extended families of West Bengal will subscribe, primarily, to the patrilineal pattern and the hypothesis was found to be true by 71 per cent of the total extended structures in the society conforming to it entirely.

The patrilineally joint structures will allow only certain kinds of lineal and affinal relations to occur in a family; nevertheless, the scope of occurrence of various kinds of lineal and affinal relations, as well as of the conjugal, parental, and sibling relations, remains very wide.[3] We may, therefore, examine the

[3]This will be realized from Formula 1.1 which gives the total possible coverage of kinship relations in the patrilineally joint structures:

$$[(E_m, E_{fu}, E_{fe}H)\ (F\ldots/B/Z\ldots)\ (M, W, S_u, D_u)], \qquad (1.1)$$

where:

(1) The first set of brackets includes the possible variations in the characteristics of the person (E) with whom the prescribed kinship relations can be drawn, and whether (E) requires any medium for that purpose. Thus, E_m= unmarried or evermarried male, and E_{fu}=unmarried female, do not require any medium; but E_{fe}=evermarried female does require her husband (H) as the medium to draw other kinship relations in the family.

(2) The second set of brackets denotes the pattern of variation in the generational and collateral extension of the patrilineal relationships. Accordingly, dots (...) against a notation indicate that it can be repeated *ad infinitum*; such as, *F* for father as *F, FF*, etc., *Z* for son as *Z, ZZ*, etc., but *B* for brother only once. A stroke (/) preceding a notation indicates that it can be preceded by the previous notations in the series; such as, *FB, FFB, FBZ, FFBZ, FBZZ, FFBZZ, BZ, BZZ*.

(3) The third set of brackets concludes the scope of variation in patrilineal relationships. Accordingly, as referring directly to the notations within the

characteristics of variation in the patrilineally joint structures of West Bengal society before bringing those extended structures into account which do not subscribe to the patrilineal pattern, fully or partly.

By the obligatory presence of at least one of the stipulated kinds of lineal and affinal relations, the configurations of the patrilineally joint structures can vary in innumerable ways. For instance, as representing only the affinal relation in the family, a mother-in-law and a daughter-in-law, or a husband's brother and a brother's wife, may constitute a patrilineal joint family. As representing only the lineal relation, another patrilineal joint family may be formed of a father's brother and a brother's son, or a father's father and a son's son. There may also be various other configurations of patrilineally joint structures according to the presence of lineal and affinal relations only, and in the absence of conjugal, parental, and sibling relations; for example, a family-unit composed of a man, his father's mother, and his father's brother's wife.

A frequent occurrence of joint structures comprising such isolated relationships only will denote an important aspect of family organization because they refer to the restricted foliage of the family tree or to the full or partial decay of some of its branches. The clue to these findings is the relative occurrence of patrilineal joint families under all possible combinations of the lineal, affinal, conjugal, parental, and sibling relations, as they are found in the structures. The number of combinations possible in this respect would be 24 since the lineal and affinal relations may occur in 3 possible ways (lineal, affinal, and lineal plus affinal) and, against each of these possiblities, the conjugal, parental, and sibling relations may occur in $2^3 = 8$ ways of their combined presence or absence. In West Bengal society in 1960–61, however, only 19 combinations were discernible; and, among them, 12 do not exist virtually, as each of them contains less than 1 per cent of the total number of patrilineal joint families. On the other hand, the majority of these families

first set of brackets or through the notations within the second set of brackets, any one of the notations M (for mother), W (for wife), S_u (for unmarried sister), or D_u (for unmarried daughter) may occur only once in a kinship notation-series; such as, E_mW, $E_{fu}M$, $E_{fe}HS$, E_mFBW, $E_{fu}BZW$, $E_{fe}HFM$, etc.

contain all the five kinship relations; and, as containing at least four out of the five kinship relations, 85 per cent of them are accounted for by only 6 combinations of these relations.

TABLE 1.10

Kinship Relations in Patrilineal Joint Structures	*Sample*	*Estimated Percentage* (±*s.e.*)
(1)	(2)	(3)
Affinal, lineal, conjugal, parental, sibling	697	64.83±1.69
Affinal, lineal, conjugal, parental	96	9.25±1.27
Affinal, conjugal, parental, sibling	112	9.17±1.23
Affinal, lineal, parental, sibling	13	1.24±0.54
Affinal, lineal, conjugal, sibling	3	0.41±0.22
Lineal, conjugal, parental, sibling	2	0.45±0.31
Affinal, conjugal, parental	56	6.47±1.23
Affinal, conjugal, sibling	20	2.12±0.68
Lineal, parental, sibling	28	2.65±0.49
Affinal, lineal, conjugal	4	0.35±0.28
Affinal, lineal, parental	3	0.72±0.62
Affinal, parental, sibling	1	0.13±0.23
Lineal, parental	7	0.54±0.19
Lineal, sibling	2	0.21±0.26
Lineal, conjugal	1	0.06±0.08
Affinal, conjugal	1	0.31±0.30
Affinal, parental	2	0.32±0.30
Lineal	7	0.55±0.35
Affinal	2	0 22±0 18
Total	1057	100.00

However, because of the patrilineal pattern, the lineal and affinal relations in these families will denote only specific variants of the classificatory relationships. A grandfather is father's father, and not mother's father; a grandmother is father's mother. A grandson or granddaughter is the son's son or the son's daughter, respectively. An uncle is the father's brother, an aunt is the father's sister (if unmarried) or the father's brother's wife (if married). A first degree cousin is the father's brother's son or the father's brother's unmarried daughter according to the sex of that person. A nephew is the brother's son, a niece is the brother's unmarried daughter; and so on with other lineal and affinal relations, as can be ascertained from Formula 1.1 in footnote 3 of this chapter. The kinship composition of the patrilineal joint families, therefore, can be delineated precisely.

But, in spite of the selected occurrence of lineal and affinal relations, the kinship composition of these families may vary extensively. For illustrative purposes, we may consider, at one extreme, the full flowering of the patrilineal joint family of a man as 'grandfather' because this is our common image of the joint family of Bengal. At the other extreme, we may, then, consider a patrilineally joint structure with only one of the relationships recorded for the former situation because it will indicate the last stage of any restricted development, or any successive course of disintegration, of the 'grandfather's' joint family. In that case, $(2^9-1)=511$ different configurations of the patrilineally joint structures are possible since the following lineal and affinal relations may or may not occur in them in any combination: grandfather, grandmother, uncle, aunt as the uncle's wife, aunt as father's unmarried sister, brother's wife, first degree male cousin, first degree male cousin's wife, and first degree female cousin.

Some of these possibilities, however, can be categorized by the total generational extensions of these families. Relatives like grandparents or grandchildren cannot occur in a family comprising less than three generation-levels. Also the corresponding collateral relatives as granduncle and grandaunt, or as grandnephew and grandniece, require a three-generational structure to occur.[4] Relatives like uncle and aunt, or nephew and niece, cannot occur in a family comprising less than 2 generations. Great grandparental or great grandavuncular relations are impossible to occur in families comprising less than four generations. Only cousins, cousins-in-law, and siblings-in-law can occur in one-generational structures; and so on. We may, therefore, examine how the patrilineal joint families of West Bengal are constituted in terms of the numbers of generations they contain.

[4]In the context of patrilineal pattern of lineal and affinal relations, granduncle = father's father's brother, grandaunt = the granduncle's wife or father's father's unmarried sister, grandnephew = brother's son's son, and grandniece = brother's son's unmarried daughter.

TABLE 1.11

Number of Generations in Patrilineal Joint Families	*Sample*	*Estimated Percentage (±s. e.)*
(1)	(2)	(3)
1	24	2.24±0.69
2	341	30.82±1.61
3	669	64.36±1.23
4	23	2.58±0.68
Total	1057	100.00

Four-generation structures are seen to occur seldom in West Bengal society; as also the one-generation structures. On the other hand, most of the patrilineal joint families represent a three-generation structure; next, a two-generation structure. Extensive possibilities are, thus, there for these families to vary according to their respective kinship composition. Out of them, the possibility that we may be particularly interested to examine is the nature and extent of variation in kinship composition of these families with reference to their 'heads' because by exercising their authority to hold the members of the respective 'families' together these persons occupy the pivotal position in family organization. The relationships they draw in respective units are, therefore, of decisive importance to the structural articulation of the families.

The 'heads' of the patrilineal joint families of West Bengal are virtually all males. In the 1960–61 sample of 1,057 families there was not a single instance of a woman being the 'head'. The 'heads' are also, almost invariably, a father; in an appreciable number of cases, a grandfather as well. Occasionally they are only a son, rarely a grandson in the family, and seldom they do not draw any parental-filial relation in the unit. On the other hand, as being both 'father and son' in a large number of cases, they are found to 'head' the patrilineal joint families although their parent(s) are there.[5]

[5]The 'head's' relationships shown in Tables 1.12–1.15 and in similar tables prepared afterwards are ascertained by following the method evolved

TABLE 1.12

'Head's' Parental-filial Position in Patrilineal Joint Families	*Sample*	*Estimated Percentage (±s.e.)*
(1)	(2)	(3)
Father and son	405	37.33±2.15
Father	255	22.21±1.69
Father and grandfather *or* only grandfather	233	24.10±1.37
Father, grandfather and son *or* grandfather and son	10	1.05±0.34
Father and grandson	9	1.20±0.43
Son only	88	8.79±0.85
Son and grandson *or* only grandson	2	0.45±0.24
No parental-filial position of the 'Head'	55	4.87±0.85
Total	1057	100.00

The progeny of a 'head' and the consorts of the male progeny, if those kins and affines are present in the family according to the patrilineal pattern, would be related collaterally amongst themselves. The 'head', however, has no collateral relatives in the family in most cases. If his collateral relatives are, at all, present in the family, they are his brother, brother's wife, and unmarried sister; less frequently, the brother's progeny or consorts of the brother's male progeny. Moreover, the second group of collateral relatives are seldom members of the family without the concurrent presence of the first group. Otherwise, they occur on stray occasions only, as do the other collateral relatives of the 'head'.[6]

by Mukherjee to record kinship distances in a family in terms of a conceptualized family matrix. Details are given in the monograph on the classification of family structures, as mentioned in the Introductory Chapter. Briefly, they are discussed in a paper [Mukherjee, 1972].

[6]The 'other collateral relatives' were found to be mostly the 'head's' first degree cousin, first degree male cousin's wife, uncle or aunt. Rarely they were as distant to the 'head' as his granduncle or grandaunt and nephew or niece once removed (namely, father's brother's son's son or his wife or his unmarried sister).

TABLE 1.13

'Head's' Collateral Relatives Present in Patrilineal Joint Families	Sample	Estimated Percentage (±s.e.)
(1)	(2)	(3)
None	645	63.32±3.06
Brother and/or brother's wife and/or unmarried sister	236	22.44±2.06
Brother's progeny and/or consort of brother's male progeny	31	2.24±0.70
Combination of above 2 categories	113	9.56±1.02
Other collateral relative(s)	19	1.23±0.44
Combination of above 2 categories	13	1.21±0.47
Total	1057	100.00

The indication is, thus, there that the extension of patrilineal joint families of West Bengal is in course of the family of procreation of the 'heads' alone. The collateral spread of the family, through the brothers of the 'heads' and of their male ancestors, is cut short in the process; and this happens in a large number of cases even when the parent(s) and grandparent(s) of the 'heads' are present in the family.

The process is substantiated by the presence or absence of the 'head's' collateral relatives in the respective sets of one, two, three, and four generation patrilineal joint families. The one-generation structures comprise a very small share of the total patrilineal joint families since they represent an untimely disappearance of the ancestral couples. They must contain the collateral relatives of the 'heads', but in overwhelming majority these structures are found to include only the siblings and/or the siblings-in-law of the 'heads'.

The two-generation structures comprise an appreciable share of the total patrilineal joint families, and are found to include the siblings, siblings-in-law, and/or the family of procreation of the brothers of the 'heads' in the majority cases. However, the other collateral relatives of the 'heads' are represented much less than for the one-generation stuctures, and there is a large number of two-generation structures without any collateral relative at all of the 'head'.

The three-generation structures comprise the main bulk of the total patrilineal joint families, and are overwhelmingly composed of only the progeny and the consorts and children of the male progeny of the 'heads'. In the remaining three-generation patrilineal joint families, the collateral relatives other than the 'head's' siblings and/or the family of procreation of the siblings occur very seldom, as for the two-generation structures.

The four-generation structures comprise as small a share of the total patrilineal joint families as the one-generation structures but for a different reason: not many persons can survive to become 'great-grandparents'.[7] However, these structures also show a pattern of variation similar to the three-generation structures except that the other collateral relatives of the 'heads' are found to occur much more frequently (but sporadically) in these families. This follows from the devolution of the family 'headship' to a son or grandson of the oldest couple; for the 'head' would draw collateral relationships beyond the sibling and first degree avuncular variety with some children and grandchildren of the oldest couple, as seen from Table 1.14.

The patrilineal joint families of West Bengal, thus, denote a central tendency towards the evolution of the 'head's' family of procreation which culminates in three-generation structures with a barely perceptible projection in the four-generation ones. The only important variation from this central tendency is noticed in the two-generation structures in which the 'head's' siblings and/or the family of procreation of his brothers occur a little

[7]On an average, a man undergoes 'effective marriage' (that is, begins to live with his wife) in West Bengal at the age of 23–34; a woman at 15–19 [NSS, 1970: 21, 98]. The man has his first child at an average age of 27–28; his wife at 19–21 [Ibid.: 54, 132]. So that, even if their first child is a son and that son's first child is also a son, the man will be 54–56 years old when he is 'father's father'; his wife, correspondingly will be 'father's mother' when she is 46–49 years old. Under the same minimum assumptions, a man will be 'father's father's father' at the age of 81–84; his wife will be 'father's father's mother' at the age of 73–77. But, according to the 1961 census data, the percentage of men in West Bengal beyond the age of 54 and 69 is 7 and 1, respectively; the same for women beyond the age of 44 and 69 is 14 and 2, respectively [GOI, 1961: 32].

TABLE 1.14

Collateral Relatives of the 'Head' of Patrilineal Joint Families	Estimated Percentage (±s.e.)			
	One-Generation Structures	Two-Generation Structures	Three-Generation Structures	Four-Generation Structures
(1)	(2)	(3)	(4)	(5)
None	—	40.27±4.97	77.17±2.46	48.19±8.33
Brother and/or brother's wife and/or unmarried sister and/or brother's male progeny and/or wives of brother's progeny	94.70±6.34	58.33±4.80	20 33±2.14	40.87±9.34
Other collateral relatives with or without above ones	5.30±6.34	1.40±1.15	2.50±1.02	10.94±6.84
Total	100.00	100.00	100.00	100.00
(Sample)	(24)	(341)	(669)	(23)

more frequently than the 'head's' family of procreation or orientation exclusively, as seen from Table 1.15.

The central tendency and the variations noticed among the patrilineal joint families of West Bengal suggest that these familes form a chronological sequence to the nuclear families we have examined earlier. The sequence we may trace according to the inevitable generational extension and attenuation of the families over time.

The nuclear family, which has been found to be usually of two-generation structures, may revert back to one-generation structures because of the disappearance of the parental couple. In that case, when one or more of the 'brothers' marry, they form a joint family which is the most frequently found one-generation patrilineal joint family in West Bengal. In course of time, the brothers will have children and the joint families would be of two-generation structures in which the 'head's' role will be as 'father, brother and uncle'. Such families, however, may also emerge from the disappearance of the parental couple in three-generation structures. So that, if there were a definite tendency in the society for the brothers to remain in the *stem* family, the familial role of the 'heads' as 'father, brother and uncle', 'father and uncle', 'brother and uncle', or only as 'uncle' would not have been so infrequent in the two-generation structures as found for West Bengal. The suggestion is, thus, there that the brothers may marry and remain together so long as only the 'head' has children in the family and assumes the role of 'father and brother'; but when the brothers have their respective families of procreation, they usually separate.

The suggestion is supported by the sequence from the commonly found nuclear structure in West Bengal which is composed of parents and children. The children marry in due course, and following the patrilineal-patrilocal pattern of family organization the daughters move over to other families while daughters from other families come to the family under reference as consorts of the sons. A joint family is thus formed in which the 'husband-father' goes on exercising his authority over the family as before, and occasionally delegates it to his only son or to one of several sons. Accordingly, in the two-generation patrilineal joint families, the familial role of the 'head' as 'father' occurs as frequently as noted earlier for his role as 'father and

TABLE 1.15*

'Head's' Familial Role in Patrilineal Joint Families (Sample in brackets against each role)		*Estimated Percentage ($\pm$s.e.) to Total distributed under*	
Central Tendency	*Variations*	*Central Tendency*	*Variations*
(1)	(2)	(3)	(4)
	One-generation structures		
×		×	
	Brother (20)		2.12±0.69
	Cousin (3)		0.04±0 05
	Brother and cousin (1)		0.08±0.13
	Two-generation structures		
Father (92)		8.86±1.97	
Son (32)		3.55±0.57	
	Son and brother (41)		3.63±0.49
	Father and brother (94)		8.30±1.04
	Father, brother and uncle (39)		2.78±0 78
	Father and uncle (11)		0.84±0.33
	Brother and uncle (22)		1.85±0.43
	Uncle (7)		0.58±0.39
	3 separate role-sets (3)		0.43±0.35
	Three-generation structures		
Grandfather and father (217)		22.72±1.60	
Grandfather (5)		0.57±0.35	
Father and son (287)		26.37±1.33	

Father, son and brother (74)		6.98±1 36
Father, son, brother, and uncle (33)		2.87±0.39
Father, son and uncle (4)		0.36±0.29
19 separate role-sets (49)		4.49±0.93
Four-generation structures		
Grandfather, father and son (8)	0.79±0.43	
Grandfather and son (1)	0.18±0.17	
Father and grandson (3)	0.07±0.04	
6 separate role-sets (11)		1.54±0.53
Totals: One-generation structures	×	2.24±0.69
Two-generation structures	12.41±1.17	18.41±0.58
Three-generation structures	49.66±1.15	14.70±0.70
Four-generation structures	1.04±0.36	1.54±0.53
Grand total	63.11±0.69	36.89±0 34

*Affinal roles of the 'heads' are not mentioned since they are specified constants to the roles mentioned. For example, the 'head' may be a 'brother-in-law' if he is a brother, a 'father-in-law' if he is a father, a 'grandfather-in-law' if he is a grandfather, 'husband's uncle' if he is an uncle, etc., with reference to a woman married into the family.

brother'; otherwise, in equal but much reduced frequency, it occurs as 'son' or 'son and brother'.

In course of time, the sons have children, and either a three-generation structure comes into being or with the disappearance of the parental couple it maintains the two-generation structure. Under the first alternative, if the 'headship' was previously located in the parental generation-level and is now retained, the family continues to operate as the family of procreation of the 'head' who assumes the familial role of 'grandfather and father' and accounts for a quarter of all patrilineal joint families in West Bengal. If, on the other hand, the 'headship' was previously located in the filial generation-level and is retained, or if the 'headship' now devolves upon one of the sons, the brothers of the 'head' leave the stem family especially if they have their own families of procreation. The family, thus, turns into the 'head's' family of orientation and procreation, with his familial role as 'father and son', which accounts for another quarter of all patrilineal joint families in West Bengal.

Under the second alternative noted above, the 'headship' is obviously held by one of the sons and, as for the corresponding three-generation structures, the brothers of the 'head' leave the stem family especially if they have their own families of procreation. So that, while the familial role of the 'head' is in almost equal frequency as 'father' or 'father and brother' (like 'son' or 'son and brother'), his role as 'uncle 'is found infrequently in the society.

The families rarely attain the four-generation structure because very few of the old men and women survive long enough to become 'great-grandparents'. In a few cases, however, when they live that long, the 'headship' of the family passes on to a son, if that has not already taken place; and the other sons move out of the stem family with their families of procreation, if they have not done so already. So that, the only consistent role of the 'head' in the four-generation structures is seen to be as 'grandfather, (father), and son', while his seven other role-sets occur as casual fluctuations.

Now, the 'head's' brothers, who move away with their own families of procreation from the stem family, do not obviously form a collateral joint family. For, in that case, such families would have been found in the society in an appreciable (if not in very large) number. These families, respectively, may be patrilineally joint in character if one or more sons of these 'brothers' have their consorts in the family. However, even if the 'brothers' set off with their nuclear families of procreation (which must occur in large number of cases), eventually they become members of their respective joint families of procreation with the 'headship' of the family retained by them or devolved upon one son for each family, who continues with the family of orientation along with his own family of procreation.

Thus, the dominant sequence that we notice in the familial organization of West Bengal is that (a) a man may be born in a nuclear or a patrilineal jont family, (b) his family of orientation may be transformed from nuclear to joint or remain as joint or wither away, and (c) his family of procreation may also be his family of orientation or separately a nuclear or a joint family; *but* if he lives for a considerable time, he dies in a joint family which is also his family of procreation. The formation of the nuclear family appears to be a passing phase in the life cycle of a man—in the course of development of his family from nuclear to joint or its regression from joint to nuclear. The women do not count in the process because they are either unmarried daughters and sisters in one family or wives and mothers in another. What the process, on the other hand, substantiates, is that the joint structures break into nuclear but that the joint family *system* survives.

The validity of this interpretation will be examined further in a subsequent chapter when we shall discuss the *trend*—both demographic and longitudinal—of variation of family structures in West Bengal over time. For the present, we should ascertain the characteristics of those extended families which do not subscribe, partly or fully, to the patrilineal pattern of family organization because they comprise 11 per cent of the total number of family-units in West Bengal, a small but an appreciable share.

IV

Virtually all the extended families which do not subscribe to the patrilineal pattern of intra-family relations, fully or partly, were also found not to conform to any other consistent pattern formation of these relations; such as, matrilineal, matripatrilocal, avunculocal, natolocal, etc. [Murdock, 1949: 17ff]. We decided, therefore, to examine how these families deviate from the patrilineal pattern of family organization which has been found to be the dominant phenomenon in West Bengal society. Now, in terms of all the intra-family relations in each of these families, we can categorize them as subscribing partly to the patrilineal or not at all to that pattern, but we cannot categorize them further. On the other hand, with respect to one family member fixed as the point of reference, we may examine the nature and extent of deviation of intra-family relations in each of these families in substantial details. We may ascertain whether that person forms a patrilineal sub-structure in the family-unit with at least one more family member or a nuclear sub-structure or has to be identified individually by failing to draw the patrilineal or the nuclear pattern with any other family member. We may ascertain afterwards various characteristics of the family members who do not belong to this sub-structure but *adhere* to it.

Strictly speaking, the choice of this point of reference is not *sui generis* to the classification and analysis of family structures because any family member can represent this point. For a dynamic appraisal of family organization, however, that person should have a meaningful role in the family as representing the base of the family tree by the sub-structure he or she forms in it. In light of the role of the 'heads' of the nuclear and patrilineal joint families which we have already ascertained, the 'heads' of these families are therefore our best choice. We find, on this basis, that the kinship composition of most of these extended families is not unpatterned. They also do not show a distinctly different pattern from the patrilineal but register one ancillary to it. In about half of these families, the 'heads' form a nuclear sub-structure; otherwise the patrilineally joint sub-structure. Seldom, these 'heads' do not form the nuclear or the patrilineal sub-structure, as seen from Table 1.16.

Also the kins and affines who adhere to the basic sub-structure register a pattern which is not anachronistic to the patrilineal pattern of intra-family relations. Half of these families contain only these 'non-patrilineal' members who are related *lineally* to the base of the family tree as the 'head's' sister, father's sister,

TABLE 1.16

Substructures Formed by 'Heads' of Extended Families which do not Conform to the Patrilineal Pattern Fully or Partly		*Sample*	*Estimated Percentage* ($\pm$*s. e.*)
(1)		(2)	(3)
Self only:	a man	18	3.09±1.23
	a woman	10	3.31±1.55
Nuclear of the form:	intersibling	2	0.70±0.65
	husband-wife	34	6.77±1.95
	parent(s)—child(ren)	194	41.34±3.17
Patrilineally joint		182	44.79±3.00
Total		440	100.00

daughter, brother's or son's or father's brother's daughter, etc., or as their progeny. Sometimes a family is found which contains only those non-patrilineal members who are related *lineally-linked affinally* to the base of the family tree, as husbands of the lineally-related non-patrilineal relatives (for example, sister's husband) or, very rarely, as kins and affines of these husbands (for example, sister's husband's brother). But, by their separate or joint occurrence, these two categories of non-patrilineal extension account for three-fifths of the total number of these families. In most of the remaining ones, the non-patrilineal members trace their relationship through the women married into these families, namely, the 'head's' wife, his brother's wife, mother, father's brother's wife, etc. They are, thus, related *affinally* to the base of the family tree.[8]

[8]The above three kinds of extension from the patrilineal pattern can be ascertained from Formulae 1.2 and 1.3 which follow from Formula 1.1 and are prepared on the same basis:

$$[(E_m, E_{fu}, E_{fe}H)\ (F\ldots/B/Z\ldots)]\ [(\overline{S}_e, \overline{D}_e)\ (Z\ldots/D\ldots)]\ [(\overline{H},\overline{W})\ (K)], \qquad (1.2)$$

$$[(E_m, E_{fu}, E_{fe}H)\ (F\ldots/B/Z\ldots)\ (\overline{M},\overline{W})]\ [(K)], \qquad (1.3)$$

where:

(1) The first set of third brackets denotes that part of the basic structure which forms the trunk of the family tree and to which the family members who record kinship relations deviated from the patrilineal pattern are grafted.

(2) The second set of third brackets denotes the *lineally* and *affinally* deviated kinship relations for the Formulae (1.2) and (1.3), respectively.

TABLE 1.17

Strain(s) of Relationship of Non-patrilineal Family Members with the Base of Family Tree	*Sample*	*Estimated Percentage* ($\pm$*s.e.*)
(1)	(2)	(3)
Lineal only	212	50.50±3.73
Lineally-linked affinal only	5	0.48±0.45
Both	43	8.87±2.26
Affinal only	149	33.39±2.90
Affinal *and* lineal and/or lineally-linked affinal	31	6.76±1.23
Total	440	100.00

The affinally related non-patrilineal members are found more frequently in those families in which the 'heads' form a non-patrilineal base to the family tree, that is, a nuclear base mainly and a non-familial base occasionally. The indication is, thus, there that the women have a more effective role in the kinship composition of family when that family is totally out of the jurisdiction of patrilineal organization; for, with a nuclear base, the affinally related non-patrilineal members refer to the kins and affines of the 'head's' wife, as seen from Table 1.18.

For all these families taken together, however, the non-patrilineal extensions are mostly with, or through, the lineally related relatives. Thus, the kinship composition of the extended families

(3) The third set of third brackets in Formula (1.2) denotes the *lineally-linked affinally* deviated kinship relations.

(4) The notations S_e and D_e in Formula (1.2) are overlined because they denote in a notation-series the *beginning* of the lineally deviated kinship relations; for example, $E_m\ F\ S_e$, $E_m\ FBDD_u$, etc.

(5) The notations H and W are overlined in Formula (1.2) because they denote in a notation-series the *beginning* of the lineally-linked affinally deviated kinship relations; for example, E_mFSH_e, $E_m\ FBDZW_e$, etc.

(6) The notations M and W are overlined in Formula (1.3) because they denote in a notation-series the *source* of the affinally deviated kinship relations; for example, E_mWM_e, E_mMB_u, $E_m\ FBWS_u$, etc.

(7) The omnibus notation (K) in both the formulae stands for any permutation and combination of the kinship notations F, M, B, S, Z, D, H, and W.

TABLE 1.18

Strains of Relationship of Non-patrilineal Family Members with the Base of Family Tree	Sample		Estimated Percentage (±s.e.)	
	Non-patrilineally Joint	Patrilineally and Non-patrilineally Joint	Non-patrilineally Joint	Patrilineally and Non-patrilineally Joint
(1)	(2)	(3)	(4)	(5)
Lineal and/or lineally-linked affinal	133	127	50.56±3.79	71.30±4.46
Affinal only	108	41	41.06±3.52	23.94±3.89
Any combination of above 2 sets	17	14	8.38±1.82	4.76±1.57
Total	258	182	100.00	100.00

of West Bengal remains essentially as patrilineal and/or lineally related non-patrilineal, that is, broadly speaking, belonging to the group of 'same blood'. Other variations from the patrilineally joint structures are met with very infrequently.

TABLE 1.19

Strain(s) of Relationship in the Extended Families	Sample	Estimated Percentage (±s.e.)
(1)	(2)	(3)
Patrilineal and/or lineally related non-patrilineal	1269	85.85±1.09
Lineally-linked affinally related non-patrilineal only	5	0.14±0.13
Both sets	43	2.52±0.55
Affinally related non-patrilineal only	149	9.56±0.91
Affinally related non-patrilineal and one of first two sets or both	31	1.93±0.43
Total	1497	100.00

We discover further, from a detailed examination of the non-patrilineal members that their presence in these families is a transitory phenomenon, as dictated by social exigencies. They are widowed (and occasionally divorced or separated) women to most of whom these are their families of orientation; to virtually all the remaining ones, these are their daughter's or sister's family. They live in these families by themselves or with their family of procreation, or their family of procreation is found there without their concurrent presence.

TABLE 1.20*

Non-patrilineal Relatives of 'Heads' of Those Extended Families Which Do not Conform to the Patrilineal Pattern Fully or Partly		*Sample*	*Estimated percentage (±s.e.)*
(1)		(2)	(3)
Widowed, divorced or separated sister		60	13.08±2.11
Sister's family of procreation:	With sister	39	7.99±1.29
	Without sister	39	8.99±1.77
Widowed, divorced or separated daughter		14	3.67±1.48
Daughter's family of procreation:	With daughter	39	7.61±1.83
	Without daughter	11	1.88±1.00
Father's widowed sister		35	10.37±1.52
Father's sister's family of procreation:	With father's sister	4	1.04±0.70
	Without father's sister	4	1.53±0.90
Mother's widowed mother		7	1.86±1.02
Mother's mother's family of procreation		4	0.90±0.64
Mother's widowed sister		9	3.85±1.41
Mother's sister's family of procreation		3	0.27±0.32
Wife's widowed mother		35	9.25±2.92
Wife's mother's family of procreation:	With Wife's mother	5	0.77±0.52
	Without wife's mother	43	7.79±1.81
Wife's evermarried sister and/or her family of procreation		14	3.37±0.97
54 combinations of above relatives and/or others		75	15.78±2.30
Total		440	100.00

*As in other tables, in case the head of the family is a female, the relationships refer to her husband.

Pursuant to the social situation, these women must fall back upon their family of orientation for shelter and sustenance and/or of their family of procreation when these two basic needs for survival are denied in their husband's family of orientation and they are not in a position to fend for themselves and their 'families'. Also, failing this alternative, they must graft themselves on to the families of other relatives (such as, of their daughters, sisters, etc.); otherwise they become totally atomized as 'non-familial unit', as we have seen earlier. Anyhow, these 'additional' family members do not lead to the development of any other form of family organization in course of time. The progeny of a few of these women may continue to remain in the families to which they had grafted themselves; the overwhelming majority of them move out after growing up. Otherwise, besides the patrilineal, we would have detected other consistent pattern formation of intra-family relations in West Bengal society or a purely random assortment of relatives in these extended families.

These families, therefore, should conform to the sequential development of the family organization we have described earlier provided they exhibit characteristics corresponding to those of the patrilineally joint structures which we have found to be distinctive in this respect. We notice, accordingly, that in consideration of the number of generations they are constituted

TABLE 1.21

	Estimated Percentage (±s.e.)			
Number of Generations in Extended Families	*Non-patrilineally Joint Families*	*Partilineally and Non-patrilineally Joint Families*	*Fully or Partly Non-patrilineally Joint Families*	*Patrilineally Joint Families*
(1)	(2)	(3)	(4)	(5)
1	1.90±1.03	—	1.05±0.58	2.24±0.69
2	41.02±3.88	26.67±4.09	34.59±3.40	30.82±1.61
3	50.56±3.78	64.11±5.89	56.63±4.01	64.36±1.23
4	6.52±2.09	9.22±3.39	7.73±2.32	2.58±0.68
Total (Sample)	100.00 (258)	100.00 (182)	100.00 (440)	100.00 (1057)

of, the fully or partly non-patrilineal joint structures do not differ sharply from the purely patrilineal structures.

The non-patrilineally joint families are more of two generations, and less of three generations, than the patrilineally and non-patrilineally joint families correspondingly. This is because of the nuclear base of the family tree of the fully non-patrilineal joint structure and because in many cases the non-patrilineal members of these families (as the 'head's' siblings, their consorts, and/or their progeny) do not refer to such a generational difference between themselves and the 'heads' which is beyond that registered by the basic sub-structure. In some cases, of course, the kins and affines adhering to the basic sub-structure extend the generational expansion of these families (as they do also in the case of the partly non-patrilineal joint families) by being the 'head's' father's sister, mother's sister, mother's mother, wife's mother, etc. As a result, the four-generation structures are seen to be represented more for these families than for the purely patrilineal ones, and it can be surmised that these families must contain, correspondingly, more of those collateral relatives of

TABLE 1.22

Presence of the 'Head's' Collateral Relatives in the Extended Families	*Estimated Percentage (±s.e.)*			
	Non-patrilineally Joint Families			*Patrilineally Joint Families*
	'Head's' Sub-structure			
	Non-familial or Nuclear	*Patrilineally Joint*	*Combined*	
(1)	(2)	(3)	(4)	(5)
None	32.79±5.28	17.41±4.40	25.90±4.66	63.32±3.06
Siblings and/or constituents of siblings' family of procreation	43.22±3.59	56.38±6.71	49.11±4.42	34.24±2.52
Others, with or without above ones	23.99±4.07	26.21±4.03	24.99±2.15	2.44±0.79
Total	100.00	100.00	100.00	100.00
(Sample)	(258)	(182)	(440)	(1057)

the 'heads' who are not their siblings or belong to the family of procreation of these siblings. However, as for the patrilineal joint families, for these families also the latter class of collateral relatives of the 'heads' are found in substantial majorities.

Obviously, the absence of collateral relatives of the 'heads' cannot be so well marked for these families as for the patrilineally joint ones because it is essentially the presence of such non-patrilineal relatives that has led to the formation of these extended structures. We notice, however, that for these families also the 'head's' siblings and/or the constituents of the family of procreation of these siblings fall out successively as we proceed along the number of generations these familes are constituted of. There is a corresponding gain in those family structures which do not contain any collateral relative of the 'heads'; that is, they contain non-patrilineal relatives referring only to the family of procreation of the 'heads' as, mostly, their daughter's family and, occasionally, the parent(s)-in-law. On the other hand, the families with 'other collateral relatives of the 'heads' register a relatively larger representation in three- and four-generation structures than in the two-generation ones for reasons stated already.

TABLE 1.23

Presence of 'Head's' Collateral Relatives in Those Extended Families Which Do not Conform to the Patrilineal Pattern, Fully or Partly	*Estimated Percentage (±s.e.)*			
	One-generation Structures	*Two-generation Structures*	*Three-generation Structures*	*Four-generation Structures*
(1)	(2)	(3)	(4)	(5)
None	—	6.81±2.63	36.17±6.20	39.58± 8.42
Siblings and/or the constituents of the siblings' family of procreation	100.00	76.77±4.71	35.94±7.21	14.97±10.01
Others, with or without above ones	—	16.42±3.53	27.89±3.29	45.45±12.68
Total (Sample)	100.00 (10)	100.00 (161)	100.00 (245)	100.00 (24)

Thus, barring certain variations *sui generis* to the manner of formation of these families, the extended families which do not conform, fully or partly, to the patrilineal pattern of intra-family relations are found to be similar in structural articulation and elaboration to the patrilineal joint families. By representing a transient formation in the society, as we have explained already, they register therefore another form of variation around the central tendency in the evolution of family organization in West Bengal society. For, in more than half of the cases they refer to the return of the 'daughters' to the 'stem families' and/or the movement of their family of procreation to these families. Also, in the remaining cases they refer to those persons and/or their 'families' to whom shelter and sustenance were not available even in their family of orientation.

The sequential development of family organization, which we have outlined earlier for the West Bengal society, is not disturbed therefore by the occurrence of those extended families which do not conform to the patrilineal pattern of intra-family relations, fully or partly.

CHAPTER TWO

Interrelations

From an examination of the composition of family-units in terms of forms of marriage, kinship relations and role-positions of the heads of the units, a pattern of *internal* variations of the West Bengal family structures in 1960-61 has emerged in Chapter 1. This pattern has emphasized the paradigm of three structural categories: non-familial unit, nuclear family, and extended family, irrespective of their further variations and consequent categorization. In this chapter, therefore, we shall examine the interrelationships between each of these three family structure categories, on the one hand, and those other categories of social stratification, on the other, which, within our resources, may unfold a pattern of *external* variations of the West Bengal family structures in the space perspective; that is, for the state as a whole at the given point of time 1960-61.

Pursuant to the overall predominance of nuclear structures in West Bengal society, we find that under any *one* kind of social stratification (for example, rural *or* urban habitation, agriculture *or* manufacture as the source of livelihood, non-manual *or* manual occupations of the people, their religion and caste-wise grouping, literacy, etc.) the incidence of nuclear families is larger or, at the least, equal to that of the extended families. The only exception was found when the family-wise joint obligations or indebtedness of the people were considered as respective kinds of social stratification. However, if we examine the *relative* incidence of the non-familial units and the nuclear and extended families, respectively, among the categories of different kinds of social stratification, distinctive variations may come to light and lead us to elicit any pattern for the West Bengal family structures in the space perspective.

Thus, beginning with the rural-urban stratification of West Bengal society, we find that although the extended family is generally hypothesized as a concomitant of the rural way of life and the nuclear fmaily of the urban, the coresident and commensal kingroups of West Bengal are predominantly nuclear in the rural areas, whether or not we consider the non-familial units along with the family-units. Contrastingly, in the urban areas there is no significant difference (even at the 10 per cent probability level) between the relative incidence of the nuclear and the extended families, with or without taking the non-familial units into account.

TABLE 2.1

Habitation	*Estimated Percentage to Total* ($\pm$*s.e.*)			
	Non-familial Unit	*Nuclear Family*	*Extended Family*	*Total* (*Sample*)
(1)	(2)	(3)	(4)	(5)
Rural	9.19±1.66	58.73±3.52	32.08±2.09	100.00 (2903)
Urban	24.15±4.89	40.87±2.05	34.98±4.98	100.00 (2031)
(considering family-units only)				
Rural		64.67±3.87	35.33±3.87	100.00 (2626)
Urban		53.88±4.07	46.12±4.07	100.00 (1493)

The non-familial units occur more frequently in the urban than in the rural areas, which are also found to occur more frequently in the cities than in the towns. There is no significant difference, however, in the proportional incidence of the nuclear families in

TABLE 2.2

Habitation	*Estimated Percentage to Total* ($\pm$*s.e.*)			
	Non-familial Unit	*Nuclear Family*	*Extended Family*	*Total* (*Sample*)
(1)	(2)	(3)	(4)	(5)
Town	15.90±0.16	42.82±3.06	41.28±2.98	100.00 (897)
City	32.53±4.44	38.88±3.54	28.59±4.01	100.00 (1134)
(considering family-units only)				
Town		50.92±3.18	49.08±3.18	100.00 (738)
City		57.63±3.54	42.37±3.54	100.00 (755)

the towns and cities. Also, the extended families are seen to occur more frequently in the towns than in the cities only if the non-familial units are taken into account; that is, the distinction is due to the very high incidence of the latter in the cities.

Within the rural areas, a classification of villages by their distance from any urban location (which is generally assumed to indicate the potentiality of urbanization) does not bring out any difference in the kinship structure of the villages either nearer the urban areas or away from them.

TABLE 2.3

Distance of Villages (in miles) from Urban Centre	*Estimated Percentage to Total (±s.e.)*			
	Non-familial Unit	*Nuclear Family*	*Extended Family*	*Total (Sample)*
(1)	(2)	(3)	(4)	(5)
10 or less	9.33±2.18	58.76±4.66	31.91±2.73	100.00 (2087)
11 or more	8.74±1.54	58.66±1.05	32.60±1.32	100.00 (816)
	(considering family-units only)			
10 or less		64.80±3.41	35.20±3.41	100.00 (1869)
11 or more		64.28±0.96	35.72±0.96	100.00 (757)

Another way to examine intra-rural variations in kinship composition would be to classify the villages in terms of the ecological zones of a state. In view of the available samples of villages and families, the smallness of the coastal and the sub-Himalayan forest belts, and their congruity with the riverine and the hill area, respectively—(as tested statistically by considering the data for the five ecological zones of West Bengal)—three areas may be considered for the present purpose: (1) riverine, including the coastal area; (2) arid plain; and (3) hill area, including the sub-Himalayan forest belt. Under this form of categorization, the nuclear families occur a little less frequently in the riverine than in the other two areas, but we do not observe any uniform pattern to coalesce the other two. For, according to the incidence of the extended families, the arid and riverine areas should then be regarded as one; just as the riverine and hill areas should be so considered according to the incidence of the non-familial units.

Also, by excluding the non-familial units, a consistently decreasing trend is noticed for the incidence of the nuclear families from the hill to the arid plain area, and then to the riverine; and a correspondingly reverse trend for the incidence of the extended families. But the trend may be due to sampling fluctuations because only between the polar ends of the hill and the riverine area a significant difference is registered for the incidence of the nuclear or the extended families.

TABLE 2.4

Ecological Zones of Rural West Bengal	*Estimated Percentage of total* (±*s.e.*)			
	Non-familial Unit	*Nuclear Family*	*Extended Family*	*Total* (*Sample*)
(1)	(2)	(3)	(4)	(5)
Hill area and sub-Himalayan forest belt	13.04±2.64	65.24±3.36	21.72±3.01	100.00 (442)
Arid plain	5.49±0.27	63.89±1.75	30.62±1.56	100.00 (838)
Riverine and coastal	11.00±0.97	55.05±2.64	33.95±1.93	100.00 (1623)
	(considering family-units only)			
Hill area and sub-Himalayan forest belt		75.02±4.29	24.98±4.29	100.00 (375)
Arid plain		67.60±2.98	32.40±2.98	100.00 (791)
Riverine and coastal		61.86±3.02	38.14±3.02	100.00 (1460)

Thus, whatever may be the nature and extent of internal variations of the rural areas (which a much larger sample than available may elicit), three segments of the state of West Bengal come up for our present consideration: the cities, towns, and the villages. If we, therefore, collate the data from Tables 2.1 and 2.2 and test the statistical significance of the collated percentage figures given in Table 2.5, we come to the following conclusions:

(1) The non-familial units clearly register an increasing trend from the villages to the towns and, then, to the cities as (v—t—c).

(2) The nuclear families record an increasing trend from the cities and/or towns to the villages as (c/t—v), since the city and

town segments of the society are not differentiated on this account whether or not the non-familial units are taken into consideration.

(3) The extended famlies definitely register an increasing trend from the villages to the towns as (v—t), but the cities behave indeterminately: they equate to the villages as (v/c—t) if the non-familial units are taken into account, but to the towns as (v—t/c) if the non-familial units are ignored.

TABLE 2.5

Habitation	Estimated Percentage to Total (±s.e.) Non-familial Unit	Nuclear Family	Extended Family	Total (Sample)	
(1)	(2)	(3)	(4)	(5)	
Village	9.19±1.66	58.73±3.52	32.08±2.09	100.00	(2903)
Town	15.90±0.16	42.82±3.06	41.28±2.98	100.00	(897)
City	32.53±4.44	38.88±3.54	28.59±4.01	100.00	(1134)
		(considering family-units only)			
Village		64.67±3.41	35.33±3.41	100.00	(2626)
Town		50.92±3.95	49.08±3.95	100.00	(738)
City		57.63±4.17	42.37±4.17	100.00	(755)

II

It follows that while the internal variations of both the rural and urban areas of West Bengal would be worth exploring, no incisive pattern of family structures can yet be discerned within them. The imprecise picture we obtain may be due to the size of samples, althogh it is reasonably large. Also, this may be due to the fact that the rural-urban difference is a *secondary* expression of its association with some other facets of the social structure with which the variations in family structures are directly associated. However, the rural-urban dichotomy, which our family structure data definitely assure, presents evidence contrary to the general belief that the ruralites live more under the extended and the urbanites more under the nuclear family organization.

Now, the rural-urban dichotomy (and even the village-town-city spectrum) may be reflected, to an extent, in the economic organization of the people. Agriculture is restricted to the villages; manufacture and the pursuits like 'service' in various kinds of establishments and independent 'profession' (of medicine, law, etc.) are largely to be found in the cities than elsewhere; and the sources of livelihood like handicrafts, trade and commerce (mainly retail trade) would be spread over the cities, towns and villages. We may, therefore, examine next the economic stratification of West Bengal society.

In order to be precise and comprehensive regarding the economic structure of a society vis-a-vis its family structures, several details of the economic activities of any and all members of the units of enquiry were collected during the 1960-61 survey and, on that basis, the affiliation of these units to particular categories of economic attributes were determined objectively in-sofar as that is possible in an interview method of survey (*vide*, Blocks 2 and 12 of aforementioned Schedules 1.0 and 1.1). Data on the principal (or only) source of livelihood of our units of enquiry were recorded under an exhaustive classification of the 'industry' (that is, the sector of the national economy) to which the member(s) of these units are engaged. In order to bring this classification into a manageable number of categories, the relative incidence of the non-familial units, nuclear families, and the extended families under all possible categories of this form of classification were tested for statistical significance and those categories which did not register any significant difference were pooled together. The process yielded ultimately 4 derived categories: 'agriculture', 'handicrafts, trade and commerce, and other ancillary activities (for example, transport and communication)', 'manufacture, service and profession', and the non-productive source of livelihood as 'dependence on others'.

We notice according to this arrangement, as given in Table 2.6, that the proportional representations of the non-familial units, nuclear families, and extended families are about the same for the 'manufacture, etc.', as we had found earlier for the cities. Correspondingly, as we had found for the villages, the proportional representation of the nuclear families is the highest and of the non-familial units the lowest in the 'agriculture' category. And the category of 'handicrafts, etc.', behaves in between the above two, especially in regard to the incidence of the non-familial units, as we had found for the towns. On the other hand, the category of 'dependence on others', which would be spread all over the society, behaves in a unique manner. It is predominantly represented by the non-familial units, while it occurs in about the same proportion for the nuclear or the extended families.

TABLE 2.6

Only or the Principal Source of Livelihood	*Estimated Percentage to Total (±s.e.)*			*Total (Sample)*	
	Non-familial Unit	*Nuclear Family*	*Extended Family*		
(1)	(2)	(3)	(4)	(5)	
Agriculture	6.62±1.48	59.90±3.56	33.48±2.33	100.00	(2225)
Handicrafts, etc.	14.49±3.34	51.34±2.81	34.17±4.25	100.00	(1484)
Manufacture, etc.	31.03±4.51	37.96±2.49	31.01±4.76	100.00	(1100)
Non-productive (dependence)	57.37±6.66	23.21±3.81	19.42±4.43	100.00	(125)
(considering family-units only)					
Agriculture		64.15±3.78	35.85±3.78	100.00	(2091)
Handicrafts, etc.		60.02±4.14	39.98±4.14	100.00	(1235)
Manufacture, etc.		55.04±4.39	44.96±4.39	100.00	(728)
Non-productive (dependence)		54.46±4.76	45.54±4.76	100.00	(65)

We notice further from Table 2.6, as we had found for the city-town-village spectrum, that the non-familial units and the nuclear families register two distinct counter trends. The relative incidence of the former increases consistently from 'agriculture' to 'handicrafts, etc.', then to 'manufacture, etc.', and finally to the non-productive source of livelihood. Correspondingly, the trend for the latter is exactly reversed, although the distinction between 'handicrafts, etc.' and 'agriculture' is now significant only at the 10 per cent probability level. We also notice that the productive sources of livelihood do not register any significant differences among them in regard to the incidence of the extended families. These categories represent *en bloc* a higher incidence of the extended families than the category of non-productive source of livelihood. Interestingly, if the non-familial units are not taken into account, the relative incidence of either the nuclear or the extended families do not register any significant difference among all the sources of livelihood—productive or non-productive.

Thus, the city-town-village spectrum is reflected by the principal (or only) source of livelihood of the non-familial units and the family-units. In fact, as we see from Table 2.7 (which collates the data in Tables 2.5 and 2.6), the two kinds of social stratification yield virtually the same result.

TABLE 2.7

Two Kinds of Social Stratification	*Estimated Percentage to Total (±s.e.)*			*Total*
	Non-familial Unit	*Nuclear Family*	*Extended Family*	
(1)	(2)	(3)	(4)	(5)
Village	9.19±1.66	58.73±3.51	32.08±2.09	100.00
Agriculture	6.62±1.48	59.90±3.56	33.48±2.23	100.00
Town	15.90±0.16	42.82±3.06	41.28±2.98	100.00
Handicrafts, etc.	14.49±3.34	51.34±2.82	34.17±4.25	100.00
City	32.53±4.44	38.88±3.54	28.59±4.01	100.00
Manufacture, etc.	31.03±4.51	37.96±2.49	31.01±4.76	100.00
Dependence on others	57.37±6.66	23.21±3.81	19.42±4.43	100.00
(considering the family-units only)				
Village		64.67±3.87	35.33±3.87	100.00
Agriculture		64.15±3.78	35.85±3.78	100.00
Handicrafts, etc.		60.02±4.14	39.98±4.14	100.00
Town		50.92±3.18	49.08±3.18	100.00
City		57.63±3.54	42.37±3.54	100.00
Manufacture, etc.		55.04±4.39	44.96±4.96	100.00
Dependence on others		54.46±4.76	45.54±4.76	100.00

III

We may, accordingly, leave aside the rural-urban differentiations and proceed with other forms of stratification relating to the economic organization of West Bengal society. Next to the principal (or only) source[1] of livelihood of our respective units

1. The principal source of livelihood of a family-unit (and of a non-familial unit) refers to the sector of the national economy in which the main or the only earner of the unit is principally engaged, and relates to his or her activity status and occupation in that context.

of enquiry, we may examine (a) the activity status of the person who (mainly or exclusively) provides for each family-unit or represents a non-familial unit, and (b) what is his or her principal or only occupation. Afterwards, we may combine these three attributes in order to ascertain any distinctive pattern of variation in family structures in West Bengal with reference to the peoples' participation in the national economy. For these three attributes are directly interlinked according to the specifications of the 1960–61 survey of family structures in West Bengal.

In terms of 'activity status', the family structures of the 'employers' and the 'self-employeds' are seen from Table 2.8 to be of the same pattern, whether or not the non-familial units are taken into account. The 'employees' are distinguished from them in two ways: (a) they form a relatively less number of extended families and more nuclear families, if the non-familial units are ignored; or (b) they are appreciably represented as non-familial units while recording a similar incidence of nuclear families as the 'employers' and the 'self-employeds'. We also notice from Table 2.8 that, like those with the non-productive sources of livelihood (Table 2.6), the 'unoccupied' category is overwhelmingly represented by the non-familial units, and in about equal but small proportions by the nuclear and extended families. Thus, the activity status distinguishes the gainfully occupied persons mainly with reference to the fact of: (a) working for others; and (b) living as non-familial units or in nuclear families.

TABLE 2.8

Activity Status of Main or Only Earner	*Estimated Percentage to Total (±s.e.)*			*Total (Sample)*	
	Non-familial Unit	*Nuclear Family*	*Extended Family*		
(1)	(2)	(3)	(4)	(5)	
Employer	7.91±2.32	48.68±3.88	43.41±3.56	100.00	(417)
Self-employed	5.48±1.79	54.18±2.98	40.34±3.32	100.00	(1685)
Employee	18.58±2.91	55.75±3.97	25.67±2.26	100.00	(2691)
Unoccupied	55.99±5.89	24.27±3.36	19.74±4.56	100.00	(141)
	(considering family-units only)				
Employer		52.86±4.01	47.14±4.01	100.00	(384)
Self-employed		58.76±3.75	41.24±3.75	100.00	(1559)
Employee		68.47±4.04	31.53±4.04	100.00	(2100)
Unoccupied		55.14±6.93	44.86±6.93	100.00	(76)

Data on occupation produce a very large number of primary categories which can be pooled into two broad categories of non-manual and manual occupations. The commonly labelled dichotomy of 'white collar' and 'blue collar' workers somewhat characterizes these two categories. Anyway, no distinction can be observed through this manner of categorization in the proportional incidence of the family structure categories by the principal occupation of the non-familial units and that of the main or only earner of the family-units.

TABLE 2.9

Principal Occupation of Main or Only Earner	*Estimated Percentage to Total (±s.e.)*			*Total (Sample)*	
	Non-familial Unit	*Nuclear Family*	*Extended Family*		
(1)	(2)	(3)	(4)	(5)	
Non-manual	12.16±1.44	53.86±2.80	33.98±2.23	100.00	(1610)
Manual	14.40±3.28	54.73±3.36	30.87±1.76	100.00	(3183)
(considering family-units only)					
Non-manual		60.42±2.97	39.58±2.97	100.00	(1382)
Manual		65.46±3.46	34.54±3.46	100.00	(2661)

The non-manual occupations, however, can be further characterized as of 'high' grade (that is, requiring a good deal of mental work), 'medium' grade (that is, requiring some mental work), and of 'low' grade (that is, requiring such mental work as can be undertaken by anyone). Correspondingly, the manual occupations can be characterized as skilled, semi-skilled, or unskilled (see the Appendix to Chapter 6 in Part 2). This form of categorization was found in earlier researches to reveal the social reality more precisely [Mukherjee, 1961a:157–67]. Accordingly, six derived categories of occupations were prepared and tested for statistically significant differences among them with reference to the proportional incidence of the non-familial units, nuclear families, and extended families. The process yielded two combined categories furnishing the significant information that the extended family structure occurs more frequently among those living on high or middle grade non-manual and skilled manual occupations and, conversely, the nuclear family structure occurs more frequently among those living on low grade non-manual and semi-skilled or unskilled manual occupations. Also, the relative incidence of the non-familial units is more in the latter than in the former combined category.

TABLE 2.10

Grading of the Principal Occupation of Main or only Earner	*Estimated Percentage to Total* ($\pm$*s.e.*)			
	Non-familial Unit	*Nuclear Family*	*Extended Family*	*Total* (*Sample*)
(1)	(2)	(3)	(4)	(5)
'High'/'middle' non-manual *or* skilled manual	8.62±1.23	49.89±3.08	41.49±2.49	100.00 (2696)
'Low' non-manual *or* semi/unskilled manual	16.74±3.60	59.60±3.68	23.66±1.57	100.00 (2097)
(considering family-units only)				
'High'/'middle' non-manual *or* skilled manual		54.60±3.43	45.40±3.43	100.00 (2392)
'Low' non-manual *or* semi/unskilled manual		71.59±3.75	28.41±3.75	100.00 (1651)

Now, if we combine the grading of occupations shown in Table 2.10 with their corresponding sources of livelihood, we can elicit more precise information which, in a large measure, will also take into account the attribute of 'activity status'. Thus, we find from Table 2.11 that the non-manual 'low' grade or semi-skilled and unskilled manual occupations under 'agriculture' denote the following characteristics: (a) comprise the largest bulk of the sample of family-units and non-familial units in view of their demographic density in the society at large; (b) refer to the sharecroppers and agricultural wage-labourers who have a distinctly important position in the economic structure of West Bengal [Mukherjee, 1957; 1961a]; and (c) record the largest incidence of the nuclear family structures as compared to all other social groups under consideration. Correspondingly, the non-manual 'high' or 'middle' grade or skilled manual occupations under 'agriculture' denote the following characteristics: (a) comprise the next largest bulk of the sample of family-units and non-familial units; (b) refer to the supervisory farmers and self-sustaining cultivators who have the complementary role to play vis-a-vis the sharecroppers and agricultural wage-labourers in West Bengal economic structure [ibid.]; and (c) record the largest incidence of the extended family structures.

We also find from Table 2.11 that, while the above two social groups account for nearly half of the total sample in view of their demographic density in West Bengal society, the distinction by the grading of occupations (irrespective of the distinction by the sources of livelihood) is maintained for the extended families whether or not the non-familial units are taken into account. On the other hand, with reference to the relative incidence of

TABLE 2.11

Principal Source of Livelihood and the Grading of Occupation as I or II		*Estimated Percentage to Total (±s.e.)*			
		Non-familial Unit	*Nuclear Family*	*Extended Family*	*Total*
(1)		(2)	(3)	(4)	(5)
Agriculture	I	4.54±0.95	52.74±3.67	42.72±3.04	100.00
Handicrafts, etc.	I	8.62±3.34	49.86±3.41	41.52±3.84	100.00
Manufacture, etc.	I	17.21±2.95	43.93±3.74	38.86±4.57	100.00
Handicrafts, etc.	II	36.96±5.99	41.64±6.43	21.40±6.06	100.00
Manufacture, etc.	II	38.84±5.73	42.28±4.23	18.88±3.25	100.00
Agriculture	II	8.40±2.39	66.03±3.14	25.57±1.85	100.00
(considering family-units only)					
Agriculture	I		55.25±3.45	44.75±3.45	100.00
Handicrafts, etc.	I		54.55±3.55	45.45±3.55	100.00
Manufacture, etc.	I		53.06±4.75	46.94±4.75	100.00
Agriculture	II		72.08±2.21	27.92±2.21	100.00
Handicrafts, etc.	II		66.05±8.73	33.95±8.73	100.00
Manufacture, etc.	II		70.28±5.09	29.72±5.09	100.00

Grading of occupations: I Non-manual 'high' or 'middle' grade, skilled manual
II Non-manual 'low' grade, semi-skilled and unskilled manual

the nuclear families, the distinction by the 'lower' occupational category of 'agriculture' vis-a-vis either occupational category of the other sources of livelihood becomes relevant when the non-familial units are taken into account, while only the grading of occupations (and not the source of livelihood categories) becomes relevant if the non-familial units are ignored.

We have commented in Chapter 1 that if we ignore the non-familial units, we would somewhat artificially truncate the total field of variation in family structures. But we have also shown in that chapter that the non-familial units are of a passing and ancillary relevance to the family organization of West Bengal society. Hence, the above findings are of significant importance to our present course of analysis, as will be confirmed later in this chapter. For the present, we may note that groups in West Bengal to denote a pattern of variation in family structures begin to emerge in terms of the economic structure of the society, which we had found for the Bengali society as early as in 1942 [Mukherjee, 1971a: 241].

IV

Let us now examine some other attributes of social stratification which are essentially 'economic' in content and could be expected on *a priori* considerations to denote variations in the incidence of the non-familial units, nuclear families, and extended families in the society. The qualifying characteristics of 'residence' of each non-familial unit and family-unit may be one of them; namely: (a) whether the residence is owned by the unit or not; (b) if owned, whether it is inherited from some person or acquired by one or more unit members; (c) if the residence is not owned, whether it is rented by the unit or provided by someone else, like, the employer of one of the family members or of the non-familial unit; and (d) whether the legal rights on the residence (owned or not) are vested on one person in each family (and on the non-familial unit exclusively) or on more than one person.

These characteristics of the attribute of 'residence' may be regarded to be related directly to any differential incidence of the non-familial units, nuclear families and extended families, for they refer to the ownership and/or utilization of the most stable form of property concerned with the operation of ccresident and commensal kingroups. No doubt, the source of livelihood, occupation and activity status are necessary for the physical existence of an individual or a kingroup. It may be argued, however, that while the livelihood characteristics reflect the societal background and other related matters, the ownership and/or utilization of the residence would, firstly, reflect the impact of these societal features on the family organization more substantially; secondly, the cumulative contribution of the societal forces generated from the past may be particularly expressed through the inheritance of residence by the units of enquiry; and, thirdly, the ownership or tenancy rights on the residence may have a significant role to play in the present context according as these rights are vested on only one individual or a number of persons jointly.

For these reasons, it is not uncommonly assumed that if the residence is owned by a unit of enquiry (and especially if it is inherited), there would be an incentive to live under the extended family organization. Alternatively, it is supposed that if the legal rights on the residence (owned or not) is vested on more than one person, the incidence of extended family structures would be greater than if the rights were vested on one person exclusively. On the other hand, very little is known or assumed regarding any difference in the incidence of the non-familial units, nuclear families, and extended families according as their residences are rented or merely provided by someone. We may, therefore, examine the association between the characteristics of 'residence' of our units of enquiry and the relative incidence of different forms of family structure.

Table 2.12 shows in this respect that: (a) the residence of the non-familial units is preponderantly as provided by someone (e.g., the employer under whom, in many cases, he or she is working as a 'domestic', an apprentice, etc.) and (b) the families living in rented buildings or apartments are relatively less prone to form the extended family structure. On the other hand, the ownership of the residence by the units of enquiry does not produce any variation in the relative incidence of nuclear or extended families (although they seldom live as non-familial units), irrespective of the ownership being inherited or acquired. Correspondingly, the legal rights of residence vested on one or a number of persons have no role to play in any differential incidence of the non-familial units, nuclear families, and extended families. Incidentally, Table 2.12 also shows that if the non-familial units are ignored, the attribute of 'residence' is irrelevant to variations in the incidence of nuclear or extende family structures.

TABLE 2.12

Residence		Estimated Percentage to Total (±s.e)			
		Non-familial Unit	Nuclear Family	Extended Family	Total (Sample)
(1)		(2)	(3)	(4)	(5)
Provided		55.44±4.17	29.12±4.04	15.44±2.69	100.00 (570)
Rented		21.62±4.28	55.44±4.29	22.94±2.76	100.00 (1517)
Either way		33.66±4.36	42.64±4.51	23.70±3.08	100.00 (2087)
Ownership:	Owned	6.68±9.15	57.34±3.46	35.98±3.15	100.00 (2847)
	Inherited	7.51±8.34	56.54±4.42	35.95±2.96	100.00 (2195)
	Acquired	6.29±9.79	57.36±3.28	36.35±3.20	100.00 (652)
Rights on residence:	Single	11.71±2.15	56.65±2.62	31.64±2.20	100.00 (3271)
	Joint	14.61±2.19	52.17±3.84	33.22±2.49	100.00 (1663)
		(considering family-units only)			
Provided			68.29±5.04	31.71±5.04	100.00 (254)
Rented			60.07±3.88	39.93±3.88	100.00 (1189)
Either way			64.27±4.21	35.73±4.21	100.00 (1443)
Ownership:	Owned		61.45±3.76	38.55±3.76	100.00 (2676)
	Inherited		60.82±5.01	39.18±5.01	100.00 (2052)
	Acquired		62.19±3.46	37.81±3.46	100.00 (624)
Rights on residence:	Single		60.87±3.37	39.13±3.37	100.00 (2888)
	Joint		62.18±3.91	37.82±3.91	100.00 (1231)

The stratification of the units of enquiry by any other property which they may possess (through inheritance or as personally acquired), and the ownership of such properties by one or more than one person, produce the same result as found regarding the residential property. Those who do not possess any such property are less prone to live in an extended family, and an appreciable number of them live as non-familial units. Otherwise, no distinction is noticed from Table 2.13 in regard to the characteristics of such properties.

The ownership of property of any kind, therefore, does not appear to be a relevant form of social stratification to appraise variations in West Bengal family structures. There is however.

TABLE 2.13

Possession of Property other than the Residence		Estimated Percentage to Total (±s.e.)			
		Non-familial Unit	Nuclear Family	Extended Family	Total (Sample)
(1)		(2)	(3)	(4)	(5)
None		18.27±2.49	56.36±4.35	25.37±2.73	100.00 (2948)
Some	Inherited	7.01±1.79	52.29±2.34	40.70±1.94	100.00 (1354)
	Acquired	9.39±1.92	46.78±2.60	43.83±2.32	100.00 (632)
	Either way	7.32±1.59	50.32±2.87	42.36±2.26	100.00 (1986)
Ownership of property	Single	5.45±1.43	52.84±2.62	41.71±2.75	100.00 (1249)
	Joint	9.07±1.50	46.54±2.36	44.39±2.18	100.00 (737)
			(considering family-units only)		
None			68.96±3.81	31.04±3.81	100.00 (2327)
Some	Inherited		56.14±3.23	43.86±3.23	100.00 (1232)
	Acquired		51.28±3.41	48.72±3.41	100.00 (560)
	Either way		54.20±3.48	45.80±3.48	100.00 (1792)
Ownership of property	Single		55.69±3.36	44.31±3.36	100.00 (1156)
	Joint		49.28±3.51	50.72±3.51	100.00 (636)

another set of societal characteristics which are essentially 'economic' in content and are not only inherited but also have to be voluntarily acquired. They may, therefore, effect variations in family structures more rigorously than the attributes of property-ownership. The fulfilment of various kinds of 'familial obligations' and repaying 'familial indebtedness' are major examples of such features in a society because they naturally devolve from the ancestor(s) to the descendants in a family but whether or not the descendants will accept the liability may depend, largely or entirely, upon them. It could be assumed, therefore, that the units of enquiry in which 'familial obligations and/or indebtedness' are acknowledged would be more prone to form the extended family organization, especially if these liabilities are inherited and/or shared jointly by a number of persons.

We find, in this respect, from Table 2.14 that relatively more non-familial units than family-units are free from any 'familial indebtedness', while it is 'inherited relatively more in the nuclear than in the extended families. Unlike the former, the latter contingency is not usually expected; however, it refers to a very small coverage of West Bengal society as evident from the sample involved. Anyhow, the most distinctive feature of both Tables 2.14 and 2.15 is that in case the familial obligations and/or indebtedness are shared jointly by more than one person, there is a marked tendency to live in an extended family. But, as seen from the samples thus involved, the societal coverage of such cases is so small as to be virtually insignificant to record variations in West Bengal family structures, even though they are relevant to explain the mechanics of family organization *per se.*

TABLE 2.14

Familial Indebtedness		*Estimated Percentage to Total (±s.e.)*				
		Non-familial Unit	*Nuclear Family*	*Extended Family*	*Total*	*(Sample)*
(1)		(2)	(3)	(4)	(5)	
Absent		21.30±2.45	48.33±3.74	30.37±2.22	100.00	(2545)
Present	Inherited	7.76±3.80	68.96±4.54	23.28±4.01	100.00	(116)
	Acquired	11.61±2.74	55.48±3.13	32.91±3.25	100.00	(2273)
	Either way	11.43±1.67	56.13±1.67	32.44±2.69	100.00	(2389)
Individual concern		11.46±2.39	56.89±1.47	31.65±2.11	100.00	(2322)
Shared jointly		10.45±4.28	29.85±3.97	59.70±5.04	100.00	(67)
		(considering family-units only)				
Absent			58.29±3.39	41.71±3.39	100.00	(2003)
Present	Inherited		74.77±3.78	25.23±3.78	100.00	(107)
	Acquired		62.77±3.58	37.23±3.58	100.00	(2009)
	Either way		64.31±3.21	35.69±3.21	100.00	(2116)
Individual concern			64.25±2.81	35.75±2.81	100.00	(2056)
Shared jointly			33.33±4.92	66.67±4.92	100.00	(60)

We find from Tables 2.14 and 2.15 that except the remarkable but insignificant instances mentioned above, the attributes of 'familial obligations and/or indebtedness' do not have any effect on the relative incidence of the non-familial units, nuclear families, and extended families, just as we had found earlier with reference to the attributes of property-ownership. It follows, therefore, that insofar as the economic aspects of social stratification is concerned, variations in West Bengal family structures are to be examined with reference to the economic structure of the society as given by the source of livelihood and the occupation on which, wholly or mainly, the respective non-familial units and family-units depend.

TABLE 2.15

Familial Indebtedness	Estimated Percentage to Total (±s.e.)			
	Non-familial Unit	*Nuclear Family*	*Extended Family*	*Total (Sample)*
(1)	(2)	(3)	(4)	(5)
Absent	16.61±3.59	55.98±4.34	27.41±1.47	100.00 (3171)
Present Inherited	9.84±4.17	56.55±4.28	33.61±3.89	100.00 (122)
Present Acquired	9.08±2.81	50.94±3.03	39.98±3.52	100.00 (1641)
Present Either way	9.30±3.60	51.30±4.26	39.40±2.18	100.00 (1763)
Individual concern	6.92±1.64	55.02±2.40	38.06±2.54	100.00 (1583)
Shared jointly	10.72±6.04	15.59±4.79	73.69±6.79	100.00 (180)
		(considering family-units only)		
Absent		67.13±3.87	32.87±3.87	100.00 (2517)
Present Inherited		62.73±3.66	37.27±3.66	100.00 (110)
Present Acquired		56.03±3.11	43.97±3.11	100.00 (1492)
Present Either way		57.49±3.59	42.51±3.59	100.00 (1602)
Individual concern		60.89±2.72	39.11±2.72	100.00 (1456)
Shared jointly		17.46±6.06	82.54±6.06	100.00 (146)

V

Corresponding to the attributes of 'economic' content, we may examine those which are regarded to be essentially 'social' in content. These attributes—ascribed by the customary, conventional, juridical, familial or personal organization in society—may be voluntary or involuntary in nature. Either way, they should be examined since they are not infrequently assumed to have a bearing on the relative incidence of the non-familial units, nuclear families, and extended families in a society. Needless to say, we shall examine those characteristics of these attributes which are particularly relevant to West Bengal society or which, in that context, may form 'residual' groups especially because the samples available for the latter do not warrant (or are found unnecessary for) the examination of any internal variation within the omnibus groupings. We should also mention that these attributes will refer directly to the 'heads' of family-units or to the non-familial units, for any intra-family variation in their respects was found to be virtually absent from the survey data.

We may, thus, begin with the 'mother tongue'—a familial and

involuntary attribute—which is categorized for the present course of analysis as Bengali or non-Bengali; and, correspondingly, the 'regional mooring'—a personal and voluntary attribute—which denotes whether the 'head' of a unit considers himself or herself to belong to West Bengal or elsewhere.[2] We find from Table 2.16 that in respect of these two attributes the non-Bengalis live in an appreciable number as non-familial units and relatively less in extended families.

TABLE 2.16

Mother Tongue and Regional Mooring of 'Head' of Uuit		*Estimated Percentage to Total (±s.e.)*			
		Non-familial Unit	*Nuclear Family*	*Extended Family*	*Total (Sample)*
(1)		(2)	(3)	(4)	(5)
Mother tongue	Bengali	11.08+1.88	53.87±4.19	35.05+2.52	100.00 (3543)
	Any other	27.11±4.35	52.42±4.12	20.47±3.23	100.00 (1391)
Consider oneself as belonging to	West Bengal	11.13±1.72	54.69±3.66	34.18±2.20	100.00 (4103)
	Elsewhere	34.04±6.32	44.42±7.21	21.54±4.80	100.00 (831)
			(considering family-units only)		
Mother tongue	Bengali		60.58±3.83	39.42±3.83	100.00 (3095)
	Any other		71.92±3.53	28.08±3.53	100.00 (1024)
Consider oneself as belonging to	West Bengal		61.55±3.45	38.45±3.45	100.00 (3576)
	Elsewhere		67.34±6.54	32.66±6.54	100.00 (543)

What we have found from Table 2.16 is, however, fairly obvious and implicit to the societal arrangements. The non-Bengalis by mother tongue do not usually consider themselves to belong to West Bengal, although there is some discrepancy in this respect as seen from the sample of non-Bengalis under regional mooring which is somewhat less than the corresponding sample under mother tongue. All the same, they are likely to have 'familial integration' elsewhere (as we shall examine in Chepter 3) and so many of them live in West Bengal like 'birds of passage', that

2. In Schedules 1.0 and 1.1 in the Appendix to Chapter 6 in Part 2, the regional mooring of a person is denoted as '*anchal* affiliation'.

is, as non-familial units or forming the nuclear coresident and commensal kingroups. For an appraisal of variations in family structures in West Bengal, these two forms of social stratification therefore, are of ancillary or marginal relevance.

But this is not the case when we examine the classification of the family-units and non-familial units in Table 2.17 by their involuntary attributes of religion and caste (which, according to the course of categorization, is customary, conventional or juridical in nature). For, these forms of social stratification are intrinsic to the West Bengal society.

In spite of the partition of Bengal at the time of creation of Pakistan in the subcontinent of India, West Bengal continued to accommodate an appreciable number of Muslims: the next largest religious community after the Hindus. There are, of course, other religious communities, like, those of the Christians, Jains, Buddhists, Sikhs, and Zoroastrians; but they can constitute only a residual group in comparison to the Hindus and the Muslims.

Within the Hindu community, the families and non-familial units can be graded according as the castes to which they are affiliated are customarily regarded as of a 'high', 'middle', or 'low' status (cf. note 4 of the Introductory chapter). During the course of analysis, however, we did not notice prima facie any difference between the 'middle' and the 'low' caste-groups in regard to the relative incidence of the non-familial units, nuclear families and extended families. We have, therefore, posed the 'high' caste Hindus vis-a-vis the other Hindu castes, which will also test the common assumption that the former category is clearly distinguished from the latter in its social organization, by being differentially influenced culturally.

Islam, in theory, does not tolerate any caste-like ranking among the Believers. But, since a long time, such categories have emerged among the Muslims in Bengali society [Gait, 1901: 165–81]. This form of social stratification can be depicted by two broad categories: (1) the 'non-functional' or 'high'-ranking Muslims who do not have any conventionally ascribed occupation of artisanship, trade, fishing, menial service, etc., of a low status; and (2) the 'functional' Muslims who are denoted by such occupations. Socially, these two categories express, respectively, a superior and an inferior status: they do not intermarry conventionally, and even interdining is looked down upon [Mukherjee, 1957: 121–24; 1971a: 266–73]. These two groupings, therefore, have been brought under examination; although for the 1960–61 survey a further categorization of the 'functional' Muslims was attempted as of 'middle' and 'low' status according as the high-ranking Muslims will interdine with the former but not with the latter. However, we did not notice any significant difference between these two categories in regard to the relative incidence of the non-familial units, nuclear families, and extended families.

Juridically, a number of Hindu castes are declared as the 'Scheduled Castes' and, correspondingly, a number of so-called aboriginal communities are declared as the 'Scheduled Tribes' in West Bengal. These two categories refer to an attribute which is also involuntarily ascriptive but it does not refer to the customary or conventional social organization as done by the attributes of religion and caste described above. Moreover, as juridically determined and governmentally administered, this attribute is expected to focus more sharply on the currently differential social positions of the West Bengal people. Therefore, the two categories of Scheduled Castes and Tribes have been posed against each other, as well as the rest of West Bengal society, in order to ascertain any differential incidence of the non-familial units, nuclear families, and extended families.

It is seen from Table 2.17 that the Hindu community is clearly distinguished from the rest in West Bengal as having a relatively larger incidence of the extended families and (unexpectedly?) of the non-familial units; but the 'high' caste Hindus do not differentiate themselves from the other Hindus in the context of family structure formation: a point which will be drastically discounted when we undertake an intensive course of analysis at the end of this chapter. The Muslim community, however, is distinguished by its 'high' rank of 'non-functional' Muslims living predominantly in nuclear families and neither in extended families nor as non-familial units. Lastly, the juridical categorization of the Scheduled Castes, Scheduled Tribes, and the rest of the society have little bearing on the differential incidence of the non-familial units, nuclear families, and extended families; although the 'tribals' tend to have a somewhat larger incidence of nuclear families than the others.

Corresponding to the attribute of the Scheduled Castes and

TABLE 2.17

Customarily, Conventionally, and Juridically Evolved Religion-caste Categories		*Estimated Percentage to Total (±s.e.)*			
		Non-familial Unit	*Nuclear Family*	*Extended Family*	*Total (Sample)*
(1)		(2)	(3)	(4)	(5)
Religious grouping	Hindu	14.95±2.25	49.62±2.78	35.43±2.56	100.00 (3929)
	Muslim	7.66±1.98	69.92±3.43	22.42±2.34	100.00 (669)
	Others	8.68±2.88	63.48±4.02	27.84±4.56	100.00 (336)
Caste-grading of Hindus	High	17.12±2.37	44.95±3.30	37.93±3.31	100.00 (1052)
	Others	14.31±2.03	50.99±2.22	34.70±2.02	100.00 (2877)
Ranking of Muslims	High	5.63±0.90	80.26±2.08	14.11±1.97	100.00 (230)
	Others	9.31±2.19	61.51±4.79	29.18±3.97	100.00 (439)
Scheduled Castes		13.80±3.50	52.70±2.88	33.50±3.66	100.00 (928)
Scheduled Tribes		8.50±3.84	62.61±4.08	28.89±4.20	100.10 (274)
All others		13.67±1.89	53.42±4.58	32.91±3.16	100.00 (3732)
			(considering family-units only)		
Religious groupings	Hindu		58.34±2.69	41.66±2.69	100.00 (3226)
	Muslim		75.72±3.67	24.28±3.67	100.10 (598)
	Others		69.51±3.82	30.49±3.82	100.00 (295)
Caste-grading of Hindus	High		54.24±3.48	45.76±3.48	100.00 (854)
	Others		59.50±2.92	40.50±2.92	100.00 (2372)
Ranking of Muslims	High		85.05±2.62	14.95±2.62	100.00 (210)
	Others		67.82±5.02	32.18±5.02	100.00 (388)
Scheduled Castes			61.14±3.42	38.86±3.42	100.00 (784)
Scheduled Tribes			68.43±4.10	31.57±4.10	100.00 (253)
All others			61.88±3.75	38.12±3.75	100.00 (3082)

Tribes, there is the juridical attribute of Backward Classes which includes the former communities and a number of other castes in addition. However, the categorization of the West Bengal family-units and non-familial units as 'backward' or not did not elicit any differential incidence of the non-familial units, nuclear families, and extended families in the society.

Thus we find that while the social stratification by mother tongue and regional mooring are of little relevance to our study, that by religion and caste as customarily and/or conventionally ordained (and not juridically determined) is of significant importance. Later, we shall refer to this form of interrelationship between social stratification and relative incidence of different forms of family structure when forming composite social groups for the course of analysis undertaken.

VI

Let us now consider a few more attributes which are 'social' and/or 'cultural' in content (in the manner 'social anthropology' is differentiated from 'cultural anthropology'), and which may have a bearing on our course of analysis. One of them is the splitting of a kingroup from the 'parent' kingroup, and the other is the distinctive movement of the 'parent' or the 'splitted' kingroup from one place to another. The former would refer to an ongoing phenomenon: the resultant of the economic, ideational and other societal forces which lead to the fission of a kingroup. The latter may reflect a crisis situation: the sudden impingement of a societal force which calls for the decision of a kingroup to move away from one place to another, and in part or as a whole. Both the attributes are voluntary in the sense that they express the decision of the unit *en bloc* or, more specifically, that of its 'head'; but their repercussions (if any) on the formation of family structures may be different.

To translate the two attributes into actual situations, we shall represent the former by the fact of leaving the 'paternal' residence of the male 'head' or that of the husband of the female 'head' since the coresident and commensal kingroups in West Bengal have been found from Chapter 1 to be neolocal or patrilineal-patrivirilocal in virtually all cases. We shall further categorize this fact as of a recent phenomenon (that is, the paternal residence has been left *within* the year from the date of enquiry) or a past incident. The second attribute will be appropriately represented by the fact of displacement of individuals and families from Pakistan (mainly the Eastern Wing of Pakistan) as due to the violent Hindu-Muslim conflicts in that region since 1946 to the date of the enquiry in 1960–61.

The displaced persons from Pakistan (and, especially, from East Pakistan) came to West Bengal in successive waves in the late 1940s and throughout the 1950s, and the bulk of them settled down on their own initiative and endeavour [Mukherjee, 1965: 109-65]. The family structures they evolved are, therefore, likely to be more or less free from temporary variations due to disequilibrations and, thus, provide us with the scope to examine a relatively stable outline of the nature and the depth of the impact of a cataclysm on their life. However, this attribute as well as the one referring to the fact of leaving the paternal residence are not found to be effective to our study.

We see from Table 2.18 that whether or not a family or non-familial unit has been displaced from Pakistan (and is now found in West Bengal) does not affect the relative incidence of the non-familial units, nuclear families, and extended families in the society. The same is the situation in regard to those who are living in their paternal residence or have left it since a year or more. Those who have left it within one year are seen to be living (a) largely as non-familial units and (b) proportionately less by forming the nuclear family than those who have not left the paternal residence or have left it for one year or more. The former may reveal a temporary phase of disequilibration and the

TABLE 2.18

'Splitting' or 'Movement' of the Unit of Enquiry	*Estimated Percentage to Total* ($\pm$*s.e.*)			
	Non-familial Unit	*Nuclear Family*	*Extended Family*	*Total (Sample)*
(1)	(2)	(3)	(4)	(5)
***Leaving paternal residence*:**				
Not left	**13.13±2.60**	**54.72±4.27**	**32.15±2.20**	**100.00 (2993)**
Left within 1 year	**41.86±7.86**	**34.88±6.87**	**23.26±6.36**	**100.00 (43)**
Left 1 year or more	**14.23±1.37**	**50.93±3.44**	**34.84±3.40**	**100.00 (1898)**
***Displacement from Pakistan*:**				
Displaced	**13.22±4.99**	**43.98±5.25**	**42.80±5.16**	**100.00 (163)**
Not displaced	**13.44±2.05**	**54.05±3.63**	**32.51±2.14**	**100.00 (4771)**
		(considering family-units only)		
***Leaving paternal residence*:**				
Not left		**62.99±3.69**	**37.01±3.69**	**100.00 (2452)**
Left within 1 year		**60.00±7.29**	**40.00±7.29**	**100.00 (25)**
Left 1 year or more		**59.38±2.68**	**40.62±2.68**	**100.00 (1642)**
***Displacement from Pakistan*:**				
Displaced		**50.68±6.28**	**49.32±6.28**	**100.00 (132)**
Not displaced		**62.44±4.02**	**37.56±4.02**	**100.00 (3987)**

the latter (or both) may suggest the stronger integrating power of the extended family structure. But the sample for this category is so small that any conclusion drawn from it would be injudicious.

From the 'socio-cultural' attributes, which give *a priori* a broad contour of the societal background of the family-units and non-familial units, we may proceed to those which are essentially 'cultural' in content. They are stably, steadily, personally, and voluntarily pursued, and are usually assumed to have a role to play in the differential formation of family structures. Education is one such attribute which for the units of enquiry may be examined in two ways: (1) the maximum level of education attained by *any* member of a family-unit; and (2) the education level of the 'head' of the family-unit. Obviously, the two ways merge into one in the case of the non-familial units. However, as regards the family-units, the first may indicate the current stage of the end-product of the efforts of the unit as a whole for the advancement of learning, while the second is relevant in the sense that the 'head' is presumed to mould the articulation of a kingroup to form a coresident and commensal family. Since the latter consideration would be incorporated in the former, the attribute of education has been analyzed in former terms.

The education of each family member and of a non-familial unit was recorded in several details during the field investigation. But, at the time of primary analysis of the data, it was found that the sample sizes for the detailed categories (that is, in regard to the vocational or technical training and 'above matriculation' levels) are too small to draw any generalized inference on their basis. The relevant forms of categorization, therefore, can only be as 'illiterate', 'literate but below the level of matriculation', and 'matriculate (that is, with or without further college and university education)'. We did not find, however, any significant difference in the relative incidence of the non-familial units, nuclear families, and extended families according to the literates' categorization as 'below matric' and 'matriculate'.

The consistently low standard errors of the mean values in Table 2.19 point out that the respective sets of units of enquiry under the classificatory schema are homogeneously constituted. So that, the absence of any significant difference by their *levels* of educational attainment indicates that this attribute is of no

TABLE 2.19

Educational Level of Any Member in Unit of Enquiry	*Estimated Percentage to Total (±s.e.)*			
	Non-familial Unit	*Nuclear Family*	*Extended Family*	*Total (Sample)*
(1)	(2)	(3)	(4)	(5)
Below matric	14.25±2.38	53.25±2.07	32.50±1.98	100.00 (1888)
Matriculate	10.14±3.02	53.19±1.96	36.67±2.15	100.00 (1075)
		(considering family-units only)		
Below matric		59.73±2.12	40.27±2.12	100.00 (1619)
Matriculate		58.07±2.25	41.93±2.25	100.00 (966)

relevance to structural variations in family organization in West Bengal society. It may be conjectured, of course, that had we examined an appreciable sample of family-units and non-familial units with a very high degree of educational attainment against the rest in the society, some significant differences between the two sets of units could be elicited in the context of variations in family structures. However, the fact that any high degree of educational attainment is a scarce phenomenon in the society at large is evident from the very small sample obtained from the 1960-61 survey. Also, the fact that the groupings in Table 2.19 are homogeneously constituted in reference to variations in family structures, and are indistinguishable with respect to a high or low level of educational attainment, suggests that these levels are of no relevance to appraise variations in family structures for the society *en bloc*. We are, thus, led to the obvious conclusion that any possible variation in West Bengal family structures due to the *degree* of educational attainment of the non-familial units and family-units is, as yet, a matter for micro-investigations into the family organization *per se*, and not for an accounting of structural variations in West Bengal families.

It follows that in regard to the attribute of education the relevant form of categorization for our present purpose will have to be merely as 'illiterate' or 'literate'. Table 2.20, prepared on this basis, shows that the literates live more under the extended family organization and less as non-familial units. The finding is contrary to the usual assumption that the 'educated' people live in nuclear families which do not suffer from any constraint due to the presence of lineal and/or affinal relations in them.

TABLE 2.20

Educational Level of the Unit of Enquiry	Estimated Percentage to Total (±s.e.) Non-familial Unit	Nuclear Family	Extended Family	Total (Sample)
(1)	(2)	(3)	(4)	(5)
Illiterate	22.17±2.18	55.50±2.89	22.33±1.96	100.00 (1971)
Literate	12.72±2.36	51.56±2.17	35.72±2.48	100.00 (2963)
	(considering family-units only)			
Illiterate		71.31±3.01	28.69±3.01	100.00 (1534)
Literate		59.07±2.88	40.93±2.88	100.00 (2585)

There may be three reasons for this kind of finding, and these reasons may operate severally or jointly: (1) the broad categorization of 'literate or not' does not really denote the role of education on variations in familial organization; (2) whatever may be the formal level of education attained, the content of education is not conducive to the inculcation of 'new' values; and (3) any distinctive 'value consideration' is irrelevant in the present context because only those families can afford the privilege of education which have an economically better-off existence and these families have been found from Table 2.11 to live proportionally more in the extended families and infrequently as non-familial units.

We had, however, collected some other data during the 1960-61 survey to denote specifically the value considerations of the people in reference to their family organization, and this we tried to do as objectively as possible in an interview method of survey. Our attention, in this context, was focussed on two issues with respect to the 'head' of each family-unit and each non-familial unit: (1) whether or not he or she considered to have a 'family' and what was the form of the family structure thus envisaged, whatever may be the form of his/her coresident and commensal kingroup (that is, a non-familial unit, a nuclear or an extended family); and (2) whether or not he or she showed any belief in the caste organization of the Hindu society (and the caste-wise ranking in Muslim society) and, if so, whether his/her caste-grading (in the case of the Hindus) or caste-wise ranking (in the case of the Muslims) was the same as that customarily or conventionally determined.

Regarding the first issue, we did not ask the persons concerned whether they, respectively, *prefer* to live in a nuclear or an extended family. Because, one's preference for a particular kind of family organization may bring out that which is up to his or her best liking, while one's consideration of some kins and affines as family-members would show whom he or she actually accepts as 'family-members'. Accordingly, as explained in the Introductory chapter, we ascertained the names of those whom they, respectively, consider to be their 'family members' and what are the kinship relations of these persons with them. This way we could objectively deduce the forms of the family structures which they consider to be their own, and compare these structures against those which they have formed, respectively, as coresident and commensal kingroups (as also obtained from Block 9 of the Schedules 1.0 and 1.1). So that, any discrepancy between the two forms of family structure for each of these persons would denote specifically his or her differential value consideration in respect of family organization.

We shall see from Chapter 3 that this form of differential value consideration occurs rarely in the rural areas. In the urban areas, it refers essentially to those living in nuclear families, whose 'familial integration' is towards an extended family organization; or to the non-familial units who want to live in a family organization of the nuclear or (more frequently) extended structure. This suggests that, instead of any alteration, the values of the people vis-a-vis their family organization are sustained in spite of the economic forces which may have compelled them to live in a different manner.

As to the second issue, we did not ask the Hindu 'heads' of family-units and the Hindu non-familial units whether they *believe* in the caste system; and, similarly, we did not ask the Muslim 'heads' of family-units and the Muslim non-familial units whether they *conform* to the caste-wise ranking in the Muslim community of West Bengal. Evidences are there that, as in regard to the joint family system, such questions usually promote violent denunciation of the caste system by the respondents. Firstly, therefore, we asked the Hindu 'heads' of family-units and the Hindu non-familial units to tell us the names of the castes to which they and their family members belong. In response to this question, they could have refused outright to furnish the information, and such a refusal might indicate a strong sentiment against the caste system. This, however, happened in no case out of the total of 4,934 units of enquiry thus concerned.

The informants may consider that stating the names of their castes is a mere formality; it does not signify their attitude towards the caste system. Next, therefore, we asked each Hindu 'head' of the family-units and each Hindu non-familial unit to grade the caste of each family member (including that of himself or herself) as 'high', 'middle', or 'low'; and, similarly, asked the Muslim 'heads' and the Muslim non-familial units to rank themselves and their family members as of 'high', 'middle', or 'low' rank. The survey data show that only in 1 per cent instances out of the total of 4934, the informants refused to grade or rank themselves and their family members; and that only in 14 per cent cases out of 4883 the grading or ranking done by them deviated from that customarily or conventionally ordained.

Additionally, we found during an intensive scrutiny of the field schedules that while none of the informants mentioned of Hindu-Muslim (and such inter-religious) or inter-caste marriages in their families, the respective surnames of the 'husbands' and 'wives' suggested the incidence of inter-caste marriages, at any rate, in one case out of all in the urban areas and one case out of all in the rural areas. Evidently, in the society at large, such incidents are rare and, even if they occur, the 'value consideration' of the persons involved leads to their suppression as not conforming to the general practice.

The conclusion thus becomes irresistible that, to date, even a meticulous attempt to ascertain the role of 'subjective' attributes like the value-considerations of the people on their family organization is of little or no relevance to the variations in West Bengal family structures. Hence, these variations, as we find from the foregoing analyses, will have to be expressed through a comprehensive accounting of the 'objective' attributes and the effective categories of: (1) the economic structure of the society, (2) its social structure as registered by the customarily or conventionally ordained religion-caste organization of the people, and (3) its cultural component given by the educational level of the 'heads' of family-units and of the non-familial units as 'literate' or 'illiterate'.

VII

The effective categories of the economic structure to register variations in family structures in West Bengal society are seen from Table 2.11 to be: (1) non-manual 'high' or 'middle' grade and skilled manual occupations in all sectors of the national economy; (2) non-manual 'low' grade and semi-skilled or unskilled manual occupations in all sectors of the national economy other than agriculture; and (3) the occupations of the second category but under agriculture, as represented by the sharecroppers and agricultural wage-labourers. The correspondingly effective categories of the 'social' structure are seen from Table 2.17 to be also three: (1) Hindus of any caste; (2) 'non-functional' upper-class Muslims; and (3) the 'functional' Muslims, with the other religious communities broadly equating to it. Lastly, we have seen from Table 2.20 that the educational level of the 'heads' of the family-units and of the non-familial units is effectively categorized in the present context as: (1) none, and (2) literate. It thus appears that a comprehensive accounting of the above attributes to appraise any differential formation of family structures would produce $(3 \times 3 \times 2) = 18$ effective categories.

This form of categorization, however, would overlook the process of interaction among the detailed categories of the attributes in reference to the course of analysis undertaken. Such as, in the present context, the Hindu caste-groups may be differentiated in reference to their educational level or location in the economic structure; the non-manual 'high' or 'middle' grade and the skilled manual occupations may be differentiated by the sectors of the national economy and/or the educational level of the 'heads' of the units of enquiry; the category of sharecroppers and agricultural wage-labourers may not operate as an isolate but in conjunction with some other detailed categories; and so on. These possible variations are of crucial importance to empirical social research, in order to unfold the social reality precisely, as we have discussed elsewhere [Mukherjee and Bandyopadhyay, 1964]. Hence, instead of depending upon the 18 *directly* available pooled categories as enumerated above, we proceeded by, first, cross-classifying all the units of enquiry in terms of the detailed categories of the attributes under reference and, then, comparing the relative incidences of the non-familial units, nuclear familes, and the extended families in them, respectively.

In this manner, 774 categories could be formed altogether; but from the 1960-61 survey data only 602 categories could be elicited. These categories were found to be of such a nature, according to the course of analysis described above, that they could be systematically pooled into three ultimately derived categories. The categories are efficient in the sense that the percentage incidences of non-familial units, nuclear families, and extended families under them register very low standard errors (*vide*, Table 2.22). However, for any course of social research the precise societal identification of the categories is no less important than their efficiency as statistical entities. In the present context, therefore, they should refer unequivocally to distinct social groups characterized by those socio-economic-cultural attributes of the 'heads' of family-units and of the non-familial units which have been found to be relevant from the foregoing course of analysis. Accordingly, the three categories are seen to be characterized as follows:

Category 1. Supervisory farmers and self-sustaining cultivators who are 'middle' or 'low' grade Hindus or 'functional' Muslims, and are literate; that is, the social group of: *Literate but socially inferior Hindu/Muslim landed gentry.*

Category 2. (1) All those supervisory farmers and self-sustaining cultivators who are not accounted for by Category 1; that is, the composite social group of: *Illiterate landed gentry and literate but socially superior Hindu/Muslim landed gentry or the landed gentry of other religious affiliation.*

(2) Sharecroppers and agricultural wage-labourers of any religion and caste, and literate or not; that is, the comprehensive social group of: *Agricultural commoners.*

(3) Those engaged in non-agricultural 'high' or 'middle' grade non-manual and skilled manual occupations, and of any religion and caste but literate; that is, the social group of: *Literate urban and not-landed rural gentry.*

(4) Those engaged in non-agricultural 'low' grade non-manual and semi-skilled or unskilled manual occupations, and are of any religion and caste, but illiterate; that is, the social group of: ***Illiterate urban and non-agricultural rural commoners.***

Category 3. (1) The 'illiterate' counterpart of sub-category 2.3; that is, the social group of: *Illiterate urban and not-landed rural gentry.*

(2) The 'literate' counterpart of sub-category 2.4; that is, the social group of: *Literate urban and non-agricultural rural commoners.*

(3) All those of any religion and caste, and literate or not, who are dependent on others in the society; that is, the residual group of: *Societal dependents.*

The three categories are seen to be composed of unequivocally defined social groups; and so they can be precisely identified in society. The categories 2 and 3 appear to be composed heterogeneously, but the heterogeneity is due to precise variations of the societal characteristics under reference. They, therefore, may suggest contrary *courses* of variation, as seen from Table 2.21.

TABLE 2.21

Category 1	*Catagory 2*	*Category 3*
(1)	(2)	(3)
Landed rural gentry, distinguished as literate Hindu or Muslim of socially inferior status (481)	Remaining landed gentry in rural areas, of any distinction (57)	
	Non-agricultural gentry—rural or urban—*but* literate (1946)	Non-agricultural gentry—rural or urban—*but* illiterate (212)
	Non-agricultural commoner—rural or urban—*but* illiterate (763)	Non-agricultural commoner—rural or urban—*but* literate (58)
	All agricultural commoners (1276)	
		Societal dependents (141)

N.B. Samples of social groups in brackets

The variations in the societal characteristics to compose the three categories may have implications on the process at work in the society to produce the nuclear family structures for different reasons; namely, *material* (as reflected by the distinction *within* a category by the 'gentry' and the 'commoner') and *ideological* (as reflected by the distinction *between* the categories by the literacy or illiteracy of the constituent groups of 'gentry' and 'commoner'). In due course, we shall touch upon these contrary courses of variation to produce the same result. For the present, we may note that they are of *subsequent* relevance to ascertain variations in family structures. For, different *functions* may institute different processes in a society, while some of these processes may lead to the *same* structural variation.

On this count, therefore, we find from Table 2.22 that the three categories are characterized, respectively, by the largest and preponderant incidence of the non-familial units *or* the nuclear families *or* the extended families. The social group representing Category 1 lives, in the majority cases, by forming extended families and seldom as non-familial units. The social groups under Category 2, on the other hand, live by mostly forming nuclear families, next the extended families, and some as non-familial units. And the social groups under Category 3 live, in the majority cases, as non-familial units, a few in nuclear families, and fewer in extended families.

TABLE 2.22

Category of Social Groups	*Estimated Percentage to Total* (±*s.e.*)			*Total*
	Non-familial Unit	*Nuclear Family*	*Extended Family*	
(1)	(2)	(3)	(4)	(5)
1	1.72±1.71	42.94±2.92	55.34±2.57	100.00
2	11.06±1.58	58.15±2.04	30.79±2.44	100.00
3	58.11±1.40	24.35±1.54	17.54±1.36	100.00
	(considering family-units only)			
1		43.68±3.77	56.32±3.77	100.00
2		65.38±2.50	34.62±2.50	100.00
3		58.14±2.62	41.86±2.62	100.00

The characteristics of the three categories become clearer if we examine the composition of their family structures by the nature of kinship relations involved. As we have discussed in Chapter 1, the nuclear family structure is involved with three kinds of intra-family relations (that is, conjugal, parental and sibling), but a nuclear family-unit may represent all three of them, any two, or any one. Correspondingly, the extended family structure is involved with five kinds of intra-family relations (that is, the above three as well as lineal and affinal), but an extended family-unit may represent only the lineal or the affinal relation, or a combination of the two, with or without the concurrent presence of the other three kinds of intra-family relations in any combination thereof. Now, we find from Table 2.23 that Category 1 is distinguished by the full-fledged representation of the extended and the nuclear family structures; Category 2 less so and particularly in respect of the nuclear families; and Category 3 is distinguished by fragmentary composition of the family-units in this respect.

TABLE 2.23

Category of Social Groups	*Estimated Percentage to Total (±s.e.)*			
	All Relations Present	*Not all Present*	*Total (Sample)*	
(1)	(2)	(3)	(4)	
	1. *Constitution of nuclear families by conjugal/parental/sibling relations*			
1	71.20±3.29	28.80±3.29	100.00	(218)
2	53.62±3.14	46.38±3.14	100.00	(2293)
3	32.86±2.80	67.14±2.80	100.00	(110)
	2. *Constitution of patrilineally extended families by lineal, affinal, and conjugal, parental sibling relations*			
1	76.04±2.81	23.96±2.81	100.00	(187)
2	62.78±3.45	37.22±3.45	100.00	(835)
3	39.67±6.54	60.33±6.54	100.00	(35)

To be sure, the absence of one or more of the scheduled intra-family relations in the nuclear and extended structures does not necessarily mean that the growth of these structures is stunted or truncated. We have discussed in Chapter 1 that a newly formed nuclear family of husband and wife will contain only the conjugal relation; if the couple has only one child, the nuclear family will contain only the conjugal and parental relations; and since the couple need not (or may not) produce any more children, the absence of the sibling relation in the family would not mean that a nuclear structure is stunted or truncated. Nevertheless, the distinctions found in the first half of Table 2.23 are worthy to note. For, if these variations were a random phenomenon in society and thus equally applicable to all the nuclear family-units in West Bengal, then: why is it that Category 1 denotes a preponderant incidence of the full-fledged nuclear structures, Category 3 just the opposite, and Category 2 does not register a significant difference in the relative incidence of the full-fledged and partially expressed nuclear structures?

The heterogeneous character of Category 2 may be particularly relevant in this context if its different segments (specified in Table 2.21) have contrary motivation or necessity to form the 'conjugal' and/or the one-child 'parental' families. The supposition seems to be buttressed by the higher incidence of the partially expressed nuclear structures in Category 3 which is largely composed in a manner analogous to Category 2. However, any such supposition calls for an intensive investigation of the 'functional variations' (that is, of familial behaviour patterns, etc.) and not just a study of structural variations in the family organization of West Bengal society.

Anyhow, that any heterogeneity in the composition of Category 2 is as yet of incipient (and not exposed) relevance to variations in family structures is suggested by the similar incidences of the full-fledged and partially denoted composition of the extended families under this category and Category 1, but not under Category 3 (*vide*, second half of Table 2.23). This is also borne out by the relative incidence of the patrilineally and non-patrilineally (including the patrilineally *and* non-patrilineally) extended family structures, and of the nature of extension of the non-patrilineally extended structures, under the above three categories. Details are given in Tables 2.24 and 2.25.

Columns (2) and (3) of Table 2.24 show that for either column a significant difference is noticed only for the values between the

TABLE 2.24

Category of Social Groups	Estimated Percentage to Total (±s.e.) Patrilineally Extended Family	Non-patrilineally Extended Family	Total (Sample)
(1)	(2)	(3)	(4)
1	64.59±2.88	35.41±2.88	100.00 (254)
2	58.99±3.58	41.01±3.58	100.00 (1189)
3	51.74±3.23	48.26±3.23	100.00 (54)

Categories 1 and 3, and not between 1 and 2 or 2 and 3. Now, if we recall from Chapter 1 the characteristics of the patrilineally extended family as representing the societal norm for West Bengal and of the non-patrilineally extended family as recording deviations from that norm, we find that in their respect there is no distinction between the Categories 1 and 2 (irrespective of the heterogeneous composition of the latter category), while the less heterogeneous Category 3 is distinguished from Category 1 but not from Category 2. Correspondingly, we notice by comparing the values of the two columns for each category that while for both the Categories 1 and 2 there is a higher incidence of the patrilineally extended structures than otherwise, there is no significant difference in the relative incidence of the two kinds of extended structures for Category 3. This means that the social groups belonging to the Categories 1 and 2 adhere more to the normative family organization than Category 3.

TABLE 2.25

Category of Social Groups	Estimated Percentage to Total (±s.e.) Only Lineally Deviated	Lineally and/or Affinially Deviated	Total (Sample)
(1)	(2)	(3)	(4)
1	64.56±5.29	35.44±5.29	100.00 (67)
2	48.82±3.69	51.18±3.69	100.00 (354)
3	18.45±8.07	81.55±8.07	100.00 (19)

On the other hand, we find from Table 2.25 that for either of the columns (2) and (3) significant differences are recorded for the values between the Categories 1 and 2, 2 and 3, and 1 and 3. Furthermore, we notice that the non-patrilineally extended structures for Category 1 are mostly 'lineally deviated', for Category 2 there is no significant difference between the 'lineally deviated' and the other kind of non-patrilineally extended structures, while for Category 3 the 'lineally deviated' structures occur seldom. Now, as we have explained in Chapter 1, the 'lineally deviated' non-patrilineally extended families contain only the widowed/divorced/separated daughters, sisters, etc. (with or without their progeny) of the male members. These 'deviant' structures, therefore, represent, wholly or mainly, the extension of the patrilineal relations in the joint families under some dire circumstances. Correspondingly, the 'affinally deviated' non-patrilineally extended families (with or without the 'lineal' deviants) register a qualitatively different form of departure from the societal norm. Here, therefore, we *may* discern any incipient variation in the family organization of some of the social groups under Category 2, which appears to find a categorical expression under Category 3.

VIII

The variations noticed in the categorization of the social groups and their association with differential incidence of some notable characteristics of the nuclear and extended family structures can, however, be explained in another way. We have seen from Chapter 1 that in West Bengal as a whole the variations in family structures (as coresident and commensal kingroups) are precisely accounted for by the kind of family organization sponsored by the 'heads' of the families in course of their life-spread; that is, according as these 'heads' grow older and finally disappear from the social scene. We have also noted that the 'heads' are almost invariably males, and the men and women of West Bengal—as in the whole of India [Mukherjee, 1971b; 48–49]—follow a distinct pattern of effective marriage and fertility (*vide*, footnote 7 of Chapter 1). Further more, it will be seen from Chapter 7 of Part 2 of this volume that in overwhelming majority the 'heads' are the seniormost persons in the respective coresident and commensal kingroups. The demographic variable of the age of the 'head', therefore, may account for the above variations in a large measure.

If the 'head' is very young (aged 19 years or less), he usually forms the 'sibling' variety of the nuclear family with his brothers and sisters or, sometimes, the extended family of one generation with his first cousins (with or without the siblings). If he is not so young (aged 20–24 years), he would usually be living with his wife and may also live with his brothers and sisters; that is, besides a small proportion of one-generation extended families, the 'heads' in this age-group live mostly in the 'conjugal' variety of the nuclear family. In the age-group of 25–29 years, the 'heads' are also 'fathers' and, thus, form two-generation nuclear structures with conjugal and parental (and, occasionally, inter-sibling relation between his children), with some incidence of two-generation collaterally extended structures with their brothers' consorts and progeny (if any).

Within the age-group of 30–44 years of the 'heads', further generational extension of the families does not usually take place. Essentially, the two-generational nuclear structures take the full-fledged form with the presence of the conjugal, parental, and sibling relations in reference to the family of procreation of the 'heads'. Also, in some cases, the two-generation collaterally extended structures persist, with the consorts and progeny of the brothers of the 'heads'.

By the time the 'heads' are in the age-group of 45–49 years, their two-generational nuclear family of procreation may become unilaterally extended families with the 'sons' bringing their wives to live in the family. The transformation would be more or less established when the 'heads' are in the age-group of 50–54 years but, as yet, three-generational unilaterally extended structures may not emerge as a common phenomenon. This takes place when the 'heads' are in the age-group of 55 or more years, have become 'grandfathers' and, in some cases, also 'great grandfathers'.

Such a sequential transformation of the family structures in West Bengal society has been described in reference to Table 1.15. Moreover, we have seen in Chapter 1 that although occurring much less frequently than the patrilineally extended families, the non-patrilineally extended families are more frequently found in reference to the 'heads' forming a 'non-familial = self only' or a nuclear base in the coresident and commensal kingroups than a patrilineally joint base (Table 1.16). Also, the patrilineally extended families are more associated with the three or four generational than one or two generational structures (Table 1.22). Furthermore, although the 'affinally deviated' non-patrilineally extended structures do not occur frequently, they are found more for those families in which the 'heads' form a 'non-familial = self only' or a nuclear base than a patrilineally joint base (Table 1.18). All these overall characteristics of variation in family structures in West Bengal society, in reference to the age of the 'heads' of the coresident and commensal kingroups, are reproduced in Table 2.26.

TABLE 2.26

Some Characteristics of the West Bengal Family Structures		*Presence of the Characteristics in Reference to the Age of the 'heads' of Coresident and Commensal Kingroups*			
		29 *or below*	30–44	45–54	55 *or more*
(1)		(2)	(3)	(4)	(5)
Larger incidence of:	Nuclear structures	yes	yes	no	no
	Extended structures	no	no	no	yes
Presence of all intra-family relations in:	Nuclear structures	no	yes	yes	yes
	Extended structures	no	no	yes	yes
Larger incidence of extended structures:	Patrilineally joint	no	no	yes	yes
	Non-patrilineally joint	yes	yes	yes	no
Larger incidence of **non-patrilineal** structures deviated:	Lineally only	yes	yes	yes	yes
	Affinally	yes	yes	yes	no

The corroboration of the tabulated alternatives in Table 2.26 is obtained from Table 2.27 in regard to the first of the four characteristics under reference, which is also of foremost importance. Moreover, Table 2.27 donotes the association between the presence of the non-familial units and their age (corresponding to the age of the 'heads' of the family-units) which is of particular relevance to interpret Table 2.22 in the present context. For we find that the non-familial units are concentrated in the age-group of 29 years or less; and, afterwards, except a small strain which persists indistinguishably by the age of the persons concerned, they form families of their own or become constituents of some family-units.

TABLE 2.27

Age of the Non-familial Units or the Heads' of Family-units	*Estimated Percentage to Total (±s.e.) for West Bengal*				
	Non-familial Unit	*Nuclear Family*	*Extended Family*	*Total (Sample)*	
(1)	(2)	(3)	(4)	(5)	
19 or less	34.49±18.76	43.10±15.67	22.41±10.52	100.00	(29)
20–24	26.04± 4.72	53.42± 6.19	20.54± 5.33	100.00	(177)
25–29	18.74± 4.79	57.18± 7.55	24.08± 4.63	100.00	(466)
30–34	8.02± 1.79	62.07± 4.33	29.91± 3.59	100.00	(751)
35–39	7.45± 1.62	61.73± 3.08	30.82± 2.16	100.00	(824)
40–44	5.50± 1.54	66.38± 3.57	28.12± 3.40	100.00	(1062)
45–49	7.21± 1.71	55.80± 2.49	36.99± 2.95	100.00	(583)
50–54	9.76± 1.81	48.16± 3.72	42.08± 4.08	100.00	(458)
55–59	8.94± 3.70	38.17± 3.30	52.89± 3.50	100.00	(240)
60–64	11.13± 2.68	38.95± 8.87	49.92±10.81	100.00	(173)
65–69	9.41± 3.09	22.36± 3.46	68.23± 3.90	100.00	(84)
70 or more	12.15± 7.96	17.42± 5.17	70.43± 4.93	100.00	(87)

It is obvious from Table 2.27 that the role of the non-familial units is ancillary to the familial organization of the society: a point we have already noted and which is of particular relevance to the present course of analysis. Later, we shall find from Table 2.29 that the age-group of 29 years or less, in which the non-familial units are mostly concentrated, has a larger representation for Category 2 and Category 3 than for Category 1, and this may partly account for the large incidence of the non-familial units in the former two categories. Anyhow, for the present, we may summarize the details of Table 2.27 in the light of the step-wise gradation of the values it contains. Table 2.28 has been prepared, accordingly, in conformity with the design in Table 2.26. It will be noticed from this table that the demographic variable of age of the 'heads' of the units of enquiry is particularly relevant when the family-units are examined exclusively, as in the second half of Table 2.28.

TABLE 2.28

Age of the Non-familial Units or the 'Heads' of Family-units	*Estimated Percentage to Total (±s.e.)*			
	Non-familial Unit	*Nuclear Family*	*Extended Family*	*Total (Sample)*
(1)	(2)	(3)	(4)	(5)
44 or less	15.79±1.28	57.91±2.62	26.30±2.74	100.00 (3309)
45–54	8.38±1.09	52.31±2.12	39.31±3.28	100.00 (1041)
55 or more	10.03±3.41	32.96±3.11	57.01±4.26	100.00 (584)
		(considering family-units only)		
44 or less		68.81±3.24	31.19±3.24	100.00 (2637)
45–54		57.09±3.01	42.91±3.01	100.00 (950)
55 or more		36.63±3.81	63.37±3.81	100.00 (532)

Now, if the Categories 1, 2 and 3 of Tables 2.21–2.25 are found to be associated, more or less, with one or another distinctive age-groups of the 'heads' of the family-units and non-familial units (as shown in Table 2.26–2.28), then we may be able to explain the variations under scrutiny to a certain extent. We find, accordingly, from Table 2.29 that Category 1 is represented more by the older 'heads' than Category 2, and Category 3 is represented more by the younger 'heads' than Category 2.

TABLE 2.29

Categories of Social Groups in Tables 2.21–2.25	*Estimated Percentage to Total under each Category of Non-familial Units and 'Heads' of Family-units belonging to Age-groups*				
	29 *or below*	30–44	45–54	55 *or more*	*Total (Sample)*
(1)	(2)	(3)	(4)	(5)	(6)
Category 1	8	44	29	19	100 (481)
Category 2	15	53	21	11	100 (4042)
Category 3	11	55	18	16	100 (411)

Let us now consolidate our earlier and current findings. We had found from Tables 2.22–2.25 that the social group denoted by Category 1 has four essential characteristics: (1) a preponderance of the full-fledged patrilineally extended structures with all the five intra-family relations (lineal, affinal, conjugal, parental, and sibling) present; (2) the secondary occurrence of the full-fledged nuclear structures with all the three intra-family relations (conjugal, parental, and sibling) present; (3) a scarce incidence of the non-patrilineally extended family structures (and especially those which are 'affinally deviated'); and (4) the rare occurrence of the non-familial units. All these characteristics may be accounted for by the current findings that: (a) 19 per cent of the 'heads' of the units under Category 1 are of age 55 years or more as against 11 and 16 per cent of the 'heads' under Category 2 and Category 3, respectively: and (b) 52 per cent of the 'heads' under Category 1 are of age 44 years or less as against 68 and 66 per cent of the 'heads' under Category 2 and Category 3, respectively. Correspondingly, therefore, these differential percentage figures may explain why more under Category 2, and the most under Category 3, we find: (1) the larger and the largest incidence of the nuclear family structures and the non-familial units; (2) the greater and the greatest occurrence of the partially expressed nuclear and extended family structures; and (3) the higher and the highest incidence of the non-patrilineally extended families as well as more and more of those which are 'affinally deviated' (with or without the 'lineal deviants').

IX

The demographic variable of age of the non-familial units and the 'heads' of family-units, however, may not completely explain away the variations we are examining. For, in reference to the relative incidence of the non-familial units, nuclear families, and extended families, the social groups comprising the Categories 1, 2, and 3 of Tables 2.22—2.25 appear to behave differently for identical age-groupings. Details are given in Table 2.30.

The extent of distinction among the Categories 1, 2 and 3 will be seen from Table 2.31 which gives the results of the *t*–test of differences in the mean values recorded in Table 2.30. It can

TABLE 2.30

Age of the Non-familial Units or the 'Heads' of Family-units	Category in Tables 2.21–2.25 (with samples)	Estimated Percentage to Total (±s.e.)			
		Non-familial Unit	Nuclear Family	Extended Family	Total
(1)	(2)	(3)	(4)	(5)	(6)
	1 (42)	8.57± 1.62	55.90± 8.67	35.53±9.36	100.00
29 or less	2 (572)	20.55± 4.07	56.83± 6.74	22.62±4.16	100.00
	3 (58)	50.22±15.69	36.86±17.42	12.92±4.39	100.00
	1 (208)	0.78± 0.29	51.49± 4 61	47.73±4.65	100.00
30–44	2 (2185)	10.63± 2.24	63.38± 3.87	25.99±2.30	100.00
	3 (244)	70.01± 5.42	18.79± 4.77	11.20±4.24	100.00
	1 (138)	1.17± 1.09	40.76± 4.49	58.07±4.23	100.00
45–54	2 (850)	6.93± 1.58	56.56± 3.61	36.51±4.35	100.00
	3 (53)	45.30±14.20	31.55± 7.24	23.15±9.92	100.00
	1 (93)	2.80± 2.43	19.00± 5.93	78.20±4.09	100.00
55 or more	2 (435)	8.32± 2.49	37.54± 2.57	54.14±3.32	100.00
	3 (56)	36.75±11.47	26.97± 9.28	36.28±7.15	100.00
		(considering family-units only)			
	1 (38)		61.14± 7.28	38.86±8.92	100.00
29 or less	2 (439)		71.53± 6.58	28.47±4.34	100.00
	3 (24)		74.04±13.28	25.96±4.50	100.00
	1 (207)		52.14± 4.34	47.86±4.04	100.00
30–44	2 (1857)		70.91± 4.02	29.09±2.69	100.00
	3 (72)		62.66± 4.38	37.34±3.67	100.00
	1 (137)		41.25± 4.56	58.75±3.97	100.00
45–54	2 (783)		60.77± 3.75	39.23±4.24	100.00
	3 (30)		57.67± 6.28	42.33±8.90	100.00
	1 (91)		19.54± 6.11	80.46±4.21	100.00
55 or more	2 (403)		40.94± 2.88	59.06±3.90	100.00
	3 (38)		42.64± 9.13	57.36±7.56	100.00

be worked out from the details given in Table 2.31 that in reference to the family-units and non-familial units, Category 1 is distinguished from Category 2 and Category 3 in 75 per cent cases for either comparison (9 cases of significant difference out of the total of 12 comparisons in each instance), while Category 2 is distinguished from Category 3 in 58 per cent cases (7 cases out of 12 comparisons). Moreover, it will be seen from the table that the respective categories are almost invariably distinguished from one another in reference to the proportional incidences of the non-familial units in them; except, interestingly, between Categories 2 and 3 for the age of the non-familial units as 29 or less, and between Categories 1 and 2 for the age of the non-familial units as 55 or more. Correspondingly, when the non-familial

TABLE 2.31

Age of the Non-familial Units or the 'Heads' of Family-units	*Comparison of Categories in Tables* 2.21–2.25	*Estimated Percentage to Total* (±*s.e.*)		
		Non-familial Unit	*Nuclear Family*	*Extended Family*
(1)	(2)	(3)	(4)	(5)
29 or less	1 and 2	++	0	0
	1 and 3	++	0	+
	2 and 3	0	0	0
30–44	1 and 2	++	+	++
	1 and 3	++	++	++
	2 and 3	++	++	++
45–54	1 and 2	++	++	++
	1 and 3	++	0	++
	2 and 3	++	++	0
55 or more	1 and 2	0	++	++
	1 and 3	++	0	++
	2 and 3	+	0	+
		(considering family-units only)		
29 or less	1 and 2		0	0
	1 and 3		0	0
	2 and 3		0	0
30–44	1 and 2		++	++
	1 and 3		0	0
	2 and 3		0	0
45–54	1 and 2		++	++
	1 and 3		+	0
	2 and 3		0	0
55 or more	1 and 2		++	++
	1 and 3		+	++
	2 and 3		0	0

N.B. '++' denotes a significant difference at 1 per cent probability level; '+' at 5 per cent probability level; '0' denotes no significant difference at these levels.

units are not taken into account (as in the second half of the table), no significant difference is observed between Category 2 and Category 3; unlike between Category 1, on the one hand, and Category 2 or Category 3, on the other.

We are, thus, led to the conclusion that while the domestic cycle of family organization (as substantiated by the demographic variable of age of the non-familial units and the 'heads' of family-units) has a perennial effect on variations in the family structures of West Bengal, the social group comprising Category 1 of Tables 2.21–2.25 (namely, the literate Hindu and Muslim supervisory farmers and self-sustaining cultivators who do not belong to the top echelon of the social hierarchy) stands out from all other social groups by adhering most strictly to the normative family organization of patrilineally extended structures. Correspondingly, the Categories 2 and 3 are much less distinguished between them, especially when the family-units *per se* are accounted for exclusively.

In this context, the distinctions noticed in the proportional incidences of the non-familial units among all the three categories is in the nature of societal arrangements we have described already. We have seen from Chapter 1 that the non-familial units are, in general, the least well-off persons, which is not the characteristic of Category 1 but of substantial segments of Category 2 and Category 3. Also, we have found in this chapter that they are the more frequently found among the 'urban commoner', the non-agricultural 'rural commoner', and those dependent on others (who, altogether, comprise Category 3) than among the 'agrarian commoner' (who form a large segment of Category 2). Moreover, the bulk of the non-familial units represents a temporary and passing phase in their younger age with reference to the family organization of West Bengal society.

X

It is seen from the above how the *external* variations of the West Bengal family structures in the space perspective (which is our task to investigate in this chapter) unfolds itself along with the *internal* variations we have examined in the last chapter. Apropos, meaningful clusters for examining the *trend* of variations in family structures over time may be elicited from the inter-relationship we have been able to establish from the 1960-61 data. Obviously, when the 'social group'-wise variations (as denoted by the Categories 1, 2 and 3 of Tables 2.21–2.25) and the age-wise variations (of the 'heads' of family-units and of the non-familial units) are given *equal* importance, instead of the former being classified *under* the latter, the clustering of the proportional incidences of the non-familial units, nuclear families, and extended families (or of the nuclear and extended families when the non-familial units are not taken into account) may not be the same as indicatced by Tables 2.30 and 2.31. However, while the nature of clustering in the two sets may not be substantially different, the former would depict the social reality more comprehensively by establishing an unconstrained inter-relationship between the internal and external variations in West Bengal family structures. We may, therefore, examine the possibilities of such clusterings from Table 2.32 for the non-familial units, Table 2.33 for the nuclear families, and Table 2.34 for the extended families.

TABLE 2.32

Estimated Percentage Distribution of Non-familial Units

'Head's' Age-wise Variation	*'Social Group'-wise Variation Denoted by*		
	Category 1	*Category 2*	*Category 3*
(1)	(2)	(3)	(4)
29 or less	8.57±1.62	20.55±4.07	50.22±15.69
30–44	0.78±0.29	10.63±2.24	70.01± 5.42
45–54	1.17±1.09	6.93±1.58	45.30±14.20
55 or more	2.80±2.43	8.32±2.49	36.75±11.47

N.B. See footnote to Table 2.34.

Table 2.32 shows that for the non-familial units the 'social group'-wise cluster formation is the dominant characteristic of variation, but their age as young (29 years or less) or old (55 years or more) also plays a critical role. This, however, as due to the nature of group-formation and the transitory existence of the non-familial units in society, has been noted already. Anyway, Tables 2.33 and 2.34 show that whether or not the non-familial units are taken into account, the cluster formations according

TABLE 2.33

Estimated Percentage Distribution of Nuclear Families

'Head's' Age-wise Variation	'Social Group'-wise Variation Denoted by		
	Category 1	Category 2	Category 3
(1)	(2)	(3)	(4)
	1. *Including non-familial units*		
29 or less	55.90±8.67	56.83±6.74	36.86±17.42
30–44	51.49±4.61	63.38±3.87	18.79± 4.77
45–54	40.76±4.49	56.56±3.61	31.55± 7.24
55 or more	19.00±5.93	37.54±2.57	26.97± 9.28
	2. *Excluding non-familial units*		
29 or less	61.14±7.28	71.53±6.58	74.04± 13.28
30–44	52.14±4.34	70.91±4.02	62.66± 4.38
45–54	41.25±4.56	60.77±3.75	57.67± 6.28
55 or more	19.54±6.11	40.94±2.88	42.64± 9.13

N.B. See footnote to Table 2.34.

TABLE 2.34

Estimated Percentage Distribution of Extended Families

'Head's' Age-wise Variation	'Social Group'-wise Variation Denoted by		
	Category 1	Category 2	Category 3
(1)	(2)	(3)	(4)
	1. *Including non-familial units*		
29 or less	35.53±9.36	22.62±4.16	12.93±4.39
30–44	47.73±4.65	25.99±2.30	11.20±4.24
45–54	58.07±4.23	36.51±4.35	23.15±9.92
55 or more	78.20±4.09	54.14±3.32	36.28±7.15
	2. *Excluding non-familial units*		
29 or less	38.86±8.92	28.47±4.34	25.96±4.50
30–44	47.86±4.04	29.09±2.69	37.34±3.67
45–54	58.75±3.97	39.23±4.24	42.33±8.90
55 or more	80.46±4.21	59.06±3.90	57.36±7.56

N.B. In Tables 2.32–2.34, the dotted lines in a row indicate that for the 'head's' age-wise variations there is significant difference between *some* but not all the values in the two clusters thus formed. Correspondingly, the dotted lines in a column indicate that for the 'social group'-wise variation there is a significant difference between the categories 1 and 3 but *not* 1 and 2, or between 1 and 2 but *not* 1 and 3.

to the two factors of variation under reference are substantially the same; but when the family-units are considered exclusively, the clusters are more clearly delineated. This point also we have underlined earlier and mentioned the particular relevance for the present purpose to consider exclusively the family-units in the society. We may, accordingly, focus our attention on the second halves of Tables 2.33 and 2.34; and, in fact consider specifically the incidence of extended families in Table 2.34. For this is generally regarded, and also ascertained in Chapter 1, to be the normative familial organization for West Bengal. Moreover, it is found to depict the cluster formations the most precisely.

However, in this context as well as in any other, we should take into account not only the *established* but also the *incipient* segregations of the proportional incidences of the units of enquiry under reference; the latter being denoted by the dotted lines in the tables. For, while examining the trend of variations in family structures over time, we must not lose sight of the processes in operation (as suggested by the incipient segregations) along with the indication of culmination of any process (as denoted by the established segregations). On this basis, therefore, the cluster-formations according to the 'social group'-wise *and* the 'head's' age-wise variations of the extended family-units in West Bengal society are reproduced in Table 2.35 in a more succinct but lopsided manner so as to specify the interacting roles of the two factors of variation.

For both the precisely identifiable 'social group' on the left side of Table 2.35 and the residual group on its right, the 'head's' age-wise variation produce three mutually distinct clusters. But when the two sets are considered jointly, the age-group of 45–54 years for the identified 'social group' equates in its value to that of the age-group of 55 or more years for the residual group. Similarly, the age-group of 44 years or less for the former equates to that of 45–54 years for the latter, while the age-group of 55 or more years for the former and 44 years or less for the latter denote two incomparably extreme situations. Proceeding with this finding, we may diagnose some such characteristics of variability in West Bengal family structures that may allow us to depict the course of cluster-formation in a still more compact form.

Let us, for this purpose, denote by the plus sign (+) a feature which is favourable to the occurrence of the extended family

TABLE 2.35

Estimated Percentage (±s.e.) of Extended Families to Total Family-units by 'Social Groups' and Age of Family 'Heads'

Literate but Socially Inferior Hindu/Muslim Landed Gentry		*All Other 'Social Groups'*	
Age	*Percentage*	*Percentage*	*Age*
44 or less	46.46±4.31	29.15±2.18	44 or less
45–54	58.75±3.97	39.37±4.24	45–54
55 or more	80.46±4.21	58.91±3.90	55 or more

structure in the society and, complementarily, that for the nuclear family structure by the minus sign (–). The precisely identified social group on the left side of Table 2.35 will, then, be consistently characterized by the plus sign as against the residual group on the right side of the table by the minus sign. Correspondingly, for both the identified and the residual social groups, the age-group of 55 years or more will be characterized by the plus and that of 29 years or less by the minus sign. And, contextually, the age-group of 45–54 years would be characterized by the zero sign (0), as representing an indeterminate or neutral situation in regard to the emergence of the extended structures and the decay of the nuclear structures. Thus conceived, the content of Table 2.35 may be schematically represented in boxes numbered I to VI as follows.

The boxes I and VI naturally denote that extreme situations are caused by both the factors of variation being jointly either favourable or unfavourable to the emergence of the extended family structures in the society. But, with respect to the intermediate situations, we find by comparing box II to box IV, and box III to box V, that in both cases the 'social group'-wise variation remains the same as 'favourable—unfavourable' but the 'head's' age-wise variation as 'neutral—favourable' is associated with a larger incidence of extended families in society than as

TABLE 2.36

	Social Groups		
Age	*Literate but Socially Inferior Hindu/Muslim Landed Gentry*	*All Others*	*Age*
		VI −−	44 or less
44 or less	III +−	V −0	45–54
45–54	II +0	IV −+	55 or more
55 or more	I ++		

'unfavourable—neutral'. The indication is thus there that the internal variations caused by the domestic cycle of family organization has a greater discriminating effect than the external variations caused by the social stratification epitomized in the identified and the residual social groups.

The indication is corroborated by the application of the technique of analysis of variance to the data in the second half of Table 2.30; that is, referring to the sample of family-units only. The results are given in Table 2.37.

The higher F-value for variation between age-groups than between the categories of social groups substantiates a point worthy of note on its own merit, as we have discussed at some length in the last chapter and recalled in this chapter. However, variations in the domestic cycle of family organization are caused by those features of the life-span of men and women in society, their age of effective marriage and fertility pattern (as described in this and the earlier chapter) which have remained virtually constant since 1900 [GOI, 1961: 32; Mukherjee, 1971b: 47–50]. Hence, firstly, their role in unfolding any trend of variation in family structures *over time* would be minimal; and, secondly,

TABLE 2.37

Analysis of Variance	*d. f.*	*Sum of Squares*	*Mean Square*	*F*
(1)	(2)	(3)	(4)	(5)
Between categories	2	270.89	135.44	25.75
Between age-groups	3	712.55	237.52	45.15
Residual (interaction)	6	31.57	5.26	
Total	11	1015.01		

Note : The percentages of extended family-units to the total of family-units, as presented in the second half of Table 2.30, were rearranged in a two-way table in terms of the social categories and the age-groups of the heads of family-units. The former criterion provides 3 classes and the latter 4, altogether yielding 12 cells. The obtained percentages in each and every cell were then transformed to degrees [Fisher and Yates, 1957: 70], and the transformed data were examined by applying the method of analysis of variance [Rao, 1965; 205–206].

whatever that role may be, it would be automatically expressed in the time-series taken into account for the longitudinal analysis.

Moreover, it would be of interest to note that when considering the data in the first half of Table 2.30, which records variations for the family-units and the non-familial units, the F-value is found to be higher for variation between the categories of social groups than between the age-groups. The results of analysis of variance, on this account, are shown in Table 2.38.

It follows that when we examine the *trend* of variation in family structures over time, and especially when the non-familial units are brought under examination as corollary to the family-units, it would be desirable to consider explicitly the three 'social group' categories which have emerged from a composite consideration of the societal attributes taken into account. We shall, therefore, follow this procedure in the next chapter to examine the trend of variation in West Bengal family structures in the 20-year period from 1946 to 1966.

However, for a comprehensive representation of the interrelations among the societal attributes in the context of variations in family structures *per se*, we may pursue the course of clustering we are presently engaged in. Accordingly, we may telescope the

TABLE 2.38

Analysis of Variance	*d.f.*	*Sum of Squares*	*Mean Square*	*F*
(1)	(2)	(3)	(4)	(5)
Between categories	2	923.38	461.69	93.65
Between age-groups	3	733.82	244.61	49.62
Residual (interaction)	6	29.56	4.93	
Total	11	1686.76		

Note : as for Table 2.37 but referring to the first half of Table 2.30, i.e., by considering the non-familial units and the family-units.

boxes II and IV of Table 2.36 into one, and the corresponding boxes III and V into another. The reconstituted boxes will, then, provide us with a simple classificatory schema without any loss of information; for the respective clusters will have a joint but unequivocal specification as seen from Table 2.36. Thus the schema, referring to both family-units and non-familial units, may be denoted by four clusters as: Cluster A = box I; Cluster B=boxes II and IV; Cluster C=boxes III and V; and Cluster D = box VI.

That the proposed clustering will precisely and comprehensively take into account the variations in West Bengal family structures in the space perspective is indicated by Table 2.39 which gives the percentage incidence of the extended families to total units over the city-town-village spectrum for each one of the four clusters.

It is seen from the table that seldom any significant difference is recorded among the mean values for each cluster, indicating thereby that variations due to rural-urban dichotomy or continuum (that is, city-town-village spectrum) have been mostly accounted for by the set of four clusters themselves. Also Table 2.40, which gives the relative incidence of all the non-familial units and family-units of West Bengal in the four clusters for the cities, towns, and villages, will be instructive in this context; for the figures denote a consistent and distinctive gradation from Cluster A to Cluster D.

In sum, then, we may consider the four clusters as the ultimate expression of variation in social stratification relevant to our

TABLE 2.39

Estimated Percentage of Extended Family-units to Total (±s.e.)
(Sample size in brackets)

Cluster	*City*	*Town*	*Village*	*West Bengal*
(1)	(2)	(3)	(4)	(5)
1. *Considering all non-familial units and family-units*				
A	100.00	96.18±5.18	77.65±4.15	78.20±4.09
	(1)	(3)	(89)	(93)
B	63.99±10.31	50.26±0.18	53.42±3.77	53.62±2.97
	(99)	(96)	(434)	(629)
C	37.85± 2.09	31.50±3.08	35.33±0.89	38.26±1.40
	(204)	(195)	(754)	(1153)
D	22.95± 2.37	21.80±2.09	23.02±3.11	25.31±2.89
	(830)	(603)	(1626)	(3059)
2. *Considering the family-units only*				
A	100.00	96.18±5.18	79.96±3.06	80.46±4.21
	(1)	(3)	(87)	(91)
B	68.04± 8.51	53.42±0.26	59.40±4.06	58.87±3.93
	(92)	(91)	(395)	(578)
C	43.10± 1.89	45.49±2.11	38.21±0.97	41.42±4.29
	(179)	(177)	(702)	(1058)
D	28.06± 3.40	32.69±1.43	25.60±2.82	29.15±2.18
	(483)	(467)	(1442)	(2392)

TABLE 2.40

Cluster	*Estimated Percentage of the Total Incidence of Non-familial and Family Units*			
	City	*Town*	*Village*	*West Bengal*
(1)	(2)	(3)	(4)	(5)
A	0.02	0.48	3.21	2.37
B	7.66	19.16	23.74	23.66
C	16.68	28.56	25.41	24.63
D	75.64	51.80	47.64	49.34
Total	100.00	100.00	100.00	100.00

study. Contextually, (a) the literate but socially inferior Hindu or Muslim landed gentry and (b) the retention of familial authority in old age are the indicators of maintaining the *status quo* according as we consider the static point and the direction of change discussed in the Introductory chapter.

CHAPTER THREE

Trend

For the State of West Bengal or its urban sector, we have data at 3 time-points: 1955–56, 1960–61 and 1965–66. Over these 10 years, the distinctive feature for West Bengal as a whole is that the relative incidence of the non-familial units drops in the first 5-year period (between 1955–56 and 1960–61) and regains its strength somewhat in the next 5-year period (between 1960–61 and 1965–66). Correspondingly, the relative incidence of the nuclear families is seen to rise in the first 5-year period and revert back to its previous strength in the next 5-year period. The incidence of the extended families tends to maintain the *status quo* except that between the two extreme time-points of 1955–56 and 1965–66 it registers a rise. Details are given in Tables 3.1 and 3.2.

TABLE 3.1

Year	*Estimated Percentage to Total* ($\pm$*s.e.*) *in West Bengal Society*				
	Non-familial Unit	*Nuclear Family*	*Extended Family*	*Total*	*Sample*
(1)	(2)	(3)	(4)	(5)	(6)
1955–56	25.11$\pm$1.21	44.81$\pm$2.03	30.08$\pm$1.75	100.00	2435
1960–61	13.44$\pm$1.93	53.66$\pm$3.60	32.90$\pm$2.28	100.00	4934
1965–66	18.20$\pm$0.72	46.89$\pm$0.67	34.91$\pm$0.73	100.00	14350

We have discussed in Chapter 6 of Part 2 that the National Sample Survey data (which have been employed to denote the time-points 1955–56 and 1965–66) were so collected that they may overestimate the relative occurrence of the non-familial units in the society and underestimate, correspondingly, that of the family-units. While

TABLE 3.2

Comparison of Time-points	Result of t-test of Difference in the Percentage Values given in Table 3.1		
	Non-familial Unit	Nuclear Family	Extended Family
(1)	(2)	(3)	(4)
1955–56 and 1960–61	++	+	0
1960–61 and 1965–66	+	0	0
1955–56 and 1965–66	++	0	+

N.B. Significance level: 1%=++; 5%=+; <5%=0.

we have also pointed out that this theoretical possibility is of little practical consequence, it strengthens the finding in Tables 3.1 and 3.2 that during and just after the Second Five-Year Plan period (which marks a phase of prosperity in Indian society) the West Bengal people lived more under family organization than either before or afterwards. In this time-span, the relative incidences of the nuclear and extended family structures do not appear to record any differential trend on their own. The variations found for the nuclear and extended families in Tables 3.1 and 3.2 are explainable as the consequence of the shift in the relative incidence of the non-familial units. For Table 3.3, which deals with the family-units only, does not register any significant difference in the percentage values at the 3 time-points for the nuclear and extended families, respectively.

TABLE 3.3

Year	Estimated Percentage to Total (±s.e.) in West Bengal Society			
	Nuclear Family	Extended Family	Total	Sample
(1)	(2)	(3)	(4)	(5)
1955–56	54.06±2.88	45.94±2.88	100.00	1734
1960–61	61.99±4.26	38.01±4.26	100.00	4119
1965–66	57.32±0.99	42.68±0.99	100.00	11037

Similar is the situation for the urban sector of West Bengal, as seen from Tables 3.4 and 3.5.

TABLE 3.4

Year	Estimated Percentage to Total (±s.e.) in Urban West Bengal				
	Non-familial Unit	*Nuclear Family*	*Extended Family*	*Total*	*Sample*
(1)	(2)	(3)	(4)	(5)	(6)
1955–56	42.07±3.98	33.44±2.10	24.49±2.21	100.00	1817
1960–61	24.15±4.89	40.87±2.05	34.98±4.98	100.00	2031
1965–66	37.64±1.06	34.94±0.98	27.42±1.48	100.00	6528
		(considering family-units only)			
1955–56		57.73±3.05	42.27±3.05	100.00	1191
1960–61		53.88±5.39	46.12±5.39	100.00	1493
1965–66		56.03±1.78	43.97±1.78	100.00	3974

TABLE 3.5

Comparison of Time-points	Result of t-test of Difference in the Percentage Values given in Table 3.4		
	Non-familial Unit	*Nuclear Family*	*Extended Family*
(1)	(2)	(3)	(4)
1955–56 and 1960–61	++	+	0
1960–61 and 1965–66	++	++	0
1955–56 and 1965–66	0	0	0
		(considering family-units only)	
1955–56 and 1960–61		0	0
1960–61 and 1965–66		0	0
1955–56 and 1965–66		0	0

N.B. Significance level: 1%=++; 5%=+; <5%=0.

For the rural sector of West Bengal, on the other hand, the situation is slightly different. This we may examine over a period of 20 years (including the 10 years for West Bengal as a whole and its urban sector), for we have now data for 5 time-points:

1946–47, 1951, 1955–56, 1960–61 and 1965–66. We have noted in Chapter 7 that any computation of standard errors of the estimated percentages from the 1946–47 data would not be efficient. Table 3.6 however, shows that the corresponding values for 1946–47 and 1951 are similar.

TABLE 3.6

Year	*Estimated Percentage to Total* (±*s.e.*) *in Rural West Bengal*				
	Non-familial Unit	*Nuclear Family*	*Extended Family*	*Total*	*Sample*
(1)	(2)	(3)	(4)	(5)	(6)
1946–47	15.94	43.76	40.30	100.00	4116
1951	16.81±3.02	38.13±4.83	45.06±3.18	100.00	900
1955–56	11.88±1.19	47.19±2.38	40.93±2.12	100.00	618
1960–61	9.19±1.66	58.73±3.52	32.08±2.09	100.00	2903
1965–66	9.70±0.53	52.11±0.70	38.19±0.78	100.00	7822
		(considering family-units only)			
1946–47		52.05	47.95	100.00	3460
1951		45.83±5.78	54.17±5.78	100.00	741
1955–56		53.56±3.19	46.44±3.19	100.00	543
1960–61		64.67±4.09	35.33±4.09	100.00	2626
1965–66		57.71±1.05	42.29±1.05	100.00	7063

Now, in the light of the results given in Table 3.7, we may interpret the figures in Table 3.6 as follows: (1) Any variation in the relative incidence of the non-familial units, nuclear families and the extended families is noticed from the Second Five-Year Plan period and not earlier. (2) Not only there has been a distinct drop in the relative incidence of the non-familial units during and after the Second Five-Year Plan period, but within the gamut of family-units also there is a trend toward an increasing incidence of the nuclear families and a decreasing incidence of the extended families.

Thus the trend of variation in West Bengal family structures cannot be interpreted merely by the higher or lower incidence of the non-familial units, as it appeared from Tables 3.1, 3.3, and 3.4 prepared with reference to West Bengal as a whole or its urban sector. The State being essentially rural (as it is true for

TABLE 3.7

Comparison of Time-points	*Result of t-test of Difference in the Percentage Values given in Table 3.6*		
	Non-familial Unit	*Nuclear Family*	*Extended Family*
(1)	(2)	(3)	(4)
1951 and 1955–56	0	0	0
1951 and 1960–61	+	++	++
1951 and 1965–66	+	++	+
1955–56 and 1960–61	0	++	++
1955–56 and 1965–66	0	++	0
1960–61 and 1965–66	0	0	+
		(considering family-units only)	
1951 and 1955–56		0	0
1951 and 1960–61		+	+
1951 and 1965–66		+	+
1955–56 and 1960–61		+	+
1955–56 and 1965–66		0	0
1960–61 and 1965–66		0	0

N.B. Significance level: 1%=++; 5%=+; <5%=0.

the whole of India), we should also examine, over time, any shift for the nuclear and the extended family organization.

II

The temporal shift in the relative incidence of the non-familial units, nuclear families, and extended families may take place in four ways: (1) change in the *nature of internal variations* of West Bengal family structures from that ascertained in Chapter 1; (2) change in the *nature of external variations* of West Bengal family structures from that ascertained in Chapter 2; (3) changes *in* those aspects of the social structure of West Bengal with which the aforementioned variations in its family structures are distinctly associated; and (4) changes in the *extent* of internal and/or external variations in West Bengal family structures with reference to one or another facet of the social structure (that is, one or another of the three 'social group' categories). Let us, first, explain why and how we may consider these possibilities in the light of our findings in the previous two chapters.

We have seen from Chapter 1 that the dominant note of West Bengal family structures is to form the *patrilineally joint family of procreation* by the 'heads' of respective units. In this process, some 'heads' may remain *sine die* in the nuclear family of procreation or pass through it into an extended family. Also, due to various exigencies, they may form the nuclear family of orientation, joint family of orientation *or* of orientation and procreation, and some non-patrilineally extended structures. As a result, a noticeable range of variation may be found in West Bengal family structures at a point in time, and at that point (1960–61, in the present instance) the incidence of the nuclear families may even be slightly higher than that of the extended families. Nevertheless, the central tendency of West Bengal family structures to evolve into patrilineally joint families of procreation is enforced.

Concurrently with this nature of internal variations in West Bengal family structures, we find from Chapter 2 a distinct characteristic of their external variations. We find that while the central tendency of internal variations is reflected by the age of the 'heads' of the non-familial units and family-units belonging to the three 'social group' categories constituted in Chapter 2, these categories have specific contributions of their own toward the variations noticed in West Bengal family structures.

Thus, Category 1—comprising the literate but socially inferior Hindu or Muslim landed gentry—is seen to have four essential characteristics: (1) a preponderance of the full-fledged patrilineal joint families with all the 5 intra-family relations (that is, lineal, affinal, conjugal, parental and sibling) present therein; (2) the secondary occurrence of the full-fledged nuclear families with all the 3 intra-family relations (that is, conjugal, parental and sibling) present therein; (3) a scarce incidence of the non-patrilineally extended families; and (4) the rare occurrence of the non-familial units.

Correspondingly, Category 2—which comprises the rest of the landed gentry, all agricultural commoner, and the non-agricultural literate gentry or illiterate commoner—is seen to be characterized primarily by the preponderance of nuclear families, next by the extended families, and lastly by the non-familial units; but the full complement of intra-family relations among them (that is, 5 for the extended and 3 for the nuclear families) and the extended families to be essentially joint patrilineally are less common in this category than in the former one.

Lastly, Category 3—which comprises the non-agricultural illiterate gentry or the literate commoner, and the societal dependents—is primarily characterized by the prevalence of the non-familial units (particularly noticeable among the non-agricultural commoner), some nuclear and a few extended families which (a) usually do not exhibit the full complement of 3 or 5 intra-family relations, respectively, and (b) the extended families tend to be patrilineally and non-patrilineally extended in about an equal strength.

Now, for each and every time-point taken into account, the three 'social group' categories may or may not be distinguished mutually by the above characteristics of variation in family structures. But if they are so distinguished (in a very large number of cases, at any rate, if not always), the indication would be there that the essential characteristic of internal variations in West Bengal family structures (as ascertained in Chapter 1) as well as their external variations (elicited in Chapter 2) are operative in the longitudinal perspective of the societal dynamics. In that case, the aforesaid possibilities 1 and 2 would be of minimal or no importance at all for the 'trend analysis' we have undertaken in this chapter; and, consequently, our attention would be drawn toward the possibilities 3 and 4 enumerated above.

It follows that if the relative incidence of the three 'social group' categories—which are respectively associated with the differential incidence of the non-familial units, nuclear families and extended families—are seen to vary over time and in the same manner as found in Tables 3.1–3.7, then the third possibility will come into prominence and, to a large extent, the temporal shift recorded by these tables may be explained as due to variations in the social structure of West Bengal and not in the family structures *per se*.

However, whether or not for the respective time-points the 'social group' categories are mutually distinguished by their specific familial characteristics elicited in Chapter 2 and summarized above, these characteristics may vary *over time* for one or another of the three categories, for the urban or the rural sector of the society, and so on. In cases of these variations in 'extent' (and not in 'nature', as distinguished under the possibilities of change enumerated as 1 and 2), the fourth possibility will come up for consideration. Another dimension of variation may thus open up, which would be of specific relevance to the 'trend analysis' undertaken in this chapter. For such questions will now be raised as: What do these variations indicate, in terms of *familial organization* and *familial integration* of the 'heads' of coresident and commensal kingroups, in the time perspective?

Hence, with this schema of four possibilities in view, we may proceed with the analysis of the trend of variation over time of the West Bengal family structures.

III

Let us begin with the non-familial units, and consider only their male component since we have already seen from Tables 1.4 and 1.5 in Chapter 1 that the female non-familial units have virtually no role to play in the family organization of West Bengal society. We have also noticed in Table 1.4 that in 1960–61 the male non-familial units were overwhelmingly unmarried or married but living away from their wives and children. The same is the situation for the other time-points as we find from Tables 3.8–3.10 which refer to the State of West Bengal, its urban sector, and its rural sector, respectively. The only exception in this arrangement is with respect to the 'social group' Category 1, but this is of little consequence as we shall explain in due course.

Besides for Category 1, Tables 3.8–3.10 elicit some interesting information when we examine the variations within the community of male non-familial units for each of the three 'social group' categories. Pursuant to the essential feature of Category 1 to be rural in character, the male non-familial units it contains are virtually all located in rural area but it is not usual for them, at any time-point, to be married but living away from their 'family' of procreation and/or orientation. In about equal strength, they are either unmarried or widowed, divorced and conjugally separated persons (Tables 3.8 and 3.10). This means that,

TABLE 3.8

Year	*Estimated Percentage of Male Non-familial Units (±s.e.) in West Bengal Society* Unmarried	Married	Widowed, etc.	Total	Sample
(1)	(2)	(3)	(4)	(5)	(6)
1. *Literate, socially inferior Hindu or Muslim landed gentry*					
1955–56	—	—	—	—	—
1960–61	58.01± 6.23	—	41.99±6.23	100.00	8
1965–66	41.85±11.05	21.46± 8.18	36.69±9.78	100.00	28
2. *Rest of landed gentry, agricultural commoner, non-agricultural literate gentry or illiterate commoner*					
1955–56	42.67± 5.22	49.24± 4.18	8.09±3.20	100.00	368
1960–61	43.78± 4.20	41.47± 4.83	14.75±2.79	100.00	499
1965–66	31.18± 2.09	61.33± 2.25	7.49±0.80	100.00	1903
3. *Non-agricultural illiterate gentry or literate commoner, societal dependents*					
1955–56	42.42±12.12	52.93±12.36	4.65±2.35	100.00	249
1960–61	21.60± 9.46	69.96± 8.82	8.44±4.12	100.00	155
1965–66	44.70± 2.88	47.59± 2.74	7.71±0.95	100.00	908

TABLE 3.9

Year	*Estimated Percentage of Male Non-familial Units (±s.e.) in Urban West Bengal* Unmarried	Married	Widowed, etc.	Total	Sample
(1)	(2)	(3)	(4)	(5)	(6)
1. *Literate, socially inferior Hindu or Muslim landed gentry*					
1955–56	—	—	—	—	—
1960–61	—	—	—	—	—
1965–66	50.00±21.60	50.00±21.60	—	100.00	8
2. *Rest of landed gentry, agricultural commoner, non-agricultural literate gentry or illiterate commoner*					
1955–56	24.43± 2.49	72.23± 2.45	3.34±1.82	100.00	329
1960–61	34.28± 6.27	56.56± 8.84	9.16±4.29	100.00	348
1965–66	24.26± 1.60	72.23± 1.51	3.51±0.46	100.00	1641
3. *Non-agricultural illiterate gentry or literate commoner, societal dependents*					
1955–56	39.37± 6.05	55.84± 6.98	4.79±1.46	100.00	234
1960–61	18.74± 9.88	72.94± 9.14	8.32±4.61	100.00	134
1965–66	31.26± 3.54	62.64± 3.20	6.10±0.59	100.00	713

TABLE 3.10

Year	Estimated Percentage of Male Non-familial Units (±s.e.) in Rural West Bengal				
	Unmarried	*Married*	*Widowed, etc.*	*Total*	*Sample*
(1)	(2)	(3)	(4)	(5)	(6)
	1. *Literate, socially inferior Hindu or Muslim landed gentry*				
1951	32.40±28.00	16.28±16.83	51.32±31.15	100.00	3
1955–56	—	—	—	—	—
1960–61	58.00± 6.26	—	42.00± 6.26	100.00	8
1965–66	40.00±12.70	15.00± 8.21	45.00±11.82	100.00	20
	2. *Rest of landed gentry, agricultural commoner, non-agricultural literate gentry or illiterate commoner*				
1951	64.49±10.54	30.99±10.56	4.52± 1.55	100.00	77
1956–56	60.51± 8.53	26.75± 5.97	12.74± 6.22	100.00	39
1960–61	54.79± 6.51	23.99± 5.81	21.22± 3.90	100.00	151
1965–66	52.67± 4.01	27.48± 3.51	19.85± 3.04	100.00	262
	3. *Non-agricultural illiterate gentry ar literate commoner, societal dependents*				
1951	65.13± 8.20	29.20±11.62	5.67± 5.82	100.00	32
1955–56	45.49±23.78	49.99±23.95	4.52± 4.48	100.00	15
1960–61	39.27±14.96	51 56±14.50	9.17± 8.34	100.00	21
1965–66	70.26± 3.84	18.97± 3.11	10.77± 2.39	100.00	195

presently at any rate, their role in the familial organization of West Bengal society is auxiliary and not instrumental which a married non-familial unit is more likely to assume in order to earn a livelihood for himself *and* his 'family'. However, this 'social group' category is the smallest of the three in size and contains only few non-familial units.

The male non-familial units belonging to Category 2—which is the largest of the three in size and contains the largest share of the non-familial units, although its essential character is to represent the nuclear family structure—are mostly married in the urban areas and unmarried in the rural areas (Tables 3.9 and 3.10). A possible distinction is, thus, indicated in the 'familial' potentiality and/or practice of the non-familial units by their rural-urban location. However, in the case of all these non-familial units no significant difference is noticed over the time-period at the 1 or 5 per cent level of significance, except on one count: for West Bengal as a whole the year 1965–66 records a higher incidence of married non-familial units (and, correspondingly, a lower incidence of unmarried male non-familial units) than in the years 1955–56 and/or 1960–61 (Table 3.8).

Lastly, the male non-familial units belonging to Category 3, which gives the largest *concentration* of non-familial units in the society, tend to behave in a manner similar to those under Category 2 which, as noted above, gives the largest *representation* of non-familial units in the society owing to its size. In Category 3 also these males are mostly married in the urban areas and unmarried in the rural areas, but the distinction for the rural areas is not so pronounced for them as it is for those belonging to Category 2. However, as for Category 2, no temporal distinction is noticed for Category 3 in the relative incidence of the male non-familial units in West Bengal as a whole or in its urban and rural sectors.

Even so, we notice an interesting phenomenon. In the urban sector of West Bengal and at the 10 per cent level of significance, there is a drop in the relative incidence of the married male non-familial units belonging to Category 2 between 1955–56 and 1960–61, and a reversal of the trend between 1960–61 and 1965–66 (Table 3.9). We have also found earlier that for the West Bengal society as a whole the above trend of reversal is sharply marked (Table 3.8). It appears, therefore, that a trend similar to that noted in Tables 3.1 and 3.4 is discernible for the male married non-familial units belonging to the 'social group' Category 2 and the urban sector of West Bengal society.

This pointer is worthy of mention because: (1) the group under reference represents the largest of all those formed by the marital status, affiliation to 'social group' categories, and the rural-urban distinction of the male non-familial units in West Bengal; and (2) as we had found from Tables 1.5 and 1.6 in Chapter 1, most of the male non-familial units live without kins or affines in order to earn a livelihood while having a 'family' elsewhere. Hence, the differential employment opportunities in rural and urban sectors of West Bengal, before and after the Second Five-Year Plan period, may partly explain how the shifts in the relative incidence of non-familial units have taken place over time, leading to changes in the family organization of society and, if at all, in the familial integration of the people thus concerned.

However, any structural analysis of the family cannot automatically *explain* the viability and dynamics of the social institution. Also, the above useful indication *towards* an explanation (which would require a functional analysis of the social institution to confirm or reject) would fail to account, directly, for the bulk of the non-familial units in West Bengal, although it may be valid for their largest grouping. We must, therefore, look beyond the internal structural variations among the non-familial units in order to ascertain comprehensively how the shifts in their relative incidence over time have been effected. In this context, the previously enumerated third possibility of social structural variations will come up for consideration. However, the distinctions noticed within the community of male non-familial units have a relevance of its own to appraise the dynamics of West Bengal family structures (and, thus, of the social institution as a whole). This we shall discuss at the end of this chapter with reference to the aforesaid fourth possibility of the extent of variations in family structures *per se*.

IV

Similar is the situation with reference to the nuclear and extended families. The structural variations within them do not yield a *sufficient* clue to explain how the shifts in their relative incidence have taken place over time, but they denote some properties which are of intrinsic merit and may be of some relevance to explain the aforesaid shifts. Accordingly, we shall examine the nuclear structures and the patrilineally joint structures which, as we have pointed out earlier, denote the dominant characteristic of extended families in West Bengal society.

Thus, we had found from Tables 1.7 and 1.10 in Chapter 1 that the majority of nuclear and patrilineally joint families in West Bengal represent 'complete' structures in the sense that: (a) the nuclear families are constituted of the conjugal, parental and sibling relations; and (b) the extended families contain the lineal, affinal, conjugal, parental, and sibling relations. But we have also found from Table 2.23 in Chapter 2 that a differential occurrence of the 'complete' nuclear or extended families is associated with the three 'social group' categories. And, now, we find from Tables 3.11 and 3.12 that this picture remains more or less the same over time and for the West Bengal society as a whole or its urban and rural sectors. Table 3.13 gives a statistical corroboration of this picture.

Substantiated by the results of the *t*-test of mean differences given in Table 3.13, we find from Tables 3.11 and 3.12 that the 'social group' Category 1 consistently represents the largest, Category 2 the next, and Category 3 the lowest incidence of 'complete' nuclear and extended family structures. The notable exceptions in this respect are for the urban sector of West Bengal

TABLE 3.11

Estimated Percentage of Nuclear Families Containing Conjugal, Parental and Sibling Relations to Total Nuclear Families (±s.e.) Under Each 'Social Group' Category and Year (Sample in brackets)

Year	*Category 1 Literate, Socially Inferior Hindu or Muslim Landed Gentry*	*Category 2 Rest of Landed Gentry, Agricultural Commoner Non-Agricultural Literate Gentry or Illiterate Commoner*	*Category 3 Non-agricultural Illiterate Gentry or Literate Commoner, Societal Dependents*
(1)	(2)	(3)	(4)
		1. *West Bengal*	
1955–56	(56) 63.96± 3.60	(684) 46.42±3.18	(142) 34.74±2.58
1960–61	(219) 71.20± 3.29	(2293) 53.62±3.14	(110) 32.86±2.80
1965–66	(1060) 77.35± 1.10	(4742) 65.51±2.10	(526) 40.55±1.89
		2. *Urban sector*	
1955–56	(5) 39.33±18.59	(472) 50.81±2.74	(119) 38.45±2.62
1960–61	(12) 48.59± 3.16	(898) 54.95±3.49	(51) 41.89±2.88
1965–66	(33) 78.85± 7.47	(1900) 63.30±1.56	(319) 42.26±3.42
		3. *Rural sector*	
1946–47	(220) 62.27	(1514) 46.83	(67) 35.82
1951	(132) 56.93± 6.71	(227) 45.88±4.35	(18) 43.67±7.69
1955–56	(51) 64.22± 5.63	(212) 45.76±3.80	(23) 33.43±8.54
1960–61	(207) 71.83± 3.30	(1395) 53.22±2.67	(59) 24.17±4.38
1965–66	(1027) 77.31± 1.11	(2842) 66.29±1.75	(207) 39.13±3.61

TABLE 3.12

Estimated Percentage of Patrilineally Joint Families Containing Lineal, Affinal, Conjugal, Parental and Sibling Relations to all Patrilineally Joint Families (±s.e.) Under each 'Social Group' Category and Year (Sample in brackets)

Year	*Category 1 Literate, Socially Inferior Hindu or Muslim Landed Gentry*	*Category 2 Rest of Landed Gentry, Agricultural Commoner Non-agricultural Literate Gentry or Illiterate Commoner*	*Category 3 Non-agricultural Illiterate Gentry or Literate Commoner, Societal Dependents*
(1)	(2)	(3)	(4)
	1. *West Bengal*		
1955–56	(84) 63.92±3.28	(394) 61.04±2.35	(57) 22.43±3.69
1960–61	(187) 76.04±5.03	(835) 62.78±2.46	(35) 39.67±4.73
1965–66	(939) 75.79±1.54	(2237) 62.35±2.04	(152) 53.62±3.92
	2. *Urban sector*		
1955–56	(10) 94.89±5.87	(295) 70.81±3.11	(48) 49.63± 8.30
1960–61	(5) 99·23±1.20	(315) 65.21±2.93	(22) 45.09±12.42
1965–66	(24) 78.38±9.72	(1029) 71.05±1.09	(84) 54.55± 4.37
	3. *Rural sector*		
1946–47	(236) 58.47	(836) 44.02	(21) 38.10
1951	(118) 51.39±8.12	(110) 42.21±6.49	(3) 0.00
1955–56	(74) 63.62±6.60	(99) 40.60±8.23	(9) 10.68±11.50
1960–61	(182) 75.20±5.15	(520) 61.71±3.72	(13) 25.30±18.04
1965–66	(915) 75.74±1.56	(1208) 58.36±1.34	(68) 52.94± 4.20

and in reference to the nuclear families for the time points 1955–56 and 1960–61. The exceptions record the prominence attained by Category 2 as against Category 1, which is in accord with the nature of structural articulations of the patrilineally joint families in the urban sector, as we shall discuss later.

In the rural sector also an exception is noticed in respect of the year 1951 and in the case of both nuclear and extended families which do not record any significant difference in the mean values among the three 'social group' categories. However, as we have already noted, there is no significant trend of variation in West Bengal family structures between 1951 and 1955–56 or, for that matter, between 1946–47 and 1955–56; that is, before the onset of the Second Five-Year Plan in independent India.

TABLE 3.13

Comparison of 'Social Group' Categories	*Reference to the Familial Characteristic*	*Result of t-test of Difference in the Percentage Values Referred Under Cols.* (1) *and* (2)			
		1951	1955–56	1960–61	1965–66
(1)	(2)	(3)	(4)	(5)	(6)
	1. *West Bengal*				
1 and 2	Table 3.11	—	++	++	++
	Table 3.12	—	0	++	++
1 and 3	Table 3.11	—	++	++	++
	Table 3.12	—	++	++	++
2 and 3	Table 3.11	—	++	++	++
	Table 3.12	—	++	++	++
	2. *Urban sector*				
1 and 2	Table 3.11	—	0	0	+
	Table 3.12	—	++	++	0
1 and 3	Table 3.11	—	0	0	++
	Table 3.12	—	++	++	+
2 and 3	Table 3.11	—	++	++	++
	Table 3.12	—	+	0	++
	3. *Rural sector*				
1 and 2	Table 3.11	0	++	++	++
	Table 3.12	0	+	+	++
1 and 3	Table 3.11	0	++	++	++
	Table 3.12	—	++	++	++
2 and 3	Table 3.11	0	0	++	++
	Table 3.12	—	+	+	0

N.B. Significance level: 1%=++; 5%=+; <5%=0; —=test not possible.

On the whole, therefore, the findings in Tables 3.11–3.13 are in conformity with the previous findings in Tables 1.7, 1.10 and and 2.23; and this suggests, again, that an examination—over time—of any variability in the relative incidence of the three 'social group' categories may explain how the shifts in the relative incidence of the West Bengal family structures have taken place in the longitudinal perspective.

And yet, more discrepancies are noticed than already pointed out for the nuclear families in the urban sector of West Bengal, namely, Categories 1 and 2 tend to register equal incidence of 'complete' nuclear families instead of Category 1 recording more than Category 2. Thus, Table 3.14 substantiates the fact that there is a longitudinal trend between 1955–56 and 1965–66 (that

TABLE 3.14

Comparison of Time-points	*Reference to the Familial Characteristic*	*Result of t-test of Difference in the Percentage Values Referred Under Cols.* (1) and (2) *for 'Social Group' Category*		
		1	2	3
(1)	(2)	(3)	(4)	(5)
	1. *West Bengal*			
1955–56 and 1960–61	Table 3.11	0	0	0
	Table 3.12	+	0	++
1960–61 and 1965–66	Table 3.11	0	++	+
	Table 3.12	0	0	++
1955–56 and 1965–66	Table 3.11	++	++	0
	Table 3.12	++	0	++
	2. *Urban sector*			
1955–56 and 1960–61	Table 3.11	0	0	0
	Table 3.12	0	0	0
1960–61 and 1965–66	Table 3.11	++	+	0
	Table 3.12	+	0	0
1955–56 and 1965–66	Table 3.11	+	++	0
	Table 3.12	0	0	0
	3. *Rural sector*			
1951 and 1955–56	Table 3.11	0	0	0
	Table 3.12	0	0	—
1955–56 and 1960–61	Table 3.11	0	0	0
	Table 3.12	0	+	0
1960–61 and 1965–66	Table 3.11	0	++	++
	Table 3.12	0	0	0
1951 and 1960–61	Table 3.11	+	0	+
	Table 3.12	+	++	—
1955–56 and 1965–66	Table 3.11	+	++	0
	Table 3.12	0*	+	++
1951 and 1965–66	Table 3.11	++	++	0
	Table 3.12	++	+	—

N.B. Significance level; 1%=++; 5%=+; 10%=0*; <10%=0; —=test not possible.

is, since the onset of the Second Five-Year Plan) toward evermore increasing incidence of the 'complete' nuclear families in Categories 1 and 2 (but not in Category 3) for West Bengal *en bloc* and its urban or rural sectors, which is particularly noticeable for Category 2.

On the other hand, we find that the rural sector of West Bengal registers an increase in the incidence of 'complete' patrilineally joint families for each one of the three 'social group' categories during this period, but for the urban sector the situation remains unchanged for any one of the three categories. The upshot is that, in reference to West Bengal *en bloc*, a similar trend as for the rural sector is noticed for Categories 1 and 3, but not for Category 2 which has a large representation in the urban sector.

Thus, an examination of the previously enumerated fourth possibility (for instance, the extent of variations in family structures *per se*) is indicated for the family-units in West Bengal; and in reference to its rural-urban distinction, as it has been for the non-familial units.

V

We have noted in reference to Table 2.23 in Chapter 2 that the absence of one or more of the scheduled intra-family relations in the nuclear or extended family structures does not necessarily mean that the growth of these families is stunted or truncated. But we have also noted that any distinct variation in this respect is worthy of investigation. Thus we have seen from Table 2.1 that, contrary to the usual belief, there are relatively more nuclear families in the rural than in the urban sector of West Bengal; and for all the available time-points also we found that to be true from Tables 3.4 and 3.6. But now we find from Table 3.11 that in both the sectors the 'complete' nuclear structures are becoming more frequent in the 'social group' Categories 1 and 2, but not in Category 3; and we may bear in mind that Category 1 is essentially a rural and, contrastingly, Category 3 an urban phenomenon. This means that, in the time perspective, not only more nuclear families are to be found in the rural than in the urban areas, but in the former they also assume evermore the 'complete' structure.

Moreover, we have seen from Table 2.1 that there is no significant difference in the relative incidence of the extended families in the rural and urban sectors of West Bengal; but we find from Table 3.12 that the patrilineally joint families with a full complement of their all possible intra-family relations is becoming more frequent in the rural than in the urban sector of the society. The suggestion is, thus, there that stabler family organizations are established contemporarily in the rural sector of West Bengal than in its urban sector.

The suggestion gathers argument if we examine the structural articulations of the patrilineal joint families in West Bengal. We have seen from Table 2.24 that the proportional incidence of these families, out of all extended families, is of about the same magnitude for the three 'social group' categories, although Category 1 definitely contains more of them than Category 3. However, Table 2.24 corroborates the earlier finding in Chapter 1 that most of the extended families in West Bengal are of this kind. Also, we have seen from Table 1.13 in Chapter 1 that most of these families have no collateral relatives of their 'heads' and, thus, register patrilineally joint families of procreation of these persons. Next, but in decisively low importance, they incorporate only the 'heads's' sibling(s) and/or the consort(s) of the male sibiling(s). In a fewer instances, they contain, additionally, the progeny of the male sibling(s) and/or the consort(s) of such progeny. And seldom they contain either exclusively the 'head's' male sibling(s)' progeny and/or their consort(s) *or* other collateral relatives of the 'head' with or without the aforementioned 'fraternal' relative(s). This arrangement of predominance of the joint family of procreation of the male 'heads' of the families, and the decreasing order of importance of different kinds of 'fraternal' or any form of collateral joint family they form, are now found to be maintained, at virtually all the time-points for the rural sector of West Bengal (and, thus, for West Bengal as a whole), but not for its urban sector. Details are given in Tables 3.15–3.19.

It will be noticed from an examination of Tables 3.15–3.19 that, contrary to the arrangement for West Bengal as a whole and its rural sector, the urban sector records, at virtually all time-points, the prevalence of the 'fraternal' joint families of the 'heads'—with or without the progeny and/or the consort(s) of

TABLE 3.15

Estimated Percentage of Those Patrilineally Joint Families which Have No Collateral Relatives of Their 'Heads' to Total of all Patrilineally Joint Families (±s.e.) Under each 'Social Group' Category and Year (Sample in brackets)

Year	Category 1 Literate, Socially Inferior Hindu or Muslim Landed Gentry		Category 2 Rest of Landed Gentry, Agricultural Commoner, Non-agricultural Literate Gentry or Illiterate Commoner		Category 3 Non-agricultural Illiterate Gentry or Literate Commoner, Societal Dependents	
(1)	(2)		(3)		(4)	
1. West Bengal						
1955–56	(84)	62.27± 6.89	(394)	53.11±5.23	(57)	63.67±12.40
1960–61	(187)	68.07± 3.58	(835)	61.12±3.81	(35)	78.75± 7.47
1965–66	(939)	65.55± 1.80	(2237)	61.02±1.42	(152)	52.73± 4.81
2. Urban sector						
1955–56	(10)	41.91±20.86	(295)	45.00±3.04	(48)	33.77±13.06
1960–61	(5)	100.00	(315)	49.75±3.61	(22)	78.13± 8.95
1965–66	(24)	70.26±12.51	(1029)	46.77±2.16	(84)	36.36± 7.64
3. Rural sector						
1946–47	(236)	55.51	(836)	61.48	(21)	47.62
1951	(118)	63.78± 6.50	(110)	58.84±7.46	(3)	100.00
1955–56	(74)	62.46± 6.96	(99)	54.48±6.13	(9)	76.59±13.96
1960–61	(182)	66.91± 3.50	(520)	66.14±4.11	(13)	80.39±14.87
1965–66	(915)	65.46± 1.82	(1208)	67.55±1.63	(68)	64.71± 5.91

TABLE 3.16

Estimated Percentage of Those Patrilineally Joint Families which Incorporate Only the 'Brother(s), Brother(s)' Wives, and/or Unmarried Sister(s)' of the 'Head' to Total of all Patrilineally Joint Families (±s e.) Under each 'Social Group' Category and Year (Sample as in Table 3.15)

Year	*Category 1* *Literate, Socially Inferior Hindu or Muslim Landed Gentry*	*Category 2* *Rest of Landed Gentry, Agricultural Commoner, Non-agricultural Literate Gentry or Illiterate Commoner*	*Category 3* *Non-agricultural Illiterate Gentry or Literate Commoner, Societal Dependents*
(1)	(2)	(3)	(4)
		1. *West Bengal*	
1955–56	10.57±2.66	25.12±3.51	22.74± 9.97
1960–61	17.76±3.61	24.77±2.64	4.03± 3.89
1965–66	17.03±1.45	22.78±1.33	26.57± 3.51
		2. *Urban sector*	
1955–56	51.91±2.32	33.58±2.66	21.18± 6.18
1960–61	0.00	30.95±2.95	0.79± 1.55
1965–66	16.21±8.85	28.95±2.57	32.73± 6.79
		3. *Rural sector*	
1946–47	21.19	26.44	28.57
1951	21.28±5.66	33.96±9.30	0.00
1955–56	10.18±2.66	23.70±4.07	23.41±13.96
1960–61	18.41±3.70	22.04±2.86	12.65± 9.22
1965–66	17.05±1.47	19.95±1.40	22.06± 4.13

TABLE 3.17

Estimated Percentage of Those Patrilineally Joint Families which Incorporate Only the 'Brother(s)' Progeny and/or the Consort(s) of Brother(s)' Male Progeny' of the 'Head' to Total of all Patrilineally Joint Families (±s.e.) Under each 'Social Group' Category and Year (Sample as in Table 3.15)

Year	Category 1 Literate, Socially Inferior Hindu or Muslim Landed Gentry	Category 2 Rest of Landed Gentry, Agricultural Commoner, Non-agricultural Literate Gentry or Illiterate Commoner	Category 3 Non-agricultural Illiterate Gentry or Literate Commoner, Societal Dependents
(1)	(2)	(3)	(4)
		1. *West Bengal*	
1955–56	0.03±0.03	5.43±3.54	1.35±1.17
1960–61	1.64±0.96	2.54±0.80	0.00
1965–66	2.79±0.45	3.90±0.60	9.08±2.73
		2. *Urban sector*	
1955–56	3.17±3.75	5.81±1.73	4.48±4.07
1960–61	0.00	3.89±1.58	0.00
1965–66	0.00	6.62±1.46	15.46±5.51
		3. *Rural sector*	
1946–47	4.66	3.35	4.76
1951	0.78±0.52	1.59±1.07	0.00
1955–56	0.00	5.36±4.13	0.00
1960–61	1.70±0.99	1.94±0.89	0.00
1965–66	2.84±0.46	2.65±0.55	4.41±2.35

TABLE 3.18

Estimated Percentage of Those Patrilineally Joint Families which incorporate both the 'Brother(s), Brother(s)' Wives and/or Unmarried Sister(s)' and the 'Brother(s)' Progeny and/or the Consort(s) of the Brother(s)' Male Progeny' of the 'Heads' to Total of the Patrilineally Joint Families (±s,e.) Under each 'Social Group' Category and Year (Sample as in Table 3.15)

Year	*Category 1* *Literate, Socially Inferior Hindu or Muslim Landed Gentry*	*Category 2* *Rest of Landed Gentry, Agricultural Commoner, Non-agricultural Literate Gentry or Illiterate Commoner*	*Category 3* *Non-agricultural Illiterate Gentry or Literate Commoner, Societal Dependents*
(1)	(2)	(3)	(4)
		1. *West Bengal*	
1955–56	22.50±5.55	9.72±3.21	10.75± 9.26
1960–61	12.13±2.17	9.10±1.04	3.44± 5.09
1965–66	12.86±1.14	9.97±0.57	7.62± 2.78
		2. *Urban sector*	
1955–56	3.01±1.38	10.99±3.02	35.61±18.70
1960–61	0.00	11.46±1.83	4.73± 7.62
1965–66	10.83±6.22	13.49±0.87	10.00± 5.17
		3. *Rural sector*	
1946–47	15.25	7.53	14.29
1951	8.69±1.27	4.12±1.82	0.00
1955–56	22.69±5.69	9.51±3.71	0.00
1960–61	12.57±2.18	8.06±1.15	0.00
1965–66	12.90±1.15	8.36±0.75	5.88± 2.73

TABLE 3.19

Estimated Percentage of Those Patrilineally Joint Families which May or May not Contain 'Fraternal' Relative(s) of the 'Head' (as Specified for Tables 3.16–3.18) but Contain Other Collateral Relative(s) to Total of All Patrilineally Joint Families (±s.e.) Under each 'Social Group' Category and Year (Sample as in Table 3.15)

Year	*Category 1* *Literate, Socially Inferior Hindu or Muslim Landed Gentry*	*Category 2* *Rest of Landed Gentry, Agricultural Commoner, Non-agricultural Literate Gentry or Illiterate Commoner*	*Category 3* *Non-agricultural Illiterate Gentry or Literate Commoner, Societal Dependents*
(1)	(2)	(3)	(4)
		1. *West Bengal*	
1955–56	4.63±3.62	6.62±2.35	1.49±1.35
1960–61	0.40±0.41	2.47±0.80	13.78±3.95
1965–66	1.77±0.41	2.33±0.34	4.00±1.52
		2. *Urban sector*	
1955–56	0.00	4.62±1.65	4.96±4.86
1960–61	0.00	3.95±1.73	16.35±4.27
1965–66	2.70±2.53	4.17±0.92	5.45±1.90
		3. *Rural sector*	
1946–47	3.39	1.20	4.76
1951	5.47±0.76	1.49±1.14	0.00
1955–56	4.67±3.65	6.95±2.72	0.00
1960–61	0.41±0.43	1.82±0.83	6.96±6.75
1965–66	1.75±0.41	1.49±0.30	2.94±2.15

the progeny of the 'brother(s)'. This, however, is not a steady and sustained phenomenon. If it were so, we would have found: (1) near about the same percentage values for the three 'social group' categories in this sector, in respect of each characteristic of structural articulations in the patrilineally joint families; and (2) the 'fraternal' joint families would mostly represent the collaterally joint families of procreation of the 'head' and his male siblings (as recorded by Table 3.18), and not a temporary affair of the 'head's' sibling(s) to be attached to his 'family' (as recorded in Table 3.16) or the fortuitous occurrence of only the progeny—and/or the consort(s) of the progeny—of the 'head's' siblings in the 'family' (as recorded in Table 3.17).

As to the first point, we notice from Tables 3.15–3.19 that the percentage values in the urban sector for Categories 1 and 3 vary widely, but the standard errors of the sharply fluctuating mean values are almost invariably found to be so high that, barring in occasional cases, the latter do not indicate any significant trend of variability. For Category 1, this is understandable and it does not matter much because this category expresses essentially a rural character and, therefore, in the urban areas it is sporadically represented and is also of marginal interest only. The significance of Category 3 for the urban sector, however, cannot be ignored although the bulk of the patrilineally joint families are concentrated in Category 2. The indication is, thus, there that in the urban sector of West Bengal the people belonging to Category 2 tend to form a steadier collateral joint family than those belonging to Categories 1 and 3, just as Category 2 registers relatively more 'complete' nuclear structures than Categories 1 and 3.

However, in the urban set-up also, none of the 'social group' categories represents a sustained propagation of the collaterally joint family of procreation of 'brothers' in order to substantiate the second point made above. Category 2 clearly registers, at all time-points, more such collaterally joint families as contain exclusively the sibling(s) of the 'head' and *not* the progeny of the male sibling(s). Category 3, on the other hand, does not register any systematic trend of occurrence of different kinds of collateral relatives of the 'head' in the temporal perspective; and Category 1, in this respect, tends to behave in-between Categories 2 and 3.

These familial properties of the collateral joint structures in the urban sector of West Bengal, as against the unilaterally joint structures there, are presented concisely in Table 3.20 which collates the relevant data from Tables 3.15–3.19.

It, thus, appears that the patrilineally joint families in the urban sector of West Bengal are in the majority cases 'stop-gap' arrangements: as if they have their full-fledged 'families' elsewhere but live here in this manner due to some extraneous causes

TABLE 3.20

Table Reference by Number	'Head's' Collateral Relatives in Patrilineal Joint Families	Percentage (±s.e.) for the Urban Sector		
		1955–56	1960–61	1965–66
(1)	(2)	(3)	(4)	(5)
	Category 1. Literate, socially inferior Hindu or Muslim landed gentry			
3.16	Sibling(s) only	51.91±2.66	0.00	16.21±8.85
3.17	Male sibling(s)' progeny	3.17±3.76	0.00	0.00
3.18	Both above	3.01±1.38	0.00	10.83±6.22
3.19	Others, with or without above ones	0.00	0.00	2.70±2.53
3.16–3.18	'Fraternal' only	58.09	0.00	27.04
3.16–3.19	Any collateral	58.09	0.00	29.74
3.15	No collateral relative	41.91±20.86	100.00	70.26±12.51
	(sample)	(10)	(5)	(24)
	Category 2. Rest of landed gentry, agricultural commoner, non-agricultural literate gentry or illiterate commoner			
3.16	'Fraternal' only	33.58±2.66	30.95±2.95	28.95±2.57
3.17	Male sibling(s)' progeny	5.81±1.73	3.89±1.58	6.62±1.46
3.18	Both above	10.99±3.02	11.46±1.83	13.49±0.87
3.19	Others, with or without above ones	4.62±1.65	3.95±1.73	4.17±0.92
3.16–3.18	'Fraternal' only	50.38	46.30	49.06
3.16–3.19	Any collateral	55.00	50.25	53.23
3.15	No collateral relative	45.00±3.04	49.75±3.61	46.77±2.16
	(sample)	(295)	(315)	(1029)
	Category 3. Non-agricultural illiterate gentry or literate commoner, societal dependents			
3.16	Sibling(s) only	21.18± 6.18	0.79±1.55	32.73±6.79
3.17	Male sibling(s)' progeny	4.48± 4.07	0.00	15.46±5.51
2.18	Both above	35.61±18.70	4.73±7.62	10.00±5.17
3.19	Others, with or without above ones	4.96±4.86	16.35±4.27	5.45±1.90
3.16–3.18	'Fraternal' only	61.27	5.52	58.19
3.16–3.19	Any collateral	66.23	21.87	63.64
3.15	No collateral relative	33.77±13.96	78.13±8.95	36.36±7.64
	(sample)	(48)	(22)	(84)

imposed by the societal forces on their familial arrangements.

Contrastingly, in the rural sector of West Bengal, we find that the bulk of the patrilineally joint families in all the three 'social group' categories represents very largely the family of procreation of the 'head' of the respective units. This tends to be the least marked in Category 2, but for this category also a mere addition of the sibling(s) of the 'head' (and *not* their progeny) registers the dominant note of the collaterally joint family structures. The same is noticed for Categories 1 and 3, while the incidence of different kinds of the collaterally joint families (as also of the unilaterally joint families, to an extent) is the most sporadic in Category 3 among all of them.

However, unlike for the unilateral joint families in the rural sector, the collaterally joint families denote a trend of variation in the longitudinal perspective between 1955–56 and 1965-66 (that is, since the onset of the Second Five Year Plan). But this trend also supports the fact that the extended family organization in the rural areas is becoming increasingly stable. For any increasing incidence is noticed steadily for Category 1 only, and that in respect of the inclusion of the sibling(s) only of the 'head' of respective family-units (and *not* the progeny of these siblings). Whereas, the presence of the 'head's' sibling(s) *and* their progeny, or of other collateral relatives of the 'head', record a decreasing incidence. In Category 2 also the exclusive presence of the 'head's' sibling(s)' progeny or of other collateral relatives (with or without the 'fraternal' relatives of the 'head') records a decline; while the collaterally joint families formed by the inclusion of the 'head's' sibling(s) only or also the family of procreation of the male sibling(s) do not register any variation over time. Lastly, Category 3, which is of a very small size in the rural sector of West Bengal, records a sporadic distribution in these respects.

These familial properties can be seen from Table 3.21 which has been prepared exactly in the same manner as Table 3.20 and, therefore, the references to Tables 3.15–3.19 are omitted herefrom.

TABLE 3.21

'Head's' Collateral Relatives in Patrilineal Joint Families	Percentage (± s. e.) for the Rural Sector			
	1951	1955–56	1960–61	1965–66
(1)	(2)	(3)	(4)	(5)
Category 1. *Literate, socially inferior Hindu or Muslim landed gentry*				
Sibling(s) only	21.28±5.66	10.18±2.66	18.41±3.70	17.05±1.47
Male sibling(s)' progeny	0.78±0.52	0.00	1.70±0.99	2.84±0.46
Both above	8.69±1.27	22.69±5.69	12.57±2.18	12.90±1.15
Others, with or without above ones	5.47±0.76	4.67±3.65	0.41±0.43	1.75±0.41
'Fraternal' only	30.75	32.87	32.68	32.79
Any collateral	36.22	37.54	33.09	34.54
No collateral relative	63.78±6.50	62.46±6.96	66.91±3.50	65.46±1.82
(sample)	(118)	(74)	(182)	(915)
Category 2. *Rest of landed gentry, agricultural commoner, non-agricultural literate gentry or illiterate commoner*				
Sibling(s) only	33.96±9.30	23.70±4.07	22.04±2.86	19.95±1.40
Male sibling(s)' progeny	1.59±1.07	5.36±4.13	1.94±0.89	2.65±0.55
Both above	4.12±1.82	9.51±3.71	8.06±1.15	8.36±0.75
Others, with or without above ones	1.49±1.14	6.95±2.72	1.82±0.83	1.49±0.30
'Fraternal' only	39.67	38.57	32.04	30.96
Any collateral	41.16	45.52	33.86	32.45
No collateral relative	58.84±7.46	54.48±6.13	66.14±4.11	67.55±1.63
(sample)	(110)	(99)	(520)	(1208)
Category 3. *Non-agricultural illiterate gentry or literate commoner, societal dependents*				
Sibling(s) only	0.00	23.41±13.96	12.65±9.22	22.06±4.13
Male sibling(s)' progeny	0.00	0.00	0.00	4.41±2.35
Both above	0.00	0.00	0.00	5.88±2.73
Others, with or without above ones	0.00	0.00	6.96±6.75	2.94±2.15
'Fraternal' only	0.00	23.41	12.65	32.35
Any collateral	0.00	23.41	19.61	35.29
No collateral relative	100.00	76.59±13.96	80.39±14.87	64.71±5.91
(sample)	(3)	(9)	(13)	(68)

VI

It should now be evident that the variations within the communities of non-familial units, nuclear families and extended families do not support the possibilities enumerated as 1 and 2, which refer to any change over time in the *nature* of internal and external variations of the West Bengal family structures. This means that the familial properties outlined in the previous two chapters, regarding the *object* and *place* perspectives of variation, hold good for the time-period taken into account. We should, accordingly, examine the possibilities enumerated as 3 and 4, the relevance of which has been suggested and indicated, respectively, by the course of 'trend analysis' undertaken so far.

The suggestion regarding the third possibility (that is, changes in the relative incidence of those social structure categories with which the internal and external variations of the family structure categories are associated) is confirmed when we examine over time the variations in the relative occurrence of the non-familial units and family-units (defined as coresident and commensal kingroups) under the three 'social group' categories for West Bengal as a whole and its urban or rural sector. Thus, we find from Table 3.22 that, at each and every time-point taken into account, both the urban and rural sectors of West Bengal are represented mainly by Category 2, but in the former the next important is Category 3 and in the latter Category 1 (which is virtually non-existent in the former). As a result, while Category 2 strikes the dominant note also in West Bengal *en bloc*, Category 1 comes up next in importance since the society is predominatly rural.

Now, we have found earlier that the essential characteristic of Category 1 is to represent, firstly, the extended family structure and, next, the nuclear; of Category 2, the nuclear and then the extended; and of Category 3, the non-familial units and then some nuclear and extended families. Hence, if at each and every time-point taken into account, the relative incidences of the non-familial units, nuclear families, and extended families in West Bengal *en bloc* and in its urban and rural sectors are found to be coincidental with the correspondingly relative magnitudes of occurrence of the three 'social group' categories, an association between the relevant aspect of the social structure and the family structure of West

TABLE 3.22

Estimated Percentage of Coresident and Commensal Kingroups Under 3 'Social Group' Categories to Total (±s.e.). (Sample in Brackets)

Year	*Category 1* Literate, Socially Inferior Hindu or Muslim Landed Gentry	*Category 2* Rest of Landed Gentry, Agricultural Commoner, Non-agricultural Literate Gentry or Illiterate Commoner	*Category 3* Non-agricultural Illiterate Gentry or Literate Commoner, Societal Dependents	*Total*
(1)	(2)	(3)	(4)	(5)
		1. *West Bengal*		
1955–56	(166) 19.10±1.80	(1714) 66.42±1.58	(555) 14.48±1.14	100
1960–61	(481) 12.69±1.84	(4042) 79.76±1.37	(411) 7.55±2.02	100
1965–66	(2390) 21.04±0.81	(10006) 67.05±0.75	(1954) 11.91±0.56	100
		2. *Urban sector*		
1955–56	(17) 1.07±0.47	(1315) 73.16±2.05	(485) 25.77±1.81	100
1960–61	(21) 1.40±0.79	(1748) 82.16±3.01	(262) 16.44±2.44	100
1965–66	(77) 1.54±0.21	(5137) 78.03±1.12	(1314) 20.43±1.21	100
		3. *Rural sector*		
1946–47	(591) 44.36	(3022) 43.42	(503) 12.22	100
1951	(332) 44.22±2.93	(491) 47.46±2.99	(77) 8.32±1.76	100
1955–56	(149) 22.87±2.19	(399) 65.01±1.89	(70) 12.12±1.27	100
1960–61	(460) 17.16±1.52	(2294) 78.81±1.78	(149) 4.03±0.52	100
1965–66	(2313) 29.57±0.97	(4869) 62.25±0.91	(640) 8.18±0.54	100

Bengal (with which the third possibility is concerned) would be indicated prima facie. This we find from Table 3.23.

For any attempt to check up the reliability of this simple table of association between the relative order of importance of the family structure categories and the dominant familial characteristics of the correspondingly graded 'social group' categories, we may note that: (1) the grading of the 'social group' categories is done from the data in Table 3.22; (2) the dominant familial characteristic of these categories, respectively, is obtained from the data in Table 2.22; and (3) the orders of importance of the family structure categories for West Bengal *en bloc* and its urban and rural sectors are obtained from Table 3.1, 3.4 and 3.6, respectively.

It may also be noted, in order that Table 3.23 may be read

precisely, that: (1) since the data for 1951 refer to the rural sector of West Bengal only, it is shown in the table within third brackets and along with the data for 1955–56; (2) in case the mean values of 2 family structure categories do not register a significant difference at the 5 per cent probability level, they are placed in the table in between the relevant grades; (3) where the nuclear family is not thus distinguished from the extended family, and the extended family from the non-familial unit, but the first category is distinguished from the third, two identities are separated by an oblique; and (4) if the mean values of 2 'social goup' categories are not found to be significantly different at the 5 per cent

TABLE 3.23

Society and Sector	*Item of Classifications*	*Relative Order of importance of the Categories of Classification, with the Dominant Familial Characteristic of each 'Social Group' in Brackets* 1	2	3
(1)	(2)	(3)	(4)	(5)
		1955–56 [1951]		
West Bengal	Family structure	Nuclear	Extended	Non-familial
	'Social group'	2 (Nuclear)	1 (Extended)	3 (Non-familial)
Urban Sector	Family structure	Nuclear & Non-familial		Extended
	'Social group'	2 (Nuclear)	3 (Non-familial)	1 (Extended)
		[Nuclear & Extended]		[Non-familial]
Rural Sector	Family structure	Nuclear	Extended	Non-familial
	'Social group'	2 (Nuclear)	1 (Extended)	3 (Non-familial)
		1960–61		
West Bengal	Family structure	Nuclear	Extended	Non-familial
	'Social group'	2 (Nuclear)	1 & 3 (Extended & Non-familial)	
Urban Sector	Family structure	Nuclear & Extended/Extended & Non-familial		
	'Social group'	2 (Nuclear)	3 (Non-familial)	1 (Extended)
Rural Sector	Family structure	Nuclear	Extended	Non-familial
	'Social group'	2 (Nuclear)	1 (Extended)	3 (Non-familial)
		1965–66		
West Bengal	Family structure	Nuclear	Extended	Non-familial
	'Social group'	2 (Nuclear)	1 (Extended)	3 (Non-familial)
Urban Sector	Family structure	Nuclear & Non-familial		Extended
	'Social group'	2 (Nuclear)	3 (Non-familial)	1 (Extended)
Rural Sector	Family structure	Nuclear	Extended	Non-familial
	'Social group'	2 (Nuclear)	1 (Extended)	3 (Non-familial)

probability level, they are placed in the table in a like manner as described for the family structure categories.

Table 3.23 shows that out of the ten comparisons between the family structure categories and the dominant familial characteristic of the correspondingly graded 'social group' categories, only in one the association is not fully maintained; for instance, in the urban sector of West Bengal and for the year 1960–61. Moreover, in this exceptional case also, it is not a matter of dissociation but of merging the identities, as we have explained before presenting the table. A close association is, thus, noticed between the relevant aspect of the social structure and the family structure of West Bengal, both in the place and time perspectives.

Following therefrom, we may examine any concordance in the increase or decrease in the relative occurrence of each 'social group' category over time and in the corresponding incidence of that family structure category which denotes the dominant familial characteristic of the 'social group' under reference. Accordingly, we have prepared Table 3.24 on the basis of the data in Tables 3.22 and the corresponding data in Tables 3.1, 3.4 and 3.6 with reference to West Bengal *en bloc* and its urban and rural sectors. The validity of Table 3.24, insofar as the relative occurrence of each 'social group' category over time is concerned, will be seen from Table 3.25; and the same for the family structure categories will be borne out by Tables 3.2, 3.5 and 3.7.

Table 3.24 shows that, out of 36 comparisons, concordance between the 'social group' category and the relevant family structure category is fully maintained in the case of 22; and in the remaining 14 cases also it is not a matter of discordance but a failure to attain full concordance. For, in the latter cases, the distinction is not as 'increase' *and* 'decrease' in the relative incidence of the corresponding categories over time, but of the lack of any 'increase' or 'decrease' in respect of one of the paired categories.

Furthermore, we notice that not only in most cases the corresponding 'social group' and family structure categories record 'increase' or 'decrease' or 'neither' in their relative incidences over time, but the rates of change are also similar. The rates of change for the 'social group' categories are constructed from Table 3.22 as, say, [(1960-61/1955-56)×100] for the percentage-values under cols. (2)–(4). For the family structure categories, the corresponding data in Tables 3.1, 3.4 and 3.6 have been computed in the same manner.

TABLE 3.24

Comparison of Time-points	*Any Change in the Relative Incidence of a 'Social Group' Category & that of Corresponding Family Structure Category*					
	Category 3	*Non-familial Unit*	*Category 2*	*Nuclear Family*	*Category 1*	*Extended Family*
(1)	(2)	(3)	(4)	(5)	(6)	(7)
			1 *West Bengal*			
1955–56 & 1960–61	decrease	decrease	increase	increase	decrease	neither
1960–61 & 1965–66	increase	increase	decrease	decrease*	increase	neither
1955–56 & 1965–66	decrease	decrease	neither	neither	neither	increase
			2. *Urban sector*			
1955–56 & 1960–61	decrease	decrease	increase	increase	neither	neither
1960–61 & 1965–66	neither	increase	neither	decrease	neither	neither
1955–56 & 1965–66	decrease	neither	increase	neither	neither	neither
			3. *Rural sector*			
1951 & 1955–56	neither	neither	increase	neither	decrease	neither
1955–56 & 1960–61	decrease	neither	increase	increase	decrease	decrease
1960–61 & 1965–66	increase	neither	decrease	decrease*	increase	increase
1951 & 1960–61	decrease	decrease	increase	increase	decrease	decrease
1955–56 & 1965–66	decrease	decrease*	neither	increase	increase	neither
1951 & 1965–66	neither	decrease	increase	increase	decrease	decrease

N.B. *denotes a significant difference at the 10% probability level only. Others are significantly different at the 5% probability level (indicated as 'increase' or 'decrease') or not even at the 10% (indicated as 'neither').

TABLE 3.25

Comparison of Time-points	Result of t-test of Difference in the Percentage Values Given in Table 3.22		
	Social Group Category 1	Social Group Category 2	Social Group Category 3
(1)	(2)	(3)	(4)
1. West Bengal			
1955–56 and 1960–61	+	++	++
1960–61 and 1965–66	++	++	+
1955–56 and 1965–66	0	0	+
2. Urban sector			
1955–56 and 1960–61	0	+	++
1960–61 and 1965–66	0	0	0
1955–56 and 1965–66	0	+	+
3. Rural sector			
1951 and 1955–56	++	++	0
1955–56 and 1960–61	+	++	++
1960–61 and 1965–66	++	++	++
1951 and 1960–61	++	++	+
1955–56 and 1965–66	++	0	++
1951 and 1965–66	++	++	0

N.B. Significance level : 1%=++; 5%=+, <5%=0

As we can see from Table 3.26, out of 17 cases in which both of the paired categories denote a significant difference of their mean values over the time-points under reference, the rates of change are very close for 13. Also, even in those 14 cases in which only one of the paired categories denotes a significant difference of its mean values over the time-points under reference, the rates of change are very close for 9; and so it is for 3 out of the remaining 5 cases in which both of the paired categories do not record any significant difference in their mean values over the time-points under reference.

Thus, in a very large measure, the temporal shifts in the relative incidence of the non-familial units, nuclear families and extended families in West Bengal *en bloc* and its urban and rural sectors are seen to be due to variations in the relevant aspect of the social structure which is denoted by the three 'social group' categories.

TABLE 3.26

Comparison of Time-points (Base=100)	*Any Change in the Relative Incidence of a 'Social Group' Category and That of Corresponding Family Structure Category*					
	Category 3	Non-Familial Unit	Category 2	Nuclear Family	Category 1	Extended Family
(1)	(2)	(3)	(4)	(5)	(6)	(7)
1. West Bengal						
1955–56 and 1960–61	52	54	120	120	66	[109]
1960–61 and 1965–66	158	135	84	91	166	[106]
1955–56 and 1965–66	82	72	(101)	(105)	[110]	116
2. Urban sector						
1955–56 and 1960–61	64	57	112	122	(130)	(143)
1960–61 and 1965–66	[124]	156	[95]	85	(110)	(78)
1955–56 and 1965–66	79	[89]	107	[104]	(144)	(112)
3. Rural sector						
1951 and 1955–56	(146)	(71)	137	[124]	52	[91]
1955–56 and 1960–61	75	[77]	121	124	33	78
1960–61 and 1965–66	203	[106]	79	88	172	119
1951 and 1960–61	48	55	166	154	39	71
1955–56 and 1965–66	67	82	[96]	110	129	[93]
1951 and 1965–66	[98]	58	131	137	67	85

N.B. Square brackets indicate that one of the paired values is not statistically significant.

Parentheses indicate that both of the paired values are not statistically significant.

This form of coincidence would be ruled out only if at other time-points the dominant and the subsequent familial properties of the three 'social group' categories are found to be different from those ascertained for 1960–61 in Table 2.22. This, however, is not the case as we find from Tables 3.27–3.29.

TABLE 3.27

Year	Non-familial Unit	Nuclear Family	Extended Family	Total	Sample
	Estimated Percentage to Total (±s.e.) for each 'Social Group' Category in West Bengal Society				
(1)	(2)	(3)	(4)	(5)	(6)
1. Literate, socially inferior Hindu or Muslim landed gentry					
1955–66	—	33.68±1.29	66.32±2.78	100.00	166
1960–61	1.72±1.71	42.94±2.92	55.34±2.57	100.00	481
1965–66	1.25±1.28	44.41±2.04	54.34±1.40	100.00	2390
2. Rest of landed gentry, agricultural commoner, non-agricultural literate gentry or illiterate commoner					
1955–56	34.92±0.39	37.37±1.50	27.71±0.68	100.00	1714
1960–61	11.06±1.58	58.15±2.04	30.79±2.44	100.00	4042
1965–66	16.57±0.56	50.96±1.42	32.47±0.25	100.00	10006
3. Non-agricultural illiterate gentry or literate commoner, societal dependents					
1955–56	60.73±1.39	24.56±1.11	14.71±1.86	100.00	555
1960–61	58.11±1.40	24.35±1.59	17.54±1.36	100.00	411
1965–66	57.34±1.09	28.34±0.95	14.32±1.72	100.00	1954

We also find, contextually, that the standard errors of the percentage values in these tables are uniformly low, as we had found in Table 2.22. We are, thus, further ensured of the deductions and inferences made in the last two chapters with reference to the entire time-period taken into account. We may also safely conclude on the redundancy of the first and second possibilities of change enumerated at the beginning of this chapter, and state that the third of the four possibilities of change is distinctly operative to reflect variations in West Bengal family structures over time.

TABLE 3.28

Estimated Percentage to Total (±s.e.) for each 'Social Group' Category in Urban Sector of West Bengal

Year	*Non-familial Unit*	*Nuclear Family*	*Extended Family*	*Total*	*Sample*
(1)	(2)	(3)	(4)	(5)	(6)
	1. *Literate, socially inferior Hindu or Muslim landed gentry*				
1955–56	—	34.14±4.01	65.86±3.07	100.00	17
1960–61	—	37.01±1.89	62.99±2.98	100.00	21
1965–66	8.61±2.89	44.83±3.20	46.56±2.50	100.00	77
	2. *Rest of landed gentry, agricultural commoner, non-agricultural literate gentry or illiterate commoner*				
1955–56	36.01±3.52	36.61±3.76	27.38±3.23	100.00	1315
1960–61	17.10±3.10	45.25±2.12	37.65±2.69	100.00	1748
1965–66	31.33±2.57	37.43±3.20	31.24±2.54	100.00	5137
	3. *Non-agricultural illiterate gentry or literate commoner, societal dependents*				
1955–56	61.00±3.01	24.42±3.66	14.58±2.71	100.00	485
1960–61	61.42±2.16	19.34±2.54	19.24±2.09	100.00	262
1965–66	63.92±2.82	24.68±2.32	11.40±3.01	100.00	1314

TABLE 3.29

Estimated Percentage of Total (±s.e.) for each 'Social Group' Category in Rural Sector of West Bengal

Year	*Non-familial Unit*	*Nuclear Family*	*Extended Family*	*Total*	*Sample*
(1)	(2)	(3)	(4)	(5)	(6)
1. *Literate, socially inferior Hindu or Muslim landed gentry*					
1946–47	0.51	37.22	62.27	100.00	591
1951	4.18±2.15	35.67±2.56	60.15±3.21	100.00	332
1955–56	—	33.22±3.23	66.78±3.72	100.00	149
1960–61	1.78±2.46	43.12±1.16	55.10±2.05	100.00	460
1965–66	1.08±0.29	44.40±0.48	54.52±1.31	100.00	2313
2. *Rest of landed gentry, agricultural commoner, non-agricultural literate gentry or illiterate commoner*					
1946–47	8.64	50.10	41.26	100.00	3022
1951	20.00±3.12	43.80±3.62	36.20±3.16	100.00	491
1955–56	9.23±2.28	55.16±3.48	35.61±2.16	100.00	399
1960–61	8.57±0.52	63.48±0.80	27.95±1.02	100.00	2294
1965–66	8.48±0.76	58.37±0.85	33.15±0.50	100.00	4869
3. *Non-agricultural illiterate gentry or literate commoner, societal dependents*					
1946–47	77.93	13.32	8.75	100.00	503
1951	65.71±4.09	18.81±4.20	15.48±4.50	100.00	77
1955–56	48.54±3.76	30.82±3.68	20.64±3.71	100.00	70
1960–61	52.75±2.36	32.47±3.42	14.78±2.33	100.00	149
1965–66	50.16±1.19	32.34±2.09	17.50±1.88	100.00	640

VII

Two questions emerge from the foregoing analysis of the trend of variation in family structures in West Bengal:

(1) What is the significance of operation of the third possibility of change in the relative incidence of the relevant social structural categories, especially when the operation of the first and second possibilities of change in the nature of variations in family structure categories is ruled out?

(2) How is the third possibility linked up with the fourth referring to the extent of variations in the family structure categories, the applicability of which to the West Bengal situation has been repeatedly indicated?

In order to answer the two questions, we should first summarize our findings so far. For this purpose, we shall take into account those items of information which record any difference by the rural-urban distinction and by the 'social group' categories because the third and fourth possibilities of change have been found to operate in their respect particularly. We could, therefore, refrain from any discussion on the global picture for the West Bengal society as a whole; but, as we shall see from Tables 3.30 and 3.31, the global picture has a specificity of its own.

However, to present comparable findings for the urban and rural sectors of West Bengal, we shall be constrained to limit our examination to the time-period of only 10 years, from 1955–56 to 1965–66, for reasons explained in the Introductory chapter. This way, we shall fail to consider the time-period of previous 10 years (from 1946–47 to 1955–56) which is applicable to our data for the rural sector of West Bengal; but we may recall that for this period we have not noticed any significantly different or noteworthy feature with reference to internal variations of the non-familial units, nuclear families, and the extended families (Tables 3.10–3.19).

Even so, in regard to the relative incidence of the 'social group' categories, we have noticed one interesting feature for the rural society of West Bengal; namely, Category 1 has been depleted in strength and Category 2 has gained in correspondence, with virtually no change effected for Category 3 (Table 3.22). This is of some significance because: (a) Category 1 is composed of 'literate, socially inferior Hindu or Muslim

TABLE 3.30

Relative Occurrence During 1955–56 and 1965–66 of:	Society and Sector	Characteristics of 'Social Groups'		
		Category 1	Category 2	Category 3
(1)	(2)	(3)	(4)	(5)
1. Categories themselves (Table 3.22)	Urban	—	First	Second
	Rural	Second	First	—
	West Bengal	Second	First	Third
2. Non-familial units (Tables 3.27–3.29)	Urban	—	Subsidiary	Dominant
	Rural	—	—	Dominant
	West Bengal	—	Subsidiary	Dominant
3. Married to unmarried non-familial units (Tables 3.8–3.10)	Urban	—	Very high	High
	Rural	—	Very low	Low
	West Bengal	—	Equal/High	Equal/High
4. Nuclear families (Tables 3.27–3.29)	Urban	Equal	Equal	Lower
	Rural	Lower	High	Lowest
	West Bengal	Lower	High	Lowest
5. 'Complete' nuclear families (Tables 3.11)	Urban	Equal/Higher	Equal/Lower	Lowest
	Rural	High	Lower	Lowest
	West Bengal	High	Lower	Lowest
6. Extended families (Tables 3.27–3.29)	Urban	Dominant	Subsidary	—
	Rural	Dominant	Subsidary	—
	West Bengal	Dominant	Subsidary	—
7. 'Complete' extended families (Table 3.12)	Urban	High	Lower	Lowest
	Rural	High	Lower	Lowest
	West Bengal	High	Lower	Lowest
8. 'Head's' family of procreation to his 'fraternal' family (Tables 3.15–3.21)	Urban	Equal/Low	Equal/Low	Low/Equal
	Rural	Very high	High	Very high
	West Bengal	High	High	Equal

N.B '—' denotes scarce incidence of the item concerned.

TABLE 3.31

Change in the Occurrence Over 1955–56 and 1965–66	Society and Sector	Characteristics of 'Social Groups' Category 1	Category 2	Category 3
(1)	(2)	(3)	(4)	(5)
1. Categories themselves	Urban	—	increase	decrease
(Table 3.22)	Rural	increase	—	decrease
	West Bengal	—	—	decrease
2. Non-familial units	Urban		—	—
(Tables 3.27–3.29)	Rural		—	—
	West Bengal		decrease	—
3. Married non-familial units	Urban		—	—
(Tables 3.8–3.10)	Rural		—	—
	West Bengal		increase	—
4. Unmarried non-familial units	Urban		—	—
(Tables 3.8–3.10)	Rural		—	—
	West Bengal		decrease	—
5. Nuclear families	Urban	increase		—
(Tables 3.27–3.29)	Rural	increase		—
	West Bengal	increase	increase	increase
6. 'Complete' nuclear families	Urban	increase	increase	—
(Table 3.11)	Rural	increase	increase	—
	West Bengal	increase	increase	—
7. Extended families	Urban	decrease	—	—
(Tables 3.27–3.29)	Rural	decrease	—	—
	West Bengal	decrease	increase	—
8. 'Complete' extended families	Urban	—	—	—
(Table 3.12)	Rural	increase	increase	increase
	West Bengal	increase	—	increase
9. 'Head's' family of procreation to his	Urban	—	—	—
'fraternal' family	Rural	—	increase	—
(Tables 3.15–3.21)	West Bengal	—	—	—

N.B. '—' denotes no change. Blank space denotes such a low incidence as to be irrelevant to record any change.

landed gentry'; (b) literacy in West Bengal was spreading over the society and was continually on the increase during this time-period as well as later; and (c) the ascriptive status of being 'socially inferior' (as well as belonging to the Hindu or Muslim religious community) would remain unchanged over this or any time-period. This shift from Category 1, therefore, could be caused only in reference to its fourth attribute of 'landed gentry', and thus would refer to the movement of an appreciable number of coresident and commensal kingroups—previously belonging to this category—to non-agricultural sources of livelihood or to the rank of 'agricultural commoner'.

Now, since this shift has not caused any change in the relative incidence of Category 3 over the time-period, the relevant coresident and commensal kingroups are not likely to refer to the component of 'non-agricultural literate commoner' of that category. Instead, they would refer to either or both of the components of 'agricultural commoner' and 'non-agricultural literate gentry' of Category 2 which has registered a corresponding effect of the change in Category 1. In due course, we shall discuss the validity of the above inference and its implications to answer the two questions we have posed. We may note, therefore, that it will not affect the merit of our present attempt if we do not consider the time-period of 1946–47 to 1955–56 on this account.

We should also note, in this context, that Table 3.29 registers an interesting feature for the rural sector of West Bengal society during this time-period; namely, while there is virtually no change to mention for Category 1, for Categories 2 and 3 a decrease is recorded (over 1946–47 to 1955–56) in the incidence of non-familial units and a corresponding increase in the incidence of nuclear families, with the extended families maintaining their relative incidence over the time-period. However, this change over the first 10 years within our reference merely denote that, in the rural sector of West Bengal, the family organization had become stabler and less number of people lived as non-familial units, but no change was effected in the formation and propagation of the extended families. Obviously, this finding has an implication corresponding to the one just mentioned and will, therefore, be discussed in due course. But it will also be realized that its exclusion from the summarized findings in Table 3.31 will not affect the merit of our present attempt.

Lastly, it should be pointed out that we have neglected the time-point 1960–61 from Table 3.31 in order to present our findings in a concise manner. This form of simplification of the 'trend analysis' should not affect the validity of the conclusions to be drawn from the data in Table 3.31 because it will be recalled from our previous discussion that the neglect of any fluctuation caused by this time-point within the period of 1955–56 to 1965–66 was not found to be of any serious concern. Anyhow, Tables 3.30 and 3.31, which reproduce a summary of the findings from our previous course of analysis, have distinctive merits of their own and will validly generate some useful conclusions to answer the two questions we have posed.

We find from the first item of information in Tables 3.30 and 3.31 that the variations in the relevant aspect of the social structure, during the 10 years ending in 1965–66, have the following dominant features: (1) The 'social group' Category 3, which is essentially an urban phenomenon, has been depleted in strength in both urban and rural areas; (2) Category 2, which is of primary importance in both urban and rural sectors, has gained in strength only in the former while maintaining *status quo* in the latter; and (3) Category 1, which is predominantly a rural phenomenon, has gained in strength in the rural sector while maintaining *status quo* in the urban. Let us examine the implications of these variations.

The 1951 and 1961 census of India show that the percentage of literates to the total population in West Bengal has increased sharply from 24 per cent in 1951 to 35 per cent in 1961; it is also known to be evermore extensive from earlier times to later dates. Therefore, the *depletion* of Category 3, which is composed of 'non-agricultural illiterate gentry or literate commoner, and societal dependents', is *not* likely to be due to an *increase* in the number of 'illiterate gentry' or 'literate commoner'. Also, under the prevailing economic situation, there is hardly any reason to believe that there has been a drastic reduction in the number of 'societal dependents' who, at any rate, form a very small share of the total constituents of this category. The indication is, thus, there that an appreciable share of the 'non-agricultural illiterate gentry' had become literate in this period and, therefore, lost their affiliation to this category.

Category 2 is composed of the 'landed gentry not affiliated to Category 1, agricultural commoner, and non-agricultural literate gentry or illiterate commoner'. Pursuant to the rapid growth of literacy in West Bengal, this category cannot increase its strength by the component of 'non-agricultural illiterate commoner'. Also, since it records an increment exclusively in the urban sector, any change effected in the components of 'landed gentry' or 'agricultural commoner' would hardly be of any relevance to the present context. Thus, the 'non-agricultural literate gentry' draws our attention to explain the gain in strength of this category in the urban sector of West Bengal; and this synchronizes with the shift we have noticed from Category 3 which is essentially an urban phenomenon.

Lastly, Category 1, which is composed of 'literate, socially inferior Hindu or Muslim landed gentry', is seen to have gained in strength in the rural sector of West Bengal, and not in the urban sector. Since the attributes of being 'socially inferior' and 'Hindu or Muslim' are immutable (as pointed out earlier), this change also is seen to be due to the spread of literacy in the 'illiterate' counterpart(s) of this 'social group' in Category 2 and/or Category 3.

Thus, the spread of literacy appears to be the primary source to affect changes in the aspect of social structure under reference; that is, among the three 'social group' categories. This we have already noted for the earlier 10 years of 1946–47 to 1955–56, but exclusively for the rural sector of West Bengal since the corresponding data for the urban sector are not available. While our inference is thus corroborated, the question follows: what is the effect of these changes on the longitudinal variations in family structures? We find several indications to answer this question from the other items of information laid down in Tables 3.30 and 3.31. Let us, therefore, examine them with reference to the paradigm of three primary family structure categories of non-familial units, nuclear families, and extended families.

The non-familial units, affiliated to any one of the three 'social group' categories, do not register any change for the urban or rural sector of West Bengal society, irrespective of the fact that (a) they are much more frequent in the urban than in the rural areas, and

(b) they represent the dominant, subsidiary, and scarce familial property, respectively, for Categories 3, 2, and 1. But, for West Bengal as a whole and exclusively for Category 2, they show a decrease in strength. Since the non-familial units in Category 2 represent the major component of all non-familial units in West Bengal (although it is of subsidiary importance to the incidence of nuclear families in this category), the indication is there that in the 10 years ending in 1965–66 the family organization is being more consolidated in the society.

A corroboration to this effect has been noted earlier in respect of the previous 10 years of 1946–47 to 1955–56 but exclusively for the rural sector of West Bengal because the corresponding data for the urban sector are not available. Moreover, we notice now for the period 1955–56 to 1965–66 that while in reference to West Bengal *en bloc* and exclusively for Category 2 most of the married non-familial units register a gain in strength, the unmarried non-familial units register a corresponding decline. Hence, in the light of our findings from Tables 3.8–3.10 on the role of married non-familial units vis-a-vis the family organization of society, we notice further a tendency toward a closer link between the two, however incipient it is. This is the beginning of the answers to the questions posed above, on the basis of which we shall later examine the familial organization and the familial integration of the West Bengal people.

Unlike the non-familial units, the nuclear families (with all the three possible intra-family relations of conjugal, parental and sibling present in them or not) have a similar order of relative incidence for the urban and rural sectors and West Bengal *en bloc*. But only for Category 1 the two sectors and the society as a whole record a gain for the nuclear families, 'complete' or not; while for Categories 2 and 3 a similar gain is recorded only for the society as a whole, that is, in their case the change records only an incipient tendency. However, for both the Categories 1 and 2, the 'complete' nuclear structures record a gain for either sector and the society as a whole; but not for Category 3. Now, we have found earlier that, along with the spread of literacy in the society, the shift of coresident and commensal kingroups has largely taken place from Category 3 to Category 2, and from Categories 3 and/or 2 to Category 1. Here is, thus, another answer to the questions posed above, which indicat that stabler (or full-fledged) nuclear families are being formed, in course of time, in Categories 2 and 1, but not particularly in Category 3.

Does this mean that, in West Bengal society, nuclearization of the joint family system is taking place? The incipient gain (only at the level of West Bengal *en bloc*) in nuclear families for Categories 2 and 3 may be explained by some of the non-familial units reverting back to a family organization, the tendency towards which has been indicated for Category 2 particularly. But this process cannot explain why Category 1, which epitomizes the incidence of extended families in society, is gaining particularly in nuclear families. On the other hand, even an appreciable gain in nuclear families in a social group, a territorial sector, or in the society as a whole does not lead us directly to the inference that the joint family organization is breaking down to a nuclear family organization. Before, therefore, we discuss the findings in Tables 3.30 and 3.31 in respect of extended families, we should clarify their background in the light of our findings in Chapter 1 and the corresponding information available for India as a whole.

Theoretically, the patrilineal joint families can spread virtually *ad infinitum*, but the common image in India (and so in West Bengal) is of a collaterally joint structure of male siblings with their wives, unmarried duaghters (if any), sons, sons' wives and unmarried children, and the married grandsons with their wives and children. This means that a distinct 'cutting off' point in the spread of patrilineal joint families in India is envisaged in the mental construct of the people concerned. But, even if the 'cutting off' point is set at that uppermost limit, 25 to 30 per cent of the coresident and commensal kingroups in the society will be nuclear in structure because of the life-expectancy, age of effective marriage, fertility pattern, and such demographic characteristics of the Indian people which are also similar for the inhabitants of West Bengal, as noted in Chapter 1 [Mukherjee, 1971b: 68–69].

In case the 'cutting off' point is set at the central tendency of each male in the society to form his joint family of procreation (which is found to be the dominant note for the West Bengal society), 51 to 55 per cent of the coresident and commensal kingroups will be nuclear [ibid.: 71]. And, if the 'cutting off' point is set at the extreme limit of operation of the join family system (namely, each male strives to form his joint family of procreation but his sons—except one—leave the 'stem' family and form eventually their own joint families of procreation), 64 to 77 per cent of the coresident and commensal kingroups in the society will be nuclear [ibid.: 73]. So, how does this bckground stimulate any valid inference from the findings in Tables 3.30 and 3.31?

We have seen from Tables 3.27–3.29 that the relative incidence of nuclear families in the three 'social group' categories and in the urban or rural sector of West Bengal denotes a position around the second of the aforementioned three 'cutting off' points. Furthermore, Table 3.32, which deals with the family-units only, shows that the coresident and commensal kingroups in Category 1 tend towards the first of the three 'cutting off points, those in Category 2 are located more around the second than those in Category 3, and those in Category 3 tend towards the third 'cutting off' point but certainly do not reach it. Thus, in no way, the present findings in respect of extended families affect our previous findings in Chapters 1 and 2 regarding the

TABLE 3.32

Year	*Estimated Percentage of Nuclear Families (±s.e.) to the Total of all (Nuclear and Extended) Families in each 'Social Group' Category*		
	Category 1	*Category 2*	*Category 3*
(1)	(2)	(3)	(4)
	1. *West Bengal*		
1955–56	(166) 33.68±2.60	(1334) 57.42±1.56	(234) 62.54±1.44
1960–61	(473) 43.68±3.77	(3482) 65.38±2.50	(164) 58.14±2.62
1965–66	(2357) 44.97±2.12	(7907) 61.08±1.28	(773) 66.44±1.39
	2. *Urban sector*		
1955–56	(17) 34.14±3.47	(983) 57.22±3.62	(191) 62.62±3.41
1960–61	(21) 37.01±2.76	(1390) 54.48±3.23	(82) 50.12±2.40
1965–66	(69) 49.06±3.10	(3345) 54.51±2.65	(560) 68.40±2.97
	3. *Rural sector*		
1946–47	(588) 37.41	(2761) 54.84	(111) 60.36
1951	(316) 37.23±3.07	(399) 54.75±3.28	(26) 54.86±4.20
1955–56	(149) 33.22±4.20	(351) 67.56±3.75	(43) 59.90±4.20
1960–61	(452) 56.10±3.42	(2092) 69.43±1.21	(82) 68.72±3.59
1965–66	(2288) 44.89±0.89	(4562) 63.78±1.28	(213) 64.89±2.21

nature of internal and external variations in West Bengal family structures.

Now, against the aforedrawn background, if we wish to examine the findings of Tables 3.30 and 3.31 on the operation of the patrilineal joint family system in West Bengal over time, we find that the extended families (with all the five possible intra-family relations of lineal, affinal, conjugal, parental and sibling present in them or not) record a decline in relative incidence for Category 1 in both urban and rural sectors and the society as a whole. On the other hand, for Category 2 alone and only at the level of the society as a whole, the extended families record a gain over time. However, for all the time-points considered respectively, and for either sector of West Bengal or for the society *en bloc*, the extended family is the dominant feature for Category 1, subsidiary for Category 2, and scarce for Category 3. Also, the incidence of 'complete' extended families is the highest in Category 1, next in Category 2, and the lowest in Category 3, irrespective of rural-urban distinction; while the previously discussed central tendency of the 'heads' of family-units to sustain (or form eventually) his joint family of procreation is of distinctive importance to the rural areas (and, thus, for the society *en bloc*), but not for the urban sector of West Bengal. The indication is, thus, there that while the nature of variation in West Bengal family structures has not yet suffered a qualitative change both in the *object* and *space* perspectives, in the *time* perspective their extent of variation has changed—especially for Category 1. Thereby, the previously enumerated fourth possibility of change has come into operation in conjunction with the third possibility of change, leading to a relatively larger incidence of nuclear families in the society and in the 'social group' Categories 1 and 2 particularly.

VIII

The operation of the fourth possibility of change, as discussed above, suggests two further possibilities: (a) the joint family system functions through the propagation of the joint family of procreation of the 'head' of the family by the persistence of the joint family structures and, increasingly, by the break-up and later formation of joint family structures; or (b) the 'sons' who break away from their fathers' joint families and form nuclear families of procreation will continue to live in nuclear families until they disappear from the social scene. In the course of 'trend analysis', therefore, we should lastly examine the feasibility of possibility (b) which specifically refers to the process of nuclearization of families in the society.

This possibility, however, refers to a behavioral phenomenon on which no deduction can be made until the practice is established. On the other hand, an inference on this account is liable to several fallacious renderings. The opinion of the non-familial units to form nuclear *or* extended families, the 'heads' of nuclear families to live as such *sine die* or strive to form extended families, or the 'heads' of extended families to behave conversely, may be casual in nature or reflect a crystallized attitude but may not be put into practice. One may, therefore, be prone to draw fallacious conclusions, as noted in this and analogous contexts [Mukherjee, 1968: 34–35, 46].

Consequently, during the 1960–61 survey, we attempted to ascertain the familial integration of the West Bengal people in an indirect manner. We did not ask for the opinion of our informants—the non-familial units and the 'heads' of family-units— on their *preference* to 'live' as such or by forming either of the two remaining categories of the paradigm of non-familial units, nuclear families, and extended families. Instead, we followed a procedure from which they could not receive any clue to what we were after and, therefore, could not bias their answers in any way. At the very beginning of our interrogation, we asked them: 'who are your family members'? From their enumeration of 'family members', the kinship relation (if any) of these 'family members' with the informants, and other details described in the Introductory chapter, we ascertained the mental construct of the 'family' of the West Bengal people.

To be sure, this construct will not exclusively, or specifically, reflect the *preference* of the informants to one or another form of family organization, for which another efficient procedure could be applied. But, surely, it will provide us with their *image* of the 'family' as formed by all possible reasons (such as, the respective informant's appreciation of familial privileges and obligations, emotional ties and preferences) which would have different orders of priority to decide ultimately the composition of the 'family' envisaged. And since their behaviour will follow from the resultant effect of all these possible reasons, we are inclined to consider that the procedure we have adopted will yield the closest possible approximation to their potential practice. Thus, valid inferences on possibility (b) may be drawn on this basis.

Table 3.33 has, therefore, been prepared which gives the percentage

TABLE 3.33

Family Structure Category	*Society and Sector*	*Estimated Percentage (±s.e.) in terms of:*	
		*Family Organization***	*Familial Integration*
(1)	(2)	(3)	(4)
Non-familial unit: Man	City*	29.87±4.38	4.67±1.52
	Town*	10.34±0.56	5.57±0.52
	Urban*	20.03±5.79	5.12±0.79
	Rural	5.35±1.51	3.62±0.86
	West Bengal*	9.51±1.83	4.05±0.72
Non-familial unit: Woman	City	2.66±0.95	1.89±0.76
	Town	5.56±0.62	4.93±0.55
	Urban	4.12±1.12	3.42±1.09
	Rural	3.84±0.31	3.75±0.28
	West Bengal	3.92±0.41	3.65±0.35
Nuclear family	City	38.88±3.54	41.61±3.56
	Town	42.82±3.06	44.67±3.12
	Urban	40.87±2.05	43.15±2.10
	Rural	58.73±3.52	58.97±3.34
	West Bengal	53.66±3.60	54.48±3.37
Patrilineally extended family	City*	16.22±2.72	37.82±3.91
	Town	27.14±1.61	30.69±1.71
	Urhan*	21.72±3.77	34.23±2.42
	Rural	24.20±1.15	25.63±1.58
	West Bengal*	23.49±1.18	28.07±1.57
Non-patrilineally extended family	City	12.37±3.29	14.01±2.33
	Town	14.14±2.04	14.14±1.38
	Urban	13.26±2.76	14.08±1.36
	Rural	7.88±1.59	8.03±1.23
	West Bengal	9.42±1.81	9.75±1.33

N.B. '*' denotes that the percentage values in cols. (3) and (4) are significantly different at the 1 or 5 per cent probability level.

'**' collated data are given in Tables 2.1 and 2.2.

distributions of the family structure categories separately in terms of the family organization (= the coresident and commensal kingroups formed by the 'heads' of family-units and none by the non-familial units) and the familial integration (=the mental construct of these persons regarding the 'family'). The distributions also refer to respective territorial sectors of West Bengal and the society *en bloc*. Now, we find from the table that the discrepancy between the two sets of distributions by family organization and familial integration is particularly noteworthy for the male non-familial units in both the cities and towns of the urban sector as well as for the West Bengal society *en bloc*. Also, a similar discrepancy is noted for the 'head' forming the patrilineally joint families in the cities and in consideration of the society as a whole.

The discrepancies noticed in Table 3.33 suggest that while more in the cities than in the towns (and, thus, in the urban sector as well as West Bengal *en bloc*) the male non-familial units are integrated towards family organization, this is not the characteristic of their conterpart in the rural areas and the female non-familial units anywhere. Those forming the nuclear or the non-patrilineally extended families do not display any discrepancy between their family organization and familial integration, but those forming the patrilineally extended family organization in the cities (and because of that in the urban sector as well as West Bengal *en bloc*) are more inclined towards the same.

Thus, a stable family organization is indicated for the rural sector of West Bengal, and for those anywhere who are living by forming the nuclear or the non-patrilineally extended families. Correspondingly, the female non-familial units are seen to have been atomized to the point of no return (insofar as the family organization of the society is concerned), as already mentioned in Chapter 1. Also, as mentioned in that chapter, a large number of those living in the urban areas (and particularly in the cities) have a 'family' elsewhere. However, a clearer picture of this incubative phase to form different forms of family organization is obtained when we examine simultaneously the family organization and familial integration of each and every person concerned, as shown in Table 3.34.

Table 3.34, which is a two-way table arranged one-way,

substantiates the findings of Table 3.33 and elicits further the following information:

(1) The mental construct of the 'family' of the male non-familial units in the urban sector tends to be more of a patrilineally extended than a nuclear family (with the non-patrilineally extended family category hardly playing a role in the context),

TABLE 3.24

Family Structure Categories According to:		*Estimated Percentage* (±*s.e.*)		
Family Organization	*Familial Integration*	*Urban*	*Rural*	*West Bengal*
(1)	(2)	(3)	(4)	(5)
Non-familial unit: Man	Non-familial	25.58±8.53	67.80±6.54	42.57±5.32
	Nuclear family	31.79±5.44	18.36±2.85	26.39±3.49
	Patrilineally extended family	40.92±9.27	12.97±4.20	29.67±5.53
	Non-patrilineally extended family	1.71±1.33	0.87±0.68	1.37±0.82
Non-familial unit: Woman	Non-familial	82.94±6.89	97.49±1.52	93.15±2.49
	Nuclear family	7.65±2.94	1.77±1.23	3.52±2.01
	Patrilineally extended family	0.34±0.57	0.37±0.27	0.36±0.26
	Non-patrilineally extended family	9.07±8.91	0.37±0.27	2.97±2.04
Nuclear family	Nuclear family	88.65±4.76	98.62±0.56	96.46±1.11
	Patrilineally extended family	10.25±4.22	1.24±0.52	3.19±1.03
	Non-patrilineally extended family	1.10±0.96	0.14±0.07	0.35±0.19
Patrilineally extended family	Nuclear family	0.10±0.19	0.00	0.03±0.05
	Patrilineally extended family	99.90±0.19	99.99±0.01	99.96±0.05
	Non-Patrilineally extended family	0.00	0.01±0.01	0.01±0.01
Non-patrilineally extended family	Nuclear family	1.64±2.79	0.00	0.66±1.07
	Patrilineally extended family	0.97±1.51	0.00	0.39±0.57
	Non-patrilineally extended family	97.39±3.30	100.00	98.95±1.22

but the preference towards a joint family organization is not established statistically.

(2) An appreciable number of those forming the nuclear family organization in the urban areas are integrated towards patrilineally extended families.

(3) Those forming the patrilineally extended or the non-patrilineally extended families in the urban or rural areas possess the same image of the 'family'.

Thus, we notice a significant tendency of the non-familial units and the 'heads' of nuclear families in the urban sector of West Bengal toward the patrilineally extended family organization:

TABLE 3.35

Family Structure Categories According to:		*Estimated Percentage (±s. e.)*	
Family Organization	*Familial Integration*	*City*	*Town*
(1)	(2)	(3)	(4)
Non-familial unit: Man	Non-familial	15.65± 5.31	53.88±2.23
	Nuclear family	32.64± 7.34	29.36±0.85
	Patrilineally extended family	49.41± 8.62	16.73±1.41
	Non-patrilineally extended family	2.30± 1.66	0.03±0.05
Non-familial unit: Woman	Non-familial	70.77±15.60	88.68±0.07
	Nuclear family	0.00	11.26±0.10
	Patrilineally extended family	0.93± 1.61	0.06±0.09
	Non-patrilineally extended family	28.30±15.60	0.00
Nuclear family	Nuclear family	80.70± 6.56	95.76±0.46
	Partilineally extended family	16.98± 6.21	4.24±0.46
	Non-patrilineally extended family	2.32± 1.61	0.00
Patrilineally extended family	Nuclear family	0.28± 0.48	0.00
	Patrilineally extended family	99.72± 0.48	100.00
	Non-patrilineally extended family	0.00	0.00
Non-patrilineally extended family	Nuclear family	3.55± 5.57	0.00
	Patrilineally extended family	2.10± 2.99	0.00
	Non-patrilineally extended family	94.35± 6.16	100.00

a picture which becomes clearer when we consider the city-town distinction of the urban sector in Table 3.35. For, in this table, all the characteristics registered in Table 3.33 and 3.34 are seen to place the towns inbetween the cities and the villages. A city-town-village spectrum is, thus, seen to represent the variations in West Bengal family structures, of which the motif is to form the patrilineal joint families of procreation—presently, eventually or potentially.

CHAPTER FOUR

Observations

In the Introductory chapter we have explained why we adopted an eclectic and elastic attitude towards the investigation of changes in family structures in West Bengal. Accordingly, in Chapter 1, we have discussed the internal variations of family structures in the 'object' dimension of our study. In Chapter 2, we have examined the interrelations of family structures with other aspects of social structural variations in the 'place' dimension of our study. In Chapter 3, we have explored the trend of internal and external variations of family structures in the 'time' dimension of our study. Thus, insofar as we are concerned with the *singularity* of a phenomenon, namely, 'family structures in West Bengal', the three chapters make a complete circuit. Its main points are summarized below:

1. The dominant note of West Bengal family structures is to evolve the patrilineally joint family of procreation of the 'heads' of respective units. A woman, in this context, is represented ancillarily as a daughter, sister, wife or mother of a man. Operatively, therefore, a man is born in a nuclear or an extended family but he usually forms a joint family of procreation and dies in it; at any rate, he strives to undergo the process. (Chapter 1).

2. Pursuant to this process, the brothers of the 'head' of a *stem* family form their respective families of procreation. Sometimes the sons of the 'head' of a *stem* family (except one to represent the family) also move out of it and form their own families. As a result, a substantial number of nuclear families are formed in the transitional phase between the joint structures which were previously the families of orientation of these 'brothers' and 'sons' and later to become their families of procreation. (Chapter 1).

3. In some instances, the 'brothers' and 'sons' of the *stem* family form collateral joint families; but the viability of the collateral structures is low, especially after the siblings have their

progeny. The parental-filial relation thus appears to be the deciding factor in family formation which, in some cases, is operative for both the families of orientation and procreation of the 'heads' who assume the joint role of 'father' and 'son' in the family. (Chapter 1).

4. The extended family organization is the most marked among those of the landed gentry who are literate Hindus or Muslims but do not belong to the highest echelon of the social hierarchy as Brahmin, Vaidya and Kayastha or non-functional Muslims. Conversely, the extended family organization is the least marked among the non-agricultural illiterate gentry, non-agricultural literate commoner, and those who depend on others in the society for their survival. (Chapter 2).

5. During the 20 years ending in 1966, the effort toward forming the joint family of procreation remains unabated. Also during the same period the association of specific social groups with the relative incidence of the joint family structures is held good. As a result, the rise in the incidence of nuclear family structures in course of these years (and particularly during 1956–66) can be largely interpreted by some shift of the socially inferior Hindu or Muslim landed gentry to non-agricultural occupations or to the rank of agricultural commoner and more by the spread of literacy among the non-agricultural gentry. (Chapter 3).

6. Over the 20 years, collateral joint families are noticeably more present in the urban than in the rural sector of West Bengal but they function as 'stop-gap' arrangements; as if the collaterals have their full-fledged families elsewhere but live 'jointly' in cities and towns due to extraneous causes imposed by the societal forces on their familial arrangements. During the same years in rural areas (and particularly during 1955–56 and 1965–66), the joint family of procreation of the 'heads' appears to be further consolidated. (Chapters 2 and 3).

7. An appreciable number of persons (mostly men) live without kins and affines. Their largest share is in the cities, next in towns, and the least in the villages. The women are usually widows with no familial mooring. The men in the urban areas are in the majority married persons; in the rural areas, unmarried. The familial mooring of the urban male non-familial units is distinctly noticed as against that of their rural counterpart, and

it appears to be more toward the joint than the nuclear family organization. (Chapters 1–3).

8. In most cases in the villages, the coresident and commensal kingroups which the 'heads' of family-units operate are in conformity with their conception of what is a family. But in the urban areas, and more in the cities than in the towns, an appreciable share of the 'heads' living under the nuclear family organization consider those persons as their family members who do not live with them but, if they did, the family would have become patrilineally joint in structure. Correspondingly, however, there is no discrepancy in the 'family organization' and the 'familial integration' of the 'heads', in either rural or urban areas, who live under the joint family organization. (Chapter 3).

9. From the *null* incidence of persons living alone as non-familial units to the flowering of joint families, and passing through a phase of nuclear formation in many instances, the motif in West Bengal is thus to form the patrilineal joint family of procreation—presently, eventually or potentially.

Beyond the above findings, further observations from this study may appear to be presumptuous. But, with respect to any phenomenon of which the 'singularity' has been analyzed, deduced and inferred, there are the succeeding aspects of *particularity* and *universality*. Obviously, for the phenomenon under reference, the former aspect would be concerned with the situation for the Indian society (of which West Bengal forms an integral part), and the latter with societies beyond the Indian and eventually for the world. Equally obvious it is that the present study can in no way generalize for either of the two aspects. However, it would be of very limited significance if we cannot draw a link among the three aspects and, thus, place our findings on a wider perspective. This, therefore, we shall try to do in this chapter, with a successive reduction of specificity in our discussion from the 'particularity' to the 'universality' of the phenomenon.

On India, we possess a good deal of research findings in the present context which have been treated elsewhere in some details and will be summarily presented here [Mukherjee, 1971b: 41–107]. Even so, in reference to the current task, we can use them merely to provide a few cues for further research on the nature and extent of variations in family structures in India. As regards any society beyond the Indian and eventually for the world, we are not in a position to suggest any specific cue: that would be presumptuous. However, certain generalizations, which we may legitimately make for the present study, would be conducive to this aspect of research. Accordingly, we shall state them subsequently.

II

We may repeat from the Introductory chapter that a nuclear family consists of *one set* of husband and wife and/or their children, so that it can contain only three kinds of kinship relation in any combination: (a) conjugal, between husband and wife; (b) parental-filial, between parents and their children; and (c) intersibling, between brother(s) and/or sister(s). A joint family, correspondingly, may or may not contain these three kinds of kinship relation, but it must contain either or both of the following two kinds: (d) lineal, between any two persons related by blood but not as (b) or (c) above; and (e) affinal, between any two persons who are related by marriage of their own or of their blood relatives.

Now, there are different kinds of joint family in India, but mostly they are patrilineal-patrivirilocal in structure. That is, a joint family contains all male progeny of the forefathers and also all their unmarried female progeny, but the married females come to live in the family of their husbands. Hence, by keeping the above definitions in mind, we find that the simplest identification of a family is in terms of forming a coresident and commensal kingroup; that is, a number of persons—who are related to one another by blood, marriage or adoption—live together and eat from the same kitchen.

There are, of course, other ways of identifying a family, which do not refer to a locally functioning societal unit; such as in terms of specific attributes of integration among a number of coresident and commensal kingroups. We mention this possibility because it brings us to the two viewpoints prevalent in India today regarding the viability of joint family organization in the society:

(1) The people are breaking away from the joint family of their forefathers and living in nuclear families of their own.

(2) The joint family is maintaining its role in the society through the 'familial integration' of the nuclear units which previously belonged to a coresident and commensal joint family.

The first viewpoint is suggested by whatever information we possess on the percentage of families living under a nuclear structure in different parts of India. Prafulla Chakrabarti, one of the two main collaborators of this study, collated the available data with reference to the minimum definition of family to form coresident and commensal kingroups. He, thus, accounts for 44,657 family-units referring to: (a) the time-period 1948–62, except in one case of 1937; and (b) 30 different groups of people living in 15 States spread over the whole of India. He found that only 5 out of these 30 groups of people have formed 35 to 39 per cent nuclear families, 9 have formed 40 to 49 per cent nuclear families, 13 have formed 50 to 59 per cent nuclear families, and the remaining 3 have formed 60, 61 and 63 per cent nuclear families. The average works out at 55 per cent nuclear to all families in India; that is, there are more nuclear than joint families in the society.

The second viewpoint has developed out of the researches of some sociologists. Desai, for example, has shown from his study of the town of Mahuva in Gujarat [Desai, 1964] that the nuclear units, which previously belonged to a joint family, maintain the 'familial integration' by helping one another at the time of marrying their 'daughters', to secure jobs for their 'sons', and so on. We have shown for West Bengal, and especially for its urban sector, that if the people are asked to report who are their family members they enumerate those relatives who, taken together, would form, in a large number of cases, the joint family. Many of these people live only with their wives (or husbands) and children; their 'familial orientation', however, is towards the joint family.

We have also found for West Bengal that three mutually distinct but analogous social groups can be identified for the predominance, minority, or scarcity of the joint family structures in the society. Furthermore, any increase in the percentage-incidence of nuclear families in West Bengal tends to be associated with the viability of these three groups characterized by the social structural attributes of religion and caste, source of livelihood and the education of the people.

It will be argued, however, that certain social groups may cling to the joint family structure but their decreasing presence in the society shows that the joint families are systematically replaced by nuclear families. It can also be argued that the persistence of familial integration or orientation in the society points to later stages of nuclearization of the joint family. In the first stage, the joint families are *irrevocably* transformed into nuclear families. In the second, the nuclear units (thus formed) maintain the familial bond by the sharing of privileges and obligations amongst themselves. In the third and the last stage, the nuclear units drift so far apart from one another that the 'joint family' is lost even in the mental horizon of the people.

These arguments prompt us to examine, first, the initial stage in the course of nuclearization of joint family structures. It involves answering three questions which may be formulated as follows:

(1) Are the joint family structures transformed into nuclear family structures?

(2) If the answer to the first question is 'yes', is there a *feed-back* to the joint family structures from the nuclear family structures?

(3) If the answer to both the questions is 'yes', what is the viability of the joint family in India?

In order to answer these three questions, we may recall from Chapter 1 the growth process of the joint family structures, and also how they can disintegrate to the point of being transformed into nuclear family structures. Let us, therefore, visualize the proliferation of a patrilineal-patrivirilocal joint family from its beginning when a man begins to live with his wife. Since the ancestors of the man are not to be considered in the present context, we shall label this pair of husband and wife as the 'root couple' of a family tree.

With respect to this 'root couple', the joint family will be formed, exclusively by generational extension, when the wife of the first son comes to live in the family, and a set of affinal relations is thus formed. The joint family will go on extending generationally, but *unilaterally* with respect to the 'root couple', through the 'sons' sons', sons' sons' sons', and so on. Correspondingly, the family will extend generationally and collaterally through a *set* of 'root couples' of 'brothers', the couples of their 'sons', the couples of their 'sons' sons', and so on. So that, unless there are selective processes at work to cut off the proliferation of the joint family at certain points of its generational and collateral expansion, it will be identical with the patrilineal kinship structure of the males in the family, with their wives in appendage.

This, obviously, is not the characteristic of family structures in India, as it is not in all those societies which contain patrilineal-patrivirilocal joint families. The course of generational extension of a joint family must be limited because the family members must die. We, thus, find for India (as for West Bengal) that one of the frequently imposed 'cutting off' points is at the extension of a family beyond three generations. This is dictated by the demographic profile of the society, which since 1911 may be summarized, as follows, on the basis of the census data and an all-India random sample survey of 84,517 evermarried men and 87,467 evermarried women regarding their marriage and fertility.

Most of the people in India marry early, in spite of the laws promulgated to prohibit child or adolescent marriage. The wives, however, come to live with their husbands at about 15–19 year of age, when their husbands are 20–24 year old. The average number of children born to a couple is four, of which the first two are born when the husband is 25-29 year old and the next two when he is 30–34 in age. Usually, of the first two children, one is a son and the other a daughter, because of the binomial probability in operation; the same is true for the next two children. We need to consider only the sons since they (and not the daughters) will propagate a patrilineal joint family. The sons, as 'brothers', are placed, on an average, in corresponding 5-year age-groups; and very few of these men and their wives live beyond the age of 64: the possibility of survival was less in earlier times. (For details, see Mukherjee, 1976: Chapter 2.)

These demographic attributes represent the central tendency in Indian society. There are, of course, variations from one region to another, one state to another, one social or cultural group to another, and one family to another. The range of variation, however, is not found to be so large as to make the average characteristics unreliable to represent the demographic profile of the society and, thus, the growth process of a joint family in India. We find, therefore, that, on an average, a 'root couple' will be formed when the man is in the age-group of 20–24 years and the woman in that of 15–19 years. This 'root couple' will attain the parental status when the husband is in the age-group of 25–29 years. It will attain the parent-in-law status, with reference to the first son's wife, when the man in the 'root couple' is 45–49 year old. It will attain the grandparental status, with reference to the first son's first son, when the man in the 'root couple' is 50–54 year old.

The family can attain the 'great grandparental' status with reference to the first son's first son's first son of the 'root couple' when the great-grandfather is 75–79 year old and the great-grandmother 70–74. These age-groups, however, are seldom reached by the Indian people even now; the prospect was worse in earlier times. Therefore, very few joint families can extend beyond the three-generation structure, and many of them will be of two or one generation only because all people are not blessed with a ripe old age.

Collaterally, however, a joint family can extend to accommodate all the surviving patrilineal kins of the males unless certain restrictions are operative in the society to limit its collateral ramifications. We may, therefore, examine some hypothetical situations in a sequence which will: (1) restrict more and more the proliferation of joint families, (2) lead in due course to the formation of nuclear units by the segmentation of joint structures, and (3) transform ultimately all joint families into nuclear ones. Let us, accordingly, begin with our idyllic image of the three-generation patrilineal-patrivirilocal joint family in India. It conjures the picture of brothers living together with their wives, sons and sons' wives, and the sons' sons and unmarried daughters. In conformity with the marriage and fertility pattern of the Indian people, which we have just described, we can draw the genealogical tree of such a family at its average extension. This is done in Diagram A.

Families of the structure shown in Diagram A were possibly rare in earlier times because they will contain those remotely placed cousins who are related as 'grandfather's brother's grandson or granddaughter'. Also they will contain granduncle and/or grandaunt, and uncles and aunts once removed. Such families are certainly rare these days as we find from family surveys in different parts of India. However, even if the societal tendency is to strive for this kind of joint famlies which denotes an uninterrupted continuation of the joint structures, about 30 per cent of all families in India would be nuclear. This will happen because of differential probability of survival of men and women

DIAGRAM A

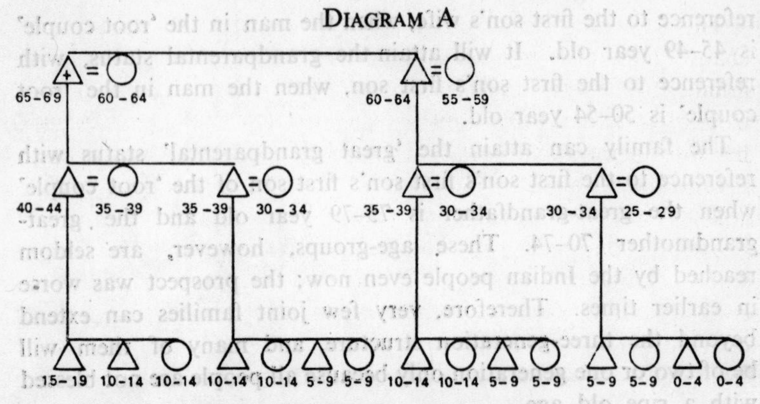

Notes : 1. The symbol △ stands for a man, ○ for a woman.
2. The sign of equality denotes a married couple.
3. A cross within a symbol denotes that the person has passed away.
4. The figures denote the 5-year age-group of each person.

of different age-groups in the family, as can be worked out from the census data from 1911 to 1961. [Mukherjee, 1971b: 66–68].

Let us assume, next, that the parental couple may pass away at an early age or at a ripe old age *but* the 'sons' couples' which will now attain the role of fraternal 'root couples', will live together so long as they have no progeny of their own. Let us also assume that if they already have their own progeny (and otherwise, when these 'root couples' will have their own progeny), they will separate with the objective of forming unilateral joint families, respectively, with their sons, sons' wives, sons' sons, and sons' unmarried daughters. The average extension of the family tree, as envisaged by this societal tendency, will be represented by the left half of Diagram A; that is, by the progeny of the 'root couple' represented by the 60–64 year old widow of the deceased male who would have belonged to the 65–69 year age-group.

In this kind of joint families there will be no granduncle, grandaunt, uncle or aunt once removed, and second degree cousins. There should be, however, grandparental and first degree uncle, aunt, and cousin relationships, and the parents-in-law, siblings-in-law, and cousins-in-law relationships, in the family. Thus the kind of joint families, which will emerge out of this societal tendency, conforms to what we come across more often these days.

This tendency, however, implies the possibility of a cyclical change in family organization by: (1) the formation of nuclear families in the intervening phase when a 'root couple' has separated from its fraternal 'root couple' but its first son has not yet brought his wife in the family; and (2) the feedback to the joint family organization from the nuclear units thus formed. The cycle, of course, may not operate invariably because there is also the possibility that the 'root couple', we are presently concerned with, had already had its son's wife in the family when the parental couple passed away. In that case, the 'root couple' will form its own joint family organization as it separates from the fraternal 'root couple' and the progeny of the latter. Thus, with or without the cyclical transformation of family organization, the persistence of the joint family in India is assured by this societal tendency as well.

However, because of differential survival probability of the family members, this tendency to maintain the joint family will lead to the emergence of 51 to 55 per cent nuclear families in India. Thus, even if half (or a little more than half) of the total number of families in the society are found to be nuclear, it will not imply that the joint structures are being transformed into nuclear structures and that too, to the point of no return to the joint family organization. So that, from the currently found rate of incidence of nuclear families in the society, we cannot infer that the joint family is disappearing from India.

Anyhow, we may conceive of further cuts in the persistence of joint family structures in order to account for still larger incidences of nuclear families in the society. For example, we had previously assumed that the 'root couples' of brothers do not wish to live together from the time they have their progeny, but had subsumed that the 'subsidiary couples' of sons of a 'root couple' will continue to live in the paternal joint family. Let us now make four assumptions on the societal tendency. The first two will stipulate that all sons of a 'root couple' set up their respective families when they (a) become parents or (b) begin to live with their wives. The last two assumptions will stipulate that instead of all the sons leaving their parental family, the last one of them will continue to live in the joint family of the 'root couple' together with his wife and children.

Obviously, the first two possibilities denote the break up of the joint family organization, and not its persistence *via* a transitional phase of formation of nuclear families. Therefore, if the sons move out of their parental families after they themselves have become parents, 84 per cent of the families in India will be nuclear; and if they move out just after they begin to live with their wives, all the families will be nuclear. Such a preponderance of nuclear families is certainly not the characteristic of the Indian society. Also, for both the possibilities, the parental couples or the widowed parents will have to live by themselves in their old age, and not with their sons. This is not a feature of India to date. We may, therefore, safely infer that a process of systematic and complete nuclearization of joint family structures is not operating in India today.

We may now examine the last two assumptions which conform to the persistence of the joint family organization but at the extreme margin of 'cutting off' the collateral ramifications of the joint structures. These two assumptions are realistic to the extent that they do not refer to the situation in which the old-age couples or the widowed parents will have to fend for themselves. Correspondingly, therefore, they refer to the persistence of the joint family organization by at least one son staying with the parents. Thus, each couple, in its turn, forms a joint family with its youngest son, his wife and his children, as shown in Diagram B in terms of the maximum extension of the family tree under the extreme condition.

In the manner of persistence of the joint family as shown in Diagram B, the family-units will not contain the relationship between 'uncle/aunt' and 'nephew/niece' and that between the

DIAGRAM B

65–69 60–64

35–39 30–34

10–14 10–14 5–9 5–9

we may make from the present study and its all-India relevance outlined in the foregoing pages. These conclusions we shall enumerate from 1 through 5.

1. *A course of analysis may lead to a valid deduction, but an inference drawn from that deduction may not be valid.* For the sequence from deduction to inference is symptomatic but not automatic. The latter may require deeper probing into the phenomenon than is usually done to draw a conclusion from the deduced results of a course of analysis.

Thus, the findings in Chapter 1 that 54 per cent of the West Bengal families in 1960–61 were nuclear, as against 33 per cent extended families and 13 per cent non-familial units, leads us to deduce correctly that, at the given 'place-time-object' dimensions, there are more nuclear than joint families. But this deduction does not lead us automatically to infer on any course of nuclearization of the joint family *system* (not of individual joint family structures). On the contrary, a consideration of the variables concomitant to the formation, propagation and destruction of family-units points out that the patrilineal-patrivirilocal joint families of procreation of the 'heads' of West Bengal families is the central tendency in the society, as it is likely for the Indian society as a whole also.

This is an inference (that is, a logical conclusion drawn from *all possible deductions* on the phenomenon under reference) which can be made from the investigations feasible at the *current state of our knowledge*. Its validity is substantiated by the findings in the subsequent two chapters, and also indicated in the foregoing pages. But it is quite contrary to the deduction which we make, firstly and correctly, from the data at hand *and* which we tend to equate to a valid inference in place of enquiring into other possible and relevant deductions. Conceptually, thus, it is useful for research to maintain a sequential but distinct relation between deduction and inference.

2. *A valid inference may attain far-reaching relevance if it is examined against other variables which are contingent to those on the basis of which the inference was drawn.* In the present instance of variations in family structures, the contingent variables will obviously refer to the social structural variations. They may appear to negate the force of inference since the deductions made on their basis are seemingly contrary to the substance of the

inference. Nevertheless, if coherence is ascertained among these deductions and that is found to fall in sequence with the nature of the inference, the consistency of the latter is further enforced.

Thus, with respect to the familial organization of Indian society, the patrilineal-patrivirilocal joint family is seen to be the 'desired' norm since the ancient times. This is noted, emphasized and even eulogized in the Hindu epics, *puranas, smrtis*, and other law books. The Moslem ethic also does not strike a different tune. And yet, the humbler sections of the society are often found in the same literatures to live in nuclear families as against the wealthier ones. The kings, noblemen, noteworthy traders, prosperous farmers, etc., are usually described to form joint families—frequently with an appreciable collateral spread, but not the wood-cutters, hunters, fishermen, pedlars, etc., in anecdotes, fables and folktales. However, the kinship bond among all these sections of the society is not reported to be different; the desire to attain large families of procreation and orientation is considered to be fairly universal. Evidently, the desire cannot always be fulfilled, while the contrary situations depicted by the nodules of the social structure emphasize the central tendency in the society and denote its dynamism regarding the aspect under reference.

The picture painted above for the past in India may require further confirmation from a content analysis of the relevant literatures. For contemporary West Bengal, however, a similar picture emerges from Chapter 2. The central tendency (which may be regarded as the *probabilistic norm* of the society since it is denoted by the high probability of its occurrence) is to live in the patrilineal-patrivirilocal joint families of procreation; but social structural differences are also clearly noticeable among the three categories which emerge in the social scene in this context. These differences yield apparently contradictory characteristics of Category 2 which is marked by the nuclear family organization. In about equal sample-strength (Table 2.21) the category is composed of the 'non-agricultural literate gentry' and the 'agricultural commoners plus the non-agricultural illiterate commoners'.

Thus, while the inference on the central tendency is valid, it leads to a crucial question: how much of the 'deviation' from it and towards the nuclear family organization is due to value differentials of the non-agricultural literate gentry, and how much is it due to the economic constraints of the other major group in the category? The question is echoed by the composition of Category 3 (Table 2.21) which registers the preponderance of the non-familial units. Accordingly, the valid inference drawn in Chapter 1 attains a particular relevance to appraise the dynamics of West Bengal family organization when the social structural variations, apparently contrary to its central tendency, are brought to account. This approach is no less important to appraise the phenomenon in the 'universal' perspective, as evident from the 'family studies' on, say, China, Korea, Japan, Philippines.

3. *A valid and relevant inference becomes efficient to portray the reality when its concomitant and contingent variables are examined over time.* For any facet of reality cannot be exposed without an appraisal of the dynamics of the situation, and any comprehensive apprehension of dynamism demands examination of the situation in the time-dimension. Hence, the deductions made from the above-mentioned variations in the longitudinal perspective would elicit such characteristics as to make the portrayal of reality evermore distinctive and comprehensive. Concurrently, therefore, they will endorse or reject the power of generalization, and so the efficiency, of the inference made earlier and found to be valid and particularly relevant in the specified context.

Thus, the findings in Chapter 3 bring out, firstly, that the role of the concomitant and contingent variables of the inference made in Chapter 1 and substantiated in Chapter 2 is maintained consistently over 20 years (1946–66); and, correspondingly, any variation noticed in the differential incidence of the family structure categories over time is due, essentially, to the variation in the relative incidence of the contingent social structure categories and not of the former set of categories on their own merit (Tables 3.22–3.29).

Secondly, the longitudinal analysis points out that as economic opportunities opened up with the onset of the Five Year Plans for India's development, there was a tendency for the male married non-familial units (comprising the bulk of the category complementary to family-units) to cease living singly and either go back to their 'families' in the rural areas or bring their 'families' to urban areas (Tables 3.8–3.10). The process is commensurate with a rise in the incidence of nuclear (but not of the extended) families in the urban areas, and of both nuclear and extended families in the rural areas (Tables 3.4–3.7). It, thus, appears that there, has been a change over time in the relative incidence of the family structure categories, and in reference to the rural-urban stratification of West Bengal society.

But it is also noticed (Tables 3.30–3.31) that the above process is linked with a depletion of the social structure category which epitomized the incidence of non-familial units (Category 3), a gain of that category in the urban areas only which records the highest relative incidence of the nuclear families (Category 2), and a gain of that category in the rural areas only which records the highest relative incidence of the extended families along with an appreciable incidence of the nuclear families (Category 1). This means that the deduction made earlier on the social structural variations to reflect family structure variations is corroborated by a set of apparently contradictory findings which, however, lead to complementary deductions.

Thirdly, we find that literacy has operated as a lever to effect changes in the relative incidence of the social structure categories reflecting family structure variations. But, does it imply that 'value-considerations' have promoted the formation of nuclear families? Alternatively, has literacy provided an added facility to utilize the economic opportunities and thus lead a stable (or stabler) family life, albeit, nuclear in structure in many instances? To be sure, in the uppermost echelons of the society, and especially in metropolitan areas, value-considerations may dictate the structure of the family. But is it a phenomenon *en masse*; at any rate, in the urban areas?

We find, in this context, that in the urban areas the joint family of orientation has registered a temporary but appreciable phase of family organization (Table 3.20). Moreover, in terms of the 'familial integration' of the people, and especially of those who live in the urban areas, the patrilineal-patrivirilocal joint families represent the present or eventual, or the potential, characteristic of West Bengal family structures (Tables 3.33–3.34).

A valid, relevant, and efficient inference can thus be drawn by examining the dynamics of family structure in terms of its 'object', 'place', and 'time' dimensions of variation; and the inference can become evermore efficient as it portrays the reality more and more precisely and comprehensively by means of intensive and extensive examinations of the concomitant and contingent variables.

4. *A valid, relevant and efficient inference unfolds the necessity to pursue empirical research on a subject instead of merely harping on (a) the theoretical generalizations which may be frequent but fallacious, or (b) hastily drawing conclusions from spontaneous deductions which may be conjectural.* This necessity is particularly underlined for a contemporary appraisal of the family as a social institution, for the subject has drawn the attention of social scientists for more than a century and thus led to many theoretical generalizations—some of which are almost regarded to be axiomatic.

From an intensive study of the 'family types in Badlapur', a village in Maharashtra, Morrison came to the conclusion:

> Types of familism in Badlapur are quite clearly related to various well defined cultural types. The data presented lead to the conclusion that the Joint and Quasi-Joint Family patterns are 'traditional middle class' village phenomena, patterns of living which are closely associated with certain multi-caste groups, certain traditional occupations, and certain educational levels. In addition, the Nuclear Family is very closely associated with both the upper and lower socio-economic and cultural groupings of the village. The Nuclear Family appears both among the better educated, more non-traditional, middle and upper status caste groupings, as well as among the lower socio-economic levels of poorer villagers. The former group reflects in its familism the influence of 'urban-industrial' non-traditional values and attitudes of modern life, whereas the latter group reflects a poverty-stricken way of life which in most cases does not permit larger family group than the nuclear. [Morrison, 1959: 67]

It will be noticed that Morrison's findings are very similar to those contained in Chapter 2 of this study, but he did not attempt to examine his findings further in the manner we did in Chapter 3 with reference to the context provided by Chapter 1. Instead, he drew conclusions which merely repeat certain theoretical generalizations on the variations in family structures as due to urbanization, industrialization, 'modernization', class-difference, etc. Such theoretical assertions are quite common, currently popular, and have been made by reputable social scientists [for example, Linton, 1952: 84; Epstein, 1962: 322; Lerner, 1963: 334]. But they may not be invariably valid as the present study points out, and which has also been noted by Goode:

> Just *how* industrialization or urbanization affects the family system, or how the family system facilitates or hinders these processes is not clear. It is doubtful that the amount of change in family patterns is a simple function of industrialization; more likely, ideological and value changes, partially independent of industrialization, also have some effect on family action. [Goode, 1963: 1–2]

We should also mention while quoting Goode that the lack of any 'ideological and value changes' *en masse*, as found in this study, need not suggest that here we are dealing with one of the Asian 'inert societies' [Mende, 1959: 26]. The fact that the people, in general, strive to form joint families of procreation need not be interpreted as 'traditionally irrational', an *interpretation* which tends to follow glibly from the peculiar inference we have drawn which, however, is found to be valid, relevant and efficient. For another set of theoretical generalizations is equally popular and frequently administered according to the schema of 'tradition to modernity' and 'irrational-rational behaviour', but which may not always be appropriate.

The fact of joint family organization or integration, as elicited from the data and the inference, may be the expression of a very rational and modern desire on the part of the people, given the meaning of rationality as the optimization of the relation between ends and means. For the overwhelming majority of the people have no savings, investments, social insurance, or old-age benefits to look after them beyond their working life. It is only their family of procreation on which they can depend to survive when they have passed the zenith of their existence.

Anyhow, whether or not the hypothesis just put forward—which would be applicable to the Indian society as a whole and also to a number of other Asian societies—is valid, it is appropriate enough to be tested by pursuing the course of empirical research. Correspondingly, several other hypotheses laid down in the preceding chapters would be worth testing, just as the main and the subsidiary inferences drawn in this study may be further confirmed or rejected from additional findings and their proper treatment.

Briefly, therefore, the theories developed in different 'place-time' contexts, or anticipatory theorizing in the light of some deductions, are no substitute for a systematic accumulation of knowledge from sustained investigations. Also, in order that the accumulation of knowledge is systematic, unequivocal, and evermore precise and comprehensive, these investigations must be based on a schema of all possible concept-formations regarding the subject under reference and a methodology appropriate to unfold the concepts. Such concepts and methods with reference to variations in family structures, on which the present study is based, have been mentioned at the beginning or during the course of this study [for example, Mukherjee, 1971b, 1972]. We may note further that, as attempted in this study, the course of investigation must not short-circuit or snap the sequential chain of 'data—analysis—deduction—inference—interpretation'. Instead, in a spiral-like progression of this chain, the investigations will bring our knowledge closer and closer to the reality. Accordingly, the inference we have drawn should be regarded as a pointer to pursue further empirical researches into the family as a social institution, and not as an end in itself.

5. *Proceeding sequentially from its validity, relevance, and gathering efficiency, any sufficient inference (as judged by its maximum efficiency) on revealing the familial properties of a society would considerably advance our knowledge on the social reality.* This proposition, however, may be overemphasized by a section of the idealists and existentialists, on one side, and derided by a section of the materialists, on the other.

Overemphasis is now less frequent and apparent than in the 1950s. The family is not contemporarily regarded as *the* medium, for socialization of individuals; nor the 'socialization and interaction process' of the family interpreted mainly in terms of 'instrumental' and 'expressive' behaviour, etc. [for example, Parsons and Bales, 1956]. Social structural variations of the family are now considered more seriously, and the economic factor in the structure, function and process of the family is now drawing more attention than ever before. Also, various other processes of socialization of the individuals (such as, economic, political, etc.) are now drawing attention of the social scientists who used to be regarded as 'biased' or 'dogmatic' in case a minority of them strayed away from the scheduled path of 'pure' sociology and ventured to examine these parameters.

However, the scale of priority has also tended to be reversed. To a section of young enthusiasts, 'family studies' have come to be of little or no significance. In fact, even such comments are made that to study 'family', 'socialization', etc.—instead of 'class', 'polarization', etc.—is to resort to escapism and end in futility. To the supporters of this viewpoint, therefore, we may quote the following from Marx and Engels who were the pioneers to bring the concepts of class, polarization in society, etc., for a precise appraisal of the social reality:

> Since we are dealing with the Germans, who do not postulate anything, we must begin by stating the first premise of all human existence, and therefore of all history, the premise namely that men must be in a position to live in order to be able to 'make history'. But life involves before everything else eating and drinking, a habitation, clothing and many other things. The first historical act is thus the production of the means to satisfy these needs, the production of material life itself....
>
> The second fundamental point is that as soon as a need is satisfied, (which implies the action of satisfying, and the acquisition of an instrument), new needs are made; and this production of new needs is the first historical act....
>
> The third circumstance which, from the very first, enters into historical development, is that men, who daily remake their own life, begin to make other men, to propagate their kind: the relation between man and wife, parents and children, the FAMILY. The family which to begin with is the only social relationship, becomes later, when increased needs create new social relations and the increased population new needs, a subordinate one (except in Germany), and must then be treated

> and analysed according to the existing empirical data, not according to 'the concept of the family', as is the custom in Germany. These three aspects of social activity are not of course to be taken as three different stages, but just, as I have said, as three aspects...which have existed simultaneously since the dawn of history and the first men, and still assert themselves in history today. [Marx, 1942: 16–18]

> According to the materialistic conception, the decisive factor in history is, in the last resort, the production and reproduction of immediate life. But this itself is of a twofold character. On the one hand, the production of the means of subsistence, of food, clothing and shelter and the tools requisite thereto; on the other, the production of human beings themselves, the propagation of the species. The social institutions under which men of a definite historical epoch and of a definite country live are determined by both kinds of production: by the stage of development of labour, on the one hand, and of the family, on the other. [Engels, 1948: 13–14]

We may also mention that Engels' emphasis on the role of the family came for a sharp criticism at one phase of its comprehension:

> But there is one inaccurate statement in Engels' preface to the first edition of the book (*The Origin of the Family, Private Property and the State*, 1884) which must be noted, as it may give rise to erroneous views on the role played by the various conditions of material life in the development of society.... The family, ..., cannot be placed on a par with labour, with material production, as a determining cause of social development.... The precise, finished, classical formulation of the main proposition of the theory of historical materialism was elaborated by Comrade Stalin in his *Dialectical and Historical Materialism.* [Marx-Engels-Lenin Institute of the Central Committee of the Communist Party of the Soviet Union (Bolsheviks) 1948: 8–9]

The critical note, however, was withdrawn later and, thus, family came to be acknowledged, again, as an important subject for study to appraise the social reality. May we, then, conclude that in this study we have neither overemphasized the role of the family as a viable and durable social entity nor derided its importance to sociological research?

PART TWO

Data and Field-work

CHAPTER FIVE

Survey

It is not usual for sociological studies, based on empirical research and depending upon the information obtained from large-scale sample surveys, to be involved with an exhaustive discussion on the data and field-work. The common practice is to briefly describe these ingredients of empirical research in the introduction to the study or in an appendix, and presume that they have been treated satisfactorily. This, however, may not be justified because too many lacunae of research may hide behind such generalities, while they can be and should be resolved. It may not also be sufficient because our knowledge on research methodology is not yet standardized or even systematized. Methods and techniques are often regarded to be inter-changeable labels, instead of the latter following from the former. Also, conceptualization as the prerequisite to any appropriate methodology is seldom considered rigorously. On these elementary considerations, therefore, it would be useful to describe, at some length, the data and the field-work of the sample surveys brought to account for the present study.

There is also the point about the design and the execution of the study itself, which is not merely a collation of the data from several sample surveys. The backgound information to design an empirical piece of research properly is lacking in many respects. A satisfactory organization, execution and appraisal of the field-work make demands which are not usually met. An appropriate analysis of the data requires facilities which are not easily forthcoming. And, all such lacunae of empirical social research are aggravated when a study is sponsored on an *ad hoc* basis, which is the common procedure in contemporary India. Hence, the experience gained from a study, which stands on its own merit but was directly involved with a large-scale sample survey and the secondary analysis of the data from several other such surveys, would be worth presenting in some details.

Moreover, the source of our limitations to empirical social research is not only the dearth of adequate information and facilities. Whether or not a piece of research has been sponsored on an *ad hoc* basis, it is usually promoted and executed through an institution where adequate expertise is available and yet it is not infrequently found that we do not pay sufficient attention to standardize the information (for example, the classificatory and the measuring variables) in order that the scope of a study is not restricted to itself. It should be amenable to secondary analysis, which may considerably help us appraise the aspect of reality under reference as the first part of this study may substantiate. Similarly, we seldom organize field-work in such a manner that the reliability of the data collected can be tested from the data-set itself. Also, our treatment and analysis of the data may lead to fallacious or imprecise deductions; and, following therefrom, the inferences drawn, and the interpretations presented, may be equivocal.

To be sure, these are all 'teething troubles' of a new undertaking: empirical social research in India (as also in many other world societies) is just about attaining its adolescence. Nevertheless, we shall not attain adulthood in this context until we have gained sufficient knowledge from the current undertakings to systematize (and, eventually, standardize) them for the future. It is, therefore, not in a spirit of castigating the aforementioned research undertakings, but to learn from our limitations, that the following chapters may be found useful.

Thus, family, religion-caste, livelihood, and education are the four major classificatory variables for the present study; and so it is for many sociological studies in the Indian context, while 'caste' may be replaced by another classificatory item (for example, 'prestige grouping') in other countries. But, how often —in India and elsewhere—attempts have been made to systematize and eventually standardize the frame of classification on their account? In this context, the details given in the appendix to Chapter 6 from the 'Instructions to Field-workers' (available in the Sociological Research Unit of the Indian Statistical Institute) may be useful.

Similarly, in how many cases any rigorous and objective attempt is made to assess the reliability and efficiency of the investigators. The general practice in contemporary India is to employ persons with postgraduate degrees in any one of the social science disciplines as field-investigators. Because of the state of the labour market, they may now be available in plenty. But, are they the right kind of persons needed for the task? In this context, the application of Mahalanobis's technique of 'inter-penetrating network of sub-samples (IPNS)' to the investigator-wise variations in survey data may be of some interest, as reproduced in Chapter 7.

Correspondingly, in the context of analysis of survey data, we are being increasingly aware of the need to apply statistical tests to ensure the validity of the deductions made and appraise the relative precision attained in making them. But, for this purpose, we usually depend on the application of the Chi-square test on bivariate frequency distributions: a test which is particularly suitable to small but duly controlled samples, as in biological research. Is it, therefore, invariably applicable to the discrete frequency distributions obtained for social research? Also, with reference to fairly large samples (which is very common in social research), the Chi-square test may elicit hardly any information additional to what is immediately noticed from the proportional distributions of the bivariate frequencies. How often, and how much, we gain, therefore, from the Chi-square test unless it is carried out meticulously by bringing in many subsequent procedures? This, however, is seldom done, while the Chi-square test is presented almost as a talisman for social research, probably because of its low cost and easy applicability.

On the other hand, the correlation and regression analysis of the data, duly or unduly quantified, tends to raise the status of empirical social research to the elite category. To be sure, under specific conditions and on the basis of a proper quantification of the data, the appropriate techniques of correlation and regression analysis can be of significant importance to appraise the social reality. But, how much may we learn just from a coefficient of correlation between two continuous variates even though it is very likely to be statistically significant because of the fairly large samples of social research? The 'social' parameters are usually (and should be by their conceptualization) related to one another in a positive or negative manner; but the coefficient of correlation between any two 'social' variables, duly quantified into continuous series, yield a value around 0.5 and seldom above 0.7. This means that less than half of the social space, purported to be represented by the two variates, would be accounted for by the value of 0.7; and the value of 0.5 would account for only one-fourth of that space. However, correlation analysis may be a prerequisite to examine the formation, consolidation and divergence of 'social groups' in the given social space defined by its 'place-time-object' dimensions; such as, to calculate discriminant functions in terms of the *net* contributions of the measuring variables reduced to unit standard deviations around zero-means for a D^2–analysis [*vide* Mukherjee and Bandyopadhyay, 1964: 259–82].

Anyhow, the identification of mutually distinct but analogous 'social groups', and recording the nature and extent of their interrelationships, are the prime considerations of social research, as we have discussed elsewhere [ibid.]. In that context, when dealing with discrete series of measuring variables, the proportionate occurrence of the classificatory categories in their respect may lead to such an identification, as it will be evident from Part 1 of this study. Accordingly, we need to deduce the respective and relevant mean values and their standard errors. The same is also required when dealing with series of continuous variates, in addition to recording their correlations. Therefore, irrespective of the merits and demerits of the two kinds of statistical tests cursorily discussed above, the point to note is that in social research the test of significance of mean differences (and, following therefrom, the tests of group-divergence) may deserve our primary attention.

Sometimes social research proceeds on a pre-conceived (but not properly tested) notions of group-constellations; but the fallacy and inadequacy of such attempts are now being evermore obvious. Hence, the calculation of sampling errors (or the standard errors) of the 'group means' becomes the first step towards ensuring the validity of the deductions to be made from a course of empirical research and, proceeding therefrom, towards the appraisal of the relative precision of the deductions made. This, however, may be quite a task in terms of expertise, time, computer cost, etc., as will be evident from the formulae to calculate the sampling errors—given in the last section of Chapter 7.

The above comments, sporadic as they are, on the data and field-work emerge from a common source: the formulation of the problem for a sociological study, its conceptualization and the appropriate methodology. In the Introductory chapter of this study we have formulated its problem, briefly discussed the concepts involved, and referred to the methodology adopted. Following therefrom, we prepared the design of research, and became involved with the collection, collation and analysis of the data—all of which comprise this part of the study. The circuit is, then, closed by the four chapters in Part 1 which incorporates the deductions made from the analysis, the inferences drawn from the deductions, and the interpretation of the facet of the social reality under reference in the light of these inferences. Now, we may venture to suggest another usefulness of discussing the back-stage manoeuvres in the form of a distinct part of the study.

Contemporary social research in India is becoming more and more empirical. Correspondingly, it is very sensitive to a proper organization and execution of the research projects, as is evident from the yearly handouts of the Indian Council of Social Science Research. But the funding sources usually stipulate the research programmes in such a manner that if x be the time (and, correspondingly, the money) allotted for the *field-work*, about $0.25x$ is allotted for *designing the study*, $0.50x$ for the *analysis of the data*, and $0.25x$ for the *write-up*; that is, a total of about $2x$. To be sure, the consideration of *'field-work'* as the yard-stick for all operations of a piece of empirical research may be fallacious and the funding sources need not invariably adopt this measure, although any estimation of the time (= mandays) involved in field-work may be more readily and accurately done than for other operations. However, even on such a rough base, our experience is that a realistic allotment of time (and, consequently, of money) would be rather as: x, x, $2x$, and x, respectively; that is, a total of about $4x$.

We trust that the following chapters will substantiate the need for a more realistic allotment of time and money than is usually forthcoming from the funding organizations. We also hope that the discussion in these chapters will bear out the responsibility of the promoting organizations to provide the essential prerequisites and expertise to plan empirical social research more efficiently than is usually the case today.

CHAPTER SIX

Design

In this chapter we shall describe the design of the study and that of the sample surveys on which it is based, showing the logical basis and reliability of generalizing from the observed samples about the universe of West Bengal society. We shall, first, describe the design of the 1960–61 survey, next give short resume of the other surveys taken into account for this study, and then indicate the common areas for all of them; so that the validity and efficiency of the design of research may be duly appreciated.

For all the surveys taken into account, our ultimate *unit of observation* was a coresident and commensal kingroup (that is, a family-unit or a non-familial unit) while the ultimate *unit of sampling* was a household (that is, a coresident and commensal group of persons who may or may not form a kingroup). This discrepancy between the two kinds of units, because of the lack of necessary background information to plan social surveys, may raise problems which we shall discuss later. Presently, let us note that in order to avoid any subjective bias in the selection of households and also to ensure the representativeness of the sample, the course of selection of the households for the 1960–61 survey was designed as follows.

The sample frame consisted of 3 primary divisions according as the households in the State of West Bengal belonged to: (1) the cities of Calcutta (including the Tollygunge Municipality which in 1953 was incorporated within the city limit) and Howrah; (2) the towns, including the remaining 'cities' of Bhatpara, Garden Reach, South Suburbs, and Kharagpur according to the 1951 census classification; and (3) the villages. The 'city households' were thus distinguished from the 'town households' because of their specific metropolitan *milieu*, while the two sets taken together represent the 'urban households' as against the third set of 'village households'.

Within the city sector of the society, Calcutta was divided into 37 contiguous segments; Howrah into 10. These segments represent the municipal wards demarcated for the 1951 census. Each of the segments was divided into a number of contiguous blocks according to the data of the Urban Frame Survey (UFS) conducted by the Indian Statistical Institute in 1959–60. From the total number of blocks thus identified in each of the 37 and 10 segments, 2 were selected at random. Then, all the households located in each of the sampled blocks were listed and the requisite number of households per block was selected at random from the respective lists.

The town and village sectors of the society were first divided in terms of the ecological characteristics of West Bengal. This was not necessary for the 'city' sector since it refers to one ecological zone only: the 'riverine plain area'. On the basis of available information, the ecological zones of West Bengal were demarcated as: (1) hill area, (2) sub-Himalayan forest belt, (3) arid plain area, (4) riverine plain area, and (5) coastal belt [*vide*, Majumdar Sastri, 1924; *Census of India* 1953: VI (IA); Chatterjee, 1957; 1951 *Census District Hand Books for West Bengal*]. The follwowing major attributes were particularly taken into consideration for this purpose: (a) natural division, (b) physical configuration, (c) soil type, (d) climate with special reference to rainfall and temperature variations, (e) river system, (f) irrigation facilities, (g) agricultural pattern, (h) population density, and (f) village arrangement (for example, size, clustering, etc.).

In order to draw the sample of 'town households', the towns falling within each ecological zone were listed, and 1 was selected at random from the respective lists. Thus, out of 3 towns in the 'hill area', Darjeeling was selected; out of 3 towns in the 'sub-Himalayan forest belt', Siliguri was selected; out of 28 towns in the 'arid plain area', Adra was selected; out of 83 towns in the 'riverine plain area', Berhampore was selected; and the only town Contai in the 'coastal belt' was automatically included in the sample.

Each of the towns, except Berhampore, was divided by the field investigators into a number of contiguous areas (=blocks), and a specified number of them was selected at random. Within each sampled block, all the households were listed and a specified number selected at random. For Berhampore, its ward-wise distinction (ignored for the other towns) was taken into account since its large size and long history were assumed to denote a more heterogeneous consistency. The 5 ward-segments, however, were subdivided into a number of contiguous blocks and the same process as for the other towns was repeated.

In order to draw the sample of 'village households', the rural sector of West Bengal was stratified by the 5 ecological zones as well as the districts falling under them either fully or partly. In other words, the 15 districts of West Bengal were distinguished by their ecological characteristics into a total of 24 strata. The objective of this 2-way stratification was to take into account any specific rural characteristic of a district along with the intrinsic characteristics of an ecological zone, and to scatter widely the villages to be selected over different areas of the State. Hence, to obtain the sample of 'village households', all the villages falling under each of these 24 strata were listed and one village was selected at random from the respective lists.

Unlike for the urban areas, the sampled villages were totally enumerated. In sociological literature on India, villages are often regarded as distinct social entities. We thought it advisable, therefore, to ascertain family structures in respect of all the households in these villages. We shall, then, subscribe to the prevailing assumption on the village as a 'unit of study' and derive whatever benefit may accrue to us thereby. At the same time, we shall be in a position to examine, with reference to the relative importance of intra-village and inter-village variations in family structures, whether from this aspect village ought to be regarded as a 'unit' or a 'variable'. This is a moot question in designing social surveys in rural India, and may have further implications for rural sociology in India [Mukherjee, 1961b].

The complete examination of all households (and, thus, all family-units and non-familial units) in the sampled villages could forbid us from bringing a larger number of villages to account on the basis of drawing samples of households within the sampled villages. But the point was also there that the transport cost rises sharply with visits to more and more villages, and more time is consumed in journeys within the rural area than from one urban area to another. Whereas, once a village is reached and accord is established by the field investigators with its inhabitants, the difference in the time expended to collect information on all or a sample of households within the relatively small compass of a village is not so large. Thus, within the limits of time and money available to us, we could have sampled only a few more villages than the 24 selected for the 1960–61 survey if we had sampled households within the selected villages. But the small gain, which we might have obtained from a somewhat wider scatter of households, would offset the possibility of testing the prevailing assumptions on our rural society. We desisted, therefore, from taking that course.

In respect of the towns and cities of West Bengal, on the other hand, their internal heterogeneity is known, as is inter-urban variations in the society. Also the stratification of cities and towns into ward-segments and/or blocks, and the sampling of blocks thereafter, were for operational purposes only; that is, to obtain a wider scatter of households in the selected urban areas. The blocks need not convey any sociological meaning by themselves. Whereas, in view of the time and money available to us, if we did not draw samples of households from the sampled blocks in the selected towns and cities of West Bengal, we would have had to reduce the total number of 'urban areas' brought forward for the 1960–61 survey. And, as such, we have taken into account the two cities of West Bengal and only five towns to represent her different regions in terms of ecological and other characteristics. Sampling of households within the sampled urban blocks was thus *sine qua non* to the design of the 1960–61 survey.

II

The exact numbers of households to be drawn at random from the sampled urban blocks are as much dependent upon the time and money available for the survey as on considerations like the specific nature of information to be collected, the safeguards to be introduced in the mechanism of investigation, etc. On the latter count, we thought it advisable to employ postgraduate degree-holders in social sciences as field investigators, and to fit them into a scheme of interpenetrating network of sub-samples—usually labelled IPNS [Mahalanobis, 1944: 380–81]. These field-workers, we expected, will understand the sociological implications of the concepts and definitions involved in the enquiry, and thus will be able to appreciate the significance of the questions to be asked to the interviewees. At the same time, IPNS will provide us with an estimate of the range of variation among these persons in respect of the collection of the same kind of information, however better equipped they may be (theoretically) than the field investigators commonly employed for socio-economic survey.

Six research assistants were, therefore, recruited: 3 anthropologists, 2 psychologists, and 1 historian. It was decided that they will be grouped into three pairs during field investigation, each pair consisting of an anthropologist and one social scientist of a different brand. So that an attempt can be made, wherever possible, to gauge any difference between anthropologists and non-anthropologists as field investigators for a social survey.

The course of selection of households in the city, town and village sector of West Bengal was, accordingly, further elaborated. For the cities of Calcutta and Howrah, and for the town of Berhampore, the sample allocation was adapted to 3-stage design: (1) A number of segments in each of the two cities, and in the town, were to be allotted at random to a pair of field investigators; (2) the blocks selected within a stratum, in the manner described earlier, will be under the joint charge of the two investigators to whom that segment was allotted; and (3) the households sampled within each of the selected blocks will be allotted in equal number, and at random, to each of the pair of investigators placed in charge of the block.

For the towns of Darjeeling, Siliguri, Adra and Contai, the course of sample allocation was to follow a 2-stage design: (1) the blocks selected in each of these towns in the manner explained earlier were to be allotted at random to a pair of investigators; and (2) the households sampled within each of the selected blocks will, then, be allotted in equal number, and at random, to each of the pair of investigators placed in charge of the block.

For the 24 sampled villages also a 2-stage design was planned: (1) the villages were to be randomized in equal number among the 3 pair of investigators, so that a sub-sample of 8 villages will be allotted to each pair; and (2) in each village the total number of households will be allotted in equal number, and at random, to each one of the pair of investigators placed in its charge.

Thus the design was to be such that the sample allocated to each of the six field investigators will comprise a network of similarly drawn random samples of the 'city households', 'town households', and 'village households'. For the respective sets of households will consist of 3 statistically valid sub-sets, with 2 replications for each one of them. They will yield, therefore, 6 valid results for any character under study, and thus represent West Bengal by 6 valid sub-samples [Mahalanobis, 1961: 4–8].

While thus evolving the design for the 1960–61 survey, a pilot enquiry was undertaken by S. Bandyopadhyay and K. Chattopadhyay in order to test the feasibility of a questionnaire-schedule incorporating the maximum possible information with respect to the objective of our study. The blocks of the schedule referred to the identification of family-unit, its structural characteristics, the forms of social stratification it is affiliated to, and the specific features of the 'social factors' it is associated with. For each block the time required to fill it in was recorded.

The experience of the pilot survey indicated that, for the present, the role of what have been labelled 'social factors' should be investigated incidentally. The collection of information, in their context, would require intensive interrogation or an altogether different type of questioning. It was also found that this aspect of the survey will prolong the interview-period to such a length that it may affect the reliability of data due to fatigue or irritation of the interviewees. These two points may be better appreciated from a list of some of those information relating to 'social factors' which were taken into account for the pilot enquiry: (1) opinion, attitude and action of family members in favour or against a common living; (2) the role of 'traditional' notions, customs and habits of the people to enforce 'norms' for different social groups with reference to the family as a social institution, and its effect on variations in family structures; (3) differential incomes of the earners in a family as affecting it in favour of cohesion or disintegration; (4) recent social legislations and constitutional provisions affecting family composition, for example, rules of inheritance and succession, age of marriage, etc.; (5) variability due to biological growth as affecting the size as well as the composition of a family; and (6) the effect of family planning propaganda and measures, made available by the Government during the plan periods to the rural and urban population of West Bengal, on family size and composition.

It was decided, therefore, that an intensive examination of the 'social factors' will be taken up in another inquiry if time and money would permit the undertaking. For the 1960–61 survey emphasis was laid on the family structure *per se* and to provide the background and initial characteristics of those items of information which may be collected in subsequent surveys in order to elicit the internal characteristics of family organization. Schedules 1.0 and 1.1, mentioned in the Introductory chapter, were accordingly designed. Their facsimile are appended to this chapter (Schedule 1.1 only in terms of its differences from Schedule 1.0).

Regarding the time which may be required to fill in the finally designed schedule, 40–45 minutes appeared to be adequate in the light of the average time taken to fill in the relevant blocks of information during the pilot enquiry. Therefore, in view of the time and money sanctioned for the study, the total number of households which could be covered was estimated at about 5,000. This figure we had to bear in mind when deciding on the size of samples to be allocated to the selected cities, towns and villages, as well as to compose the interpenetrating network of sub-samples of the field investigators. It was noticed that the 1951 census records a total of 3,043 households for the 24 sampled villages. About 2,000 households could, therefore, be drawn as samples for the cities of Calcutta and Howrah as well as for the 5 sampled towns.

We decided to sample 5 'city households' per field investigator per block so as to obtain 10 households from each city block. Thus, according to the previously described stratification of Calcutta and Howrah by 37 and 10 segments, and the selection of 2 blocks from each segment, the total sample of 'city households' was to be 940: Calcutta represented by 740 households and Howrah by 200. It was further decided that, field investigators' batch-wise, Calcutta was to be represented by 2 batches of 240 households each, and by the third batch of 260 households; for one of the 37 strata could be allotted to one batch of field investigators only. Howrah, likewise, was to be represented by 2 batches of 60 households each and by the third batch of 80 households; for one of the 10 strata could be allotted to only one batch of field investigators. In all, therefore, Calcutta was to be represented by 6 sub-samples of 120–130 households each, and Howrah by 6 sub-samples of 30–40 households each. Together, the 'city' sector of West Bengal was to be represented by 6 sub-samples of 150–170 households each.

It was considered advisable that an investigator surveys a minimum of 10 households per town in order that the investigator-wise comparison of the sub-samples can be done with some degree of reliability. It was also regarded to be sufficient in the light of our resources that an investigator surveys 30 households, at the maximum, per town. The range was kept in view to meet the internal heterogeneity of respective towns. Hence, with the assumption that all the 6 investigators will be in each town, 60–180 households were to be surveyed per town. The procedure to fix the actual sample size was as follows.

Contai was regarded to be adequately represented by a sample of 60 households because its population size is much smaller than that of other towns. Also, although classified as a town since 1931, Contai in 1960 was still in a transitional phase of emerging into an urban area from a cluster of villages. The sample households in each of the other towns, except Berhampore, were to be scattered over 6 blocks, after these blocks have been drawn at random from their total numbers within respective townships. In Berhampore, 2 blocks were to be drawn at random from each of its 5 wards in the same manner as adopted for the two cities. Each of the 3 pairs of field investigators, then, was to survey 2 blocks in a town, except for Berhampore. For this town the 10 sampled blocks were to be randomly allocated to the three pairs as 4, 4, and 2, respectively.

Accordingly, it was further decided that each field investigator will be allotted 5 households per block for Contai, 9 households per block for Berhampore, and 15 households per block for Darjeeling, Siliguri and Adra. The 5 sampled towns were to contribute, therefore, a total of 780 households to the allotted sample of 1,720 households for the urban sector of West Bengal. Also, field investigators' batch-wise, the 'town households' of West Bengal were to be represented by 3 valid sets. Two of them would comprise 272 households each; the third, 236 households. Six sub-samples of 'town households' would, thus, be obtained; each sub-sample comprising 118–136 households.

For the rural sector, the 24 villages were scheduled to be allocated equally, at random, to the 3 pairs of field investigators. So that, after the enumeration of all the households in these villages and the drawing of half-samples between the two in each pair of investigators, the rural sector of West Bengal was expected to be represented by 3 sets of about 971, 1,020, and 1,052 households, or by 6 sub-samples of about 500 households each. The variation in the number of households per pair of field investigators and in reference to each one of them would be due to the unequal number of households in the sets of 8 villages allotted to respective pairs.

Correspondingly, the urban sector of West Bengal was designed to be represented by 3 sets of about 575 households each, or by 6 sub-samples of about 287 households each. Thus, West Bengal was to be represented by 3 sets of about 1,600 households each, or by 6 sub-samples of about 800 households each.

III

We had prepared the design for multi-stage stratified random sampling in such a manner that it will be efficient in two ways: (1) it will represent West Bengal society objectively and comprehensively since the households, the ultimate sampling units, were drawn at random with equal probability given to the selection of urban and rural areas and their constituent blocks, etc.; and (2) the precision at which West Bengal society is to be represented will be indicated by the variations found among the valid estimates of the items of information as obtained from the investigator-wise distribution of the households. The design, however, had to be amended on account of the inherent weakness in the organization of an *ad hoc* survey.

Although the field investigators agreed at the time of their appointment to remain in office until the phase of investigation was over, all of them (except one) failed to honour the agreement. Fresh from the university, they were sincere and well equipped for the task. Also their performance was satisfactory, as it will be evident from the next chapter. They had not reckoned, however, with their temperamental suitability to this kind of arduous and monotonous assignment: a factor which is ruled out when dealing with a tested team of field-workers who can be employed for one survey after another. One of our 6 investigators left after the survey of the two cities and one village; 4 left by the time the survey in four towns and twenty villages additionally was over; and only P. Chakrabarti remained with us for the remaining town of Darjeeling and the villages Dumriguri Chhat and Algarah Bazar.

We had planned to survey the last three areas at the final stage of our field-work. Darjeeling and Algarah Bazar refer to a cultural *milieu* which is sharply different from that in the rest of West Bengal. Also we would require interpreters to communicate with the majority of their inhabitants in local dialects and language. Therefore, we thought it advisable to take up these two areas after our investigators (all Bengalees) had become fully accustomed to the course of investigation by working with their own cultural *milieu*. Since the village Dumriguri Chhat is situated at the foot of the hills leading to Darjeeling, it was planned to be surveyed when the field team moves over to this region. Furthermore, we had planned to survey the village Kaylapara before the survey of the aforesaid town and two villages but after the survey of the other villages, towns and the cities. As representing the 'coastal belt' of the State, Kaylapara is situated in an almost inaccessible island. Except during a few months in the winter, transport to this village was virtually impossible to arrange unless one was willing to face grave risks. And now we had to alter the design of field-work in tune with the emergent exigencies.

K. Chattopadhyay and S. Bandyopadhyay conducted the field investigation of Kaylapara with the assitance of P. Chakrabarti and B. Ray. Dumriguri Chhat and Algarah Bazar were surveyed by Ray and Chakrabarti, respectively, with the assistance of the local people. Bandyopadhyay organized the survey of Darjeeling by employing 4 local people as field investigators and one as field supervisor. These individuals were graduates from Calcutta University and connected with local organizations. They had sustained and intimate contact with the resident of the town, as had the interpreters in Algarah Bazar.

While the field design was thus revised to meet the limitations inherent in an *ad hoc* survey, it did not affect the comparability of different sectors of West Bengal, namely, the first aspect of the 1960–61 survey design. Of course, the second aspect concerning inter-investigator comparisons and formation of a number of independent estimates of the items of information could not be rendered as effective as previously planned. Nonetheless, the scheme of interpenetrating network of sub-samples was applied in its full measure to the 'city' sector of West Bengal and in a certain manner to the 'town' and 'village' sectors also. For the latter, we rearranged the batches of field investigators in two's and three's, and reallocated the remaining sampled villages among them, in order that by maintaining the process of randomization of households within the sampled villages and among the members of the batch to which they were allocated, we could still subscribe to the IPNS scheme. For the 'town' sector of West Bengal, since the field-design was further disturbed by the leave of absence of one or another investigator during the period of field-work, we adopted a more direct procedure of sample allocation. Each investigator working in a town was allotted 2 sampled blocks at random in order to survey 10–25 households in a block, so that the total sample for each of the 3 towns (except Contai) was fixed at 200 households and for Contai at 80. Thus, 5 sub-samples for the respective sectors and the state of West Bengal could be obtained satisfactorily in order to appraise the reliability of survey data. Details are given in Table 6.1.

TABLE 6.1

*Sector of West Bengal**	*Final Allocation of Samples Per Investigator*						
	1	2	3	4	5	6	*Total*
(1)	(2)	(3)	(4)	(5)	(6)	(7)	(8)
'City'	160	160	160	160	150	150	940
'Town'	160	160	140	110	—	110	680
Urban	320	320	300	270	150	260	1620
Rural	465	325	449	449	228	514	2430
Total	785	645	749	719	378	774	4050

*The 'town' sector excludes Darjeeling (200 sampled households), and the 'rural' sector excludes the villages Kaylapara, Dumriguri Chhat, and Algarah Bazar (a total of 467 households).

IV

For purposes of longitudinal comparison we had selected the years 1956, 1951 and 1946–47 for the backward projection of the findings from the 1960–61 survey, and the year 1965–66 for forward projection. Comparative data for 1965–66 we could obtain from the 20th Round of the National Sample Survey (conducted during July 1965–June 1966), for 1956 from the 10th Round (conducted during December 1955–May 1956), and for 1951 from the 2nd and 3rd Rounds (conducted during April–June and August–November, 1951, respectively). For 1946–47, we relied upon the survey conducted by the Indian Statistical Institute, Calcutta, in order to submit two reports to the Government of West Bengal [ISI, 1951; 1952].

All these surveys were undertaken to meet ends other than the study of family structures. Moreover, to none of them the 'universe' was West Bengal. The 1946–47 survey referred to undivided Bengal (presently, West Bengal and Bangladesh). The National Sample Surveys are designed to supply information for India as a whole or her 4 regions: north, south, east and west. West Bengal, in that context, is one of the States in Eastern India. However, these surveys can give us a fairly representative, reasonable comparable, and adequate coverage of data in reference to the objective of our study.

The rural sector of West Bengal was thus represented by 463, 95 and 103 randomly selected villages for the time-points 1965–66, 1956 and 1951, respectively, comprising 7,582, 568 and 795 randomly selected households within the three sets of villages. The designs adopted for the selection of villages and households were similar for the aforementioned rounds of the National Sample Survey [NSS, 1953: 4, 17; 1954: 7, 25; 1960: 20] and may be represented by the following statement on the design of the 20th Round [NSS, 1965: 3]:

> The sample design is a stratified two-stage one, where contiguous tehsils homogeneous with respect to geographical, climatic and crop considerations are grouped to form strata. Villages, the first stage units, are selected with probability proportional to size (pps) systematically in the form of 4 independent interpenetrating sub-samples from each stratum, and house-

holds, the second stage units for socio-economic enquiries... are selected systematically with equal probability within the selected first stage units.... The sample design has been made self-weighting at State level for all the household enquiries.

For the 1946–47 survey the design to represent rural Bengal was as follows [ISI, 1952: 1]:

In the first stage of the enquiry the entire province (undivided Bengal) was divided into 1,247 square zones, each approximately of 64 sq. miles. Out of these 476 were selected at random with the help of random numbers. Each zone, thus selected, was divided on the map into 64 cells of one mile square. One such cell from each zone was again picked at random, and all households falling within such cells were surveyed.... In the second stage...a definite proportion of the families was selected at random from sample units of the first stage, 80,710 families in the first stage now giving a sub-sample of about 10,000 families (a proportion of about 12½ per cent from each zone).

In this case, therefore, West Bengal villages had to be distinguished from East Bengal (now Bangladesh) villages since the partition of Bengal took place later than the period of this survey and, therefore, the state boundary of West Bengal (which is taken into account for the National Sample Surveys) was irrelevant in those days. After the necessary scrutiny and categorization of the villages surveyed, the 1946–47 data referred to a toal of 3,654 randomly selected households for the State of West Bengal, although the total number was expected to be 3,680 as reported at the time of the survey. The slight discrepancy between the two figures is mainly due to the fact that the boundary between West Bengal and East Pakistan was not so well defined in the first two years after the partition of the British province of Bengal as it is today.

Thus, although the designs for these surveys varied somewhat among themselves, they present fairly representative data for the backward and forward projections of the findings from the 1960–61 survey in regard to the rural sector of West Bengal. A point, however, is worthy of note in this context. The course of sampling for the National Sample Surveys went up to households within a village; that for the 1946–47 survey ignored villages altogether. Therefore, the representative character of the data for our purpose may suffer if in respect of variations in family structures the villages were to be regarded as 'units' and not as 'variables', the question we had raised earlier. From the 1960–61 data, however, we had ascertained that inter-village variation in family structures is not less (if not greater) than intra-village variation. We have no reason to doubt, therefore, the representative character of our comparative data with reference to the rural sector of West Bengal.

For the urban sector our comparative data are relatively scarce. The 1946–47 survey referred to rural Bengal only. The 2nd Round of the National Sample Survey was restricted to rural India. The 3rd Round took notice of urban India for the first time, but this initial attempt covered such a small sample that it was representative at the all-India level only [NSS, 1954: 18–19]. Therefore, in reference to the urban sector of West Bengal, the backward projection of the findings from 1960–61 survey can refer to only 1956 and the forward projection to 1965–66.

The 10th Round of the National Sample Survey (1956) provides us with 1,671 sampled households from Calcutta, Howrah, and 41 towns of West Bengal. From the 20th Round (1965–66) we can obtain a sample of 6,186 households from the 2 cities and 82 towns. In either case, thus, the size of sample is adequate. Also, the designs for these two rounds of the National Sample Survey of urban India was such that they will fairly represent the urban sector of West Bengal. Similar to that for the 10th Round [NSS, 1960: 21–22], the design for the 20th Round was as follows [NSS, 1965: 7]:

> The design is a stratified two-stage one, where strata are formed on the basis of the population of towns and cities within each state; and urban blocks, the first stage units, are selected pps systematically in the form of 4 independent interpenetrating sub-samples, and households, the second stage units, are selected systematically with equal probability. The NSS-UFS frame has been used for all cities and towns whose population in 1961 was 50,000 or more (Sector 1) and for about half the number of the remaining towns (Sector 2) and the 1961 census frame has been used in the rest of the Sector 2 towns. The

sample design has been made self-weighting at Sector level within each State.

V

However, the comparability of data from the all-Bengal and National Sample Surveys with those from the 1960–61 survey may suffer on two counts: (1) variable definition of 'household', the ultimate unit of sampling, and (2) variable coverage of family-units and non-familial units within the sampled households.

The definition of household for the 1960–61 survey was the same as for the surveys of 1965–66, 1956 and 1946–47. It referred to 'those persons who *usually* and *regularly* lived together and ate from the same kitchen'. For the 1951 survey a specified time-period was introduced in the definition, namely, 'persons who may have resided and taken their meals in the households for 16 days or more during a period of 30 days immediately preceding the date of enquiry should be deemed as members of the household' [NSS, 1951: 4]. Purely on this account, therefore, it may be apprehended that the estimated occurrence of different family structures in West Bengal will be different for 1951 from the same for other time-periods.

This follows from the manner in which the design of our study has been evolved. One of its premises is that the members of a locally functioning family-unit are identified, in the first instance, with reference to the structure of the household which locates the coresident and commensal kingroup. Hence, if the household structures for 1951 are different from those for other time-periods owing to the difference in defining the household, the variation noted in the incidence of different family structures over time may be due to this factor.

It was ascertained, however, that even if the attributes of coresidence and commensality are specified by different measures of time-periods, the probable variation thus introduced in the structure of the respective households occurs infrequently. Moreover, this variation is of a random order within the society at large. For the persons left out from certain households and consequently from certain family-units, under a stringent stipulation of the time-period, are incorporated in certain others. As a result, the quantitative disturbance in the pattern of distribution of family structures in the society is rather marginal or insignificant. This can be seen from Table 6.2 which gives the analysis of the 1951 data obtained from the 2nd and 3rd Rounds of the National Sample Survey combined together.

TABLE 6.2

Coresident and Commensal Kingroups=Family-units and Non-familial Units in West Bengal in 1951	*Percentage to Total Coresident and Commensal Kingroups (±s.e.), Formed According as Their Constitutent Members Lived Together Prior to the Date of Investigation for:*		
	16 Days or More in Last 30 Days	*6 Months or More in Last 12 Months*	*Throughout the Previous Year*
(1)	(2)	(3)	(4)
'Non-familial'	12.40±1.24	12.53±1.73	13.33±1.93
Nuclear	45.10±3.61	46.58±3.70	47.98±3.89
Patrilineally joint	25.88±2.49	26.09±2.35	25.87±2.61
Non-patrilineally joint *or* Non-patrilineally and patrilineally joint	16.62±0.18	14.80±0.11	12.82±0.08
Total (Sample)	100.00 (739)	100.00 (733)	100.00 (704)

On the first count, therefore, we may be assured that the data brought to account from different surveys will be comparable for our study. The second brings in complications. Pursuant to the objective of those surveys and unlike that of the 1960–61 survey, their ultimate unit of observation was a household and not a family or non-familial unit. As a result, the occurrence of additional family-units in the households may be underestimated and that of the non-familial units overestimated. For, according as the 'heads' of households draw kinship relations with one or more members of their respective units, it would be readily ascertained whether or not they form locally functioning family or non-familial units and what is the form of family structure they represent, respectively. But, as to those members in a household who do not draw any kinship relation with their 'head', they would all be returned as non-familial units unless such relations are recorded in the household schedules for two or more of them, as it was stipulated for the 1960–61 survey.

This possibility may affect comparability of the time-series data in reference to the relative incidence of family and non-familial units and different family structure categories. The possibility, however, is more in theory than in practice, as it will be seen from Table 6.3 which refers to the 1960–61 survey.

TABLE 6.3

*Sector of West Bengal**	*Estimated Number of Coresident and Commensal untis =Households*	*Estimated Number of Family-units and Non-familial Units*	*Ratio of Col. (3) to Col. (2)*
(1)	(2)	(3)	(4)
City	599158	724981	1.21
Town	1148499	1194310	1.04
Rurban	3560749	3596286	1.01
Rural	1502488	1504605	1.00
All rural	5063237	5100891	1.01
Total	6810894	7020182	1.03

*'Rurban' sector refers to villages within a distance of 10 miles from a town or city; 'rural' to villages beyond the distance of 10 miles from a town or city; and 'all rural' to all villages in West Bengal. The estimates exclude the 'hill area' of West Bengal.

It is seen from Table 6.3 that there are some city-households which contain, respectively, more than one family or non-familial unit, but such composite family-households are rare in towns and virtually absent in villages. Moreover, it is common knowledge that the composite family-households are usually formed by the occurrence of domestics who seldom occur as more than one in a household and, even if they do, they need not be related by blood or marriage. Even so, we examined scrupulously each and every household schedule obtained from the 1946–47, 1951, 1956 and 1965–66 surveys in order to ascertain whether it contains additional family-units and/or non-familial units. The possibility of error in their respective and total estimations is, therefore, likely to be virtually nil for the rural sector of West Bengal and negligible for the urban sector.

Now, in addition to the comparability of the time-series data, there is the question of their coverage of information to meet the objective of our study. It will be seen from Chapter 3 in Part 1 that they have been employed to denote: (1) the categories of family structure to which the respective family-units belong; and (2) the composite social structure categories to which the respective family and non-familial units are affiliated. All items of information relevant to these two courses of categorization were available from the questionnaire-schedules and the written instructions to the investigators for each survey. We could, therefore, classify the family-units for the time-series in exactly the same way as done for the 1960–61 data.

In one respect, however, the comparative data did not meet our requirement fully, namely, the caste and grade-wise categorization of Hindu and Muslim households which we have seen from Chapters 2 and 3 of Part 1 to have a bearing upon the social structural affiliation of the family structure categories. The National Sample Survey organization, which conducts 'sample surveys on a nation-wide basis for collecting various socio-economic data required for planning and other purposes by the Central and State Ministries, Planning Commission, and other interested organizations' [NSS, 1965: 1], had discontinued since 1961 the previous practice of collecting caste-data for the households surveyed. The data on Scheduled Castes and Tribes, or the Backward Classes, which this organization continues to collect diligently, were not found to have direct relevance to variations in family structures in West Bengal (Chapter 2, Part 1). Hence, the forward projection of the 1960–61 findings to 1965–66 could not but be less precise because the 'socially inferior' Hindu and Muslim family and non-familial units had to be identified from the caste and grade-wise surnames and the information regarding the Scheduled Castes and Backward Classes in the household schedules. This is the only limitation to our comparative data which we could not avoid.

VI

We have described in considerable details the design of the 1960–61 survey, and discussed the merits of the comparable data from other surveys, because in the words of Parsons 'a barrier has grown out of the fact that a major structural aspect of a large-scale society cannot be observed in a single program of field research' [Parsons, 1954: 177]. We wish to point out, therefore, how a programme of field research on the family as a major structural aspect of a large-scale society like West Bengal can be organized, what difficulties we may encounter in assuming that charge, and how such difficulties may be resolved.

To be sure, ours is not the only venture in the field. Also, it could have been better designed and executed if we had the requisite amount of time and money, and the desired flow of men and auxiliary data. Such as, within the 'town' and 'village' sectors of West Bengal, we should have had replicated the sampling of towns and villages within each stratum; but that would have cost us more time and money than what were allotted to us. We could have strictly enforced the IPNS scheme in these sectors if we had access to a permanent field organization. Our projection of the basic findings from the 1960–61 survey also could have been more precise and elaborate by going down to intra-sectoral levels of the society if we had requisite data for comparison.

Such expectations, however, hardly ever come to be true: some may, all do not. In the present context, therefore, they are beside the point. In reality, however streamlined is the design of a survey theoretically, it may be further improved, on one side, and, on the other, amendments to it become inevitable because of operational exigencies. Hence, the appropriate point with respect to the 1960–61 survey may not be that its design was not more efficient or that the IPNS scheme had to be revised during field-work. Instead, the point to note is whether the design is efficient enough in reference to the time, money and men available for its execution, and whether the limitations imposed upon it by the operational exigencies were attended to in the best possible manner so as to fulfil the objective of our study.

The point that the comparative data are not more precise and extensive than they are found to be is also not of specific relevance to this study. The appropriate issue, in the present context, is the extent to which we have made the best possible use of whatever comparative data are available, and whether or not we have integrated them satisfactorily so as to evolve a proper design to meet our objective. We do not claim to have evolved and executed a *perfect* design to fulfil our objective: a claim which can never be fulfilled.

Consequently, in reference to the *best possible* design in the given circumstances, we may draw the attention of relevant authorities to the needs of the situation and thus prepare the ground for evermore efficient design for the same or similar studies. Evidently, it is only in this sequence that empirical research may uphold its worth and be fruitful.

Appendix

DIFFERENCES IN THE FACSIMILE OF SCHEDULES 1.1 and 1.0 (Facsimile of Schedule 1.0 appears between pages 214–15.)

1. Schedule 1.1 refers to:
   'Any other household member's family/non-familial unit'
2. The 'Instructions' at the top of Schedule 1.0 are repeated for Schedule 1.1, with the addition of the following:
   'This schedule refers to such household members who are marked 'X' under col. (5) in sub-block 9.2 of a Schedule 1.0. Use only one Schedule 1.1 for those who are related to one another by kinship terms; otherwise, use separate Schedules 1.1 for each non-related person.'
3. Blocks 1–2 and 4–12 of Schedule 1.1 are composed exactly as for Schedule 1.0.
4. (a) Block 3 is labelled 'Unit's Head/Ego' in Schedule 1.1 instead of 'Unit's Head/Substitute/Ego' in Schedule 1.0.
   (b) Instead of 9 items of information in Block 3 of Schedule 1.0, there are 6 items of information in that block of Schedule 1.1.
   (c) Items 4–6 of Block 3 of Schedule 1.1 are the same as items 7–9 of Block 3 of Schedule 1.0.
   (d) The items 1–3 of Block 3 of Schedule 1.1 are the following:
      1. Have you any relative in this household? yes—1/No—0.
      2. If yes, who is 'Head' amongst you?
      3. If none is Head, who is the eldest?

RANKING OF HINDU CASTES

'*Uchcha-varna'* (*high*) *caste Hindu*: Agradani Brahman, Baidya, Brahmin, Barna Brahman, Babhan (Bhumihar Brahman), Chatri, Goswami, Kayastha (Karan, Kastha), Rajput Brahmin.

'Jal-chal' (*middle*) *caste Hindu*: Agaria, Agarwalla, Aghori, Aguri, Barai, Barjibi, Barui, Chasa-dhoba, Dalia, Dhanuk, Gareri (Gadariya), Gaura (Goala of Orissa), Gandhabanik, Goala (Abhir, Ahir, Bagal, Gop, Jadav, Pallav), Gurung, Halia, Halia-dhoba, Halwai, Kahar, Kangsakara (Kansari), Kapali, Karmakar (Kamar), Kasarwani, Khandait, Kshtriya, Kumbhakar (Kumor), Koiri, Kuri, Kurmi (Kumbhi, Krumbhi, Kurum, Kurnmanik, Kurmi-Kshatriya), Lala (Lalli), Magar (Mangar), Mahisya, Malakar, Modok (Moira), Murmi (Tamang), Napit, Nabasakh group, Rai, Samkhakara (Sankhari), Satgop (Gopa), Satsudra, Satchasi, Sunuwar, Tambuli, Tanti (Tantubaya), Tili (abandoned oil trade).

'Jal-achal' (*low*) *caste Hindu*: Abasan (Namasudra), Agnia (Dhimal), Agrahari, Amat, Arja, Asur, Bagdi (Bygra-Kshatriya, Bholla, Danda-Manjhi, Dulia, Dule, Kusumetia, Let, Manjhi, Matia, Tentulia), Bahelia, Baisnab (Bairagi), Baiti (Baoti, Barna Tamuli, Chumari, Chuniya, Chunkar), Banik (Bania), Bantar, Bauri, Behara, Beldar, Bhat, Bhogta, Bhuinmali (Bhusandar), Bhuiyan, Bhumij, Bind (Binta, Binti, Brinti), Birbangsi, Byadh (Abdal, Babajia, Badia, Mir Sikari, Supuria, Shandar), Chamar (Charmakar, Dhekaru, Rabidas, Ruidas, Rishi, Satnami), Chandal, Chang (Limbu), Chang-nama (Namosudra), Chasa, Chasati, Chatrisa (Barnasankar), Chaupal, Chhimba, Chik (Barik), Chitrakar, Dai, Dabgar, Damai (Dami, Damyi, Darzo), Danjongpa (Bhotia), Darzi, Das, Dejong (Bhotia), Desi (Rajbangsi), Deyara, Dhami, Dhangar, Dhari, Dhemal (Dhimal, Dungsai, Later), Dhimar, Dhoba (Dhobi, Razak, Sukladas), Dhuliya, Doai (Chalanta), Dom (Dhangar, Hari, Muddafarash), Dosad (Dushad), Drukpea (Bhotia), Gamta, Ghandmali, Ganral (Namosudra), Garo, Gaur banik, Ghani, Ghantra, Ghasi, Ghusuria, Gokha, Gola, Gond, Gonrhi, Giri (Gosain), Gorait, Halalkhor, Hari (Bhusan, Birbangsi, Birghoria, Harsantan), Ho, Horohon, Jalia-Kaibarta, Janior (Khambhu), Jalla-Kshatriya (Jhalo-Malo), Jimbar (Khambu), Julha, Jugi (Jogi, Nath, Mahatma), Kadar, Kalita (Kolita), Kalu, Kalwar,

F. S.: First Phase

	Adhesion*				
-j)	If [Σ(F & M)—Σ(Z & D)], is		j	(i+j)	Position of each person in family matrix*
. (9) – (11)]	Positive i	Negative i′	[(as for col. (11)]	[col. (13) + col.(15)]	
2)	(13)	(14)	(15)	(16)	(17)
					1/2/3/4/5
					1/2/3/4/5
					1/2/3/4/5
					1/2/3/4/5
					1/2/3/4/5
					1/2/3/4/5
					1/2/3/4/5
					1/2/3/4/5
					× × ×
					1/2/3/4/5
					1/2/3/4/5
					1/2/3/4/5
					1/2/3/4/5
					1/2/3/4/5
					1/2/3/4/5
					1/2/3/4/5
					1/2/3/4/5
					× × ×
	n	n′	l	k	F.S. (5)
					1/2/3/4/5
					1/2/3/4/5
					1/2/3/4/5
					1/2/3/4/5
					× × ×
	n	n′	l	k	F.S. (5)

Muslim group		Belongs or not to		General and vocational/ technical education-level
ing	Rank*	Backward class	Scheduled castes/tribes	
	(12)	(13)	(14)	(15)
/X	1/2/3/X	1/2	0/1/2	0/1/2/3/4/5/6/7/8/9/X/Y
/X	1/2/3/X	1/2	0/1/2	0/1/2/3/4/5/6/7/8/9/X/Y
/X	1/2/3/X	1/2	0/1/2	0/1/2/3/4/5/6/7/8/9/X/Y
/X	1/2/3/X	1/2	0/1/2	0/1/2/3/4/5/6/7/8/9/X/Y
/X	1/2/3/X	1/2	0/1/2	0/1/2/3/4/5/6/7/8/9/X/Y
/X	1/2/3/X	1/2	0/1/2	0/1/2/3/4/5/6/7/8/9/X/Y
/X	1/2/3/X	1/2	0/1/2	0/1/2/3/4/5/6/7/8/9/X/Y
/X	1/2/3/X	1/2	0/1/2	0/1/2/3/4/5/6/7/8/9/X/Y
/X	1/2/3/X	1/2	0/1/2	0/1/2/3/4/5/6/7/8/9/X/Y
/X	1/2/3/X	1/2	0/1/2	0/1/2/3/4/5/6/7/8/9/X/Y
/X	1/2/3/X	1/2	0/1/2	0/1/2/3/4/5/6/7/8/9/X/Y
/X	1/2/3/X	1/2	0/1/2	0/1/2/3/4/5/6/7/8/9/X/Y
/X	1/2/3/X	1/2	0/1/2	0/1/2/3/4/5/6/7/8/9/X/Y
/X	1/2/3/X	1/2	0/1/2	0/1/2/3/4/5/6/7/8/9/X/Y

)

Occupation		Relation to *jat* occupation	Activity status	Place of work
Grade	Rank*			
(10)	(11)	(12)	(13)	(14)
1/2/3/X	1/2/3/4/5/6/X	0/1/2/3/4/5/X/Y	1/2/3/4/X	1/2/3/X
1/2/3/X	1/2/3/4/5/6/X	0/1/2/3/4/5/X/Y	1/2/3/4/X	1/2/3/X
1/2/3/X	1/2/3/4/5/6/X	0/1/2/3/4/5/X/Y	1/2/3/4/X	1/2/3/X
1/2/3/X	1/2/3/4/5/6/X	0/1/2/3/4/5/X/Y	1/2/3/4/X	1/2/3/X
1/2/3/X	1/2/3/4/5/6/X	0/1/2/3/4/5/X/Y	1/2/3/4/X	1/2/3/X
1/2/3/X	1/2/3/4/5/6/X	0/1/2/3/4/5/X/Y	1/2/3/4/X	1/2/3/X

Kami (Nepali), Kandari (Patni), Kandh, Kandra (Kadma), Kanjar, Kantai (Rajbangsi), Kaora, Karal (Rajbangsi), Karali, Karenga (Koranga), Kaur, Keot (Keyot), Khaira, Kharia, Khatic, Kisan, Koch, Kol, Konai, Konwar, Kora (Kuda, Kura), Korwa, Kotal, Kshatriya-Kaibarta, Kurariar, Laheri, Lalbegi, Lopa-Bhotia, Lhori-Bhotia, Lombu (Chang, Tsang), Lodha, Lohar, Lupta-Mahisya, Magh, Mahar, Mahli, Mal, Mala, Malar (Malhar), Mallah, Malo, Malpaharia, Matia, Matial, Maulik (Naiya), Mehtar, Muchi (Mochi), Mura, Murung (Mru), Musahar, Nagbangsi, Nagesai, Namabrahman (Namosudra), Namabrahmo (Namosudra), Namanapit (Namosudra), Namasudra (Chandal), Nat, Nuniya, Pal (Paliya), Pan (Panika, Chik-Barik, Pab, Panik, Paur, Pauwa, Sawasi), Pariah (Parhiya), Pasi, Patni (Kandari, Lupta-Mahisya, Patuni, Patauni, Adi-Mahisya, Manjhi), Pator, Patra, Pod (Pundra, Podmaraj, Paundra), Rabidas (Ruidas), Rabha, Rajbangsi (Desi, Kantai, Rajbangsi-Kshatriya), Rajwar, Razak, Sadhubanik (Shaha), Sannyasi, Saundika (Sunri), Saha, Sarki (Nepali), Sonar, Subarnabanik, Sukladas, Sunri (Saundika, Saundika-Kshatriya, Sondia), Sutarwala, Sutradhar (Chhutar, Biswakarma-Brahmin), Teli (Kolu), Tiyar, Toto, Turi, Vaisya-saha, Vaisya-basak, Yakha-Thumba (Limbu).

There may be more synonyms of the castes mentioned in the list. There may also be other caste names not mentioned in the list. In either case, their equivalence to the castes recorded above would determine their respective ranks.

CLASSIFICATION OF OCCUPATIONS

Non-manual high grade: Accountant, Actuarist, Advocate, Agents (executive), Agronomist, Allopathic surgeon/physician, Archaeologist, Architect, Archivist, Assistant Station Master, Assistant Superintendent, Astrologer, Attorney, Auditor, Author, Ayurvedic surgeon/physician, Barrister, Biologist, Botanist, Captain (ship and boat), Chemical Engineer, Chemist, Civil Engineer, Clinical Specialist, Collector, Columnist, Commercial Artist, Contractor, Decorative Designer, Demonstrator, Dentist, Deputy Collector, Deputy Magistrate, Director, Economist, Editor, Electrical Engineer, Farmer (crops, dairy), Flight Engineer, Flight Navigator, Forest Ranger, Geologist, Hakim physician, Head of the Department in Government and non-Government institution,

Historian, Homeopathic physician/surgeon, Horticulturist, Inspector in Government and non-Government offices and institutions, Interpreter, Journalist, Judge, Junior officers in Government and non-Government offices and institutions, Lecturer, Legislator, Librarian, Magistrate, Manager, Mathematician, Mechanical Engineer, Metallurgical Engineer, Meteorologist, Mining Engineer, Modeller, Office Superintendent, Optician, Overseer, Painter, Pathologist, Pharmacist, Philosopher, Physicist, Physiologist, Pilot (ship and aircraft), Pleader, Political Scientist, Politician, Postmaster, Professor, Priest, Psychologist, Rearer (livestock and poultry), Radio Engineer, Sculptor, Secondary School Teacher, Section Officer, Secretary, Senior Officers in Government and non-Government offices and institutions, Ship Engineer, Solicitor, Sound Engineer, Statesman, Station Master, Station Superintendent, Statistician, Teachers in research/technical/technological institutions, Technologist, Translator, Veterinarian physician/surgeon, Wholesale dealer, Yunani physician, Zoologist. Other Engineers, professional artists, physical/biological/medical/health/agricultural and social scientists, deck officers; and other professional/technical and similar non-manual occupations not specified above but which do not correspond to or are similar to the occupations of middle or low grade.

Non-manual middle grade: Accounts clerk, Actor, Assistant Postmaster, Aratdar, Auctioneer, Bill Collector, Book-keeper, Brakesman, Broker, Canvasser, Cashier, Coach, Compounder, Dancer, Draughtsman, Estate and Security Agent, Field Investigator, Forester, Health Visitor, House-keeper, Insurance Agent, Laboratory Assistant, Law Assistant, Matron, Middle School Teacher, Midwife, Moneylender, Mukteer, Musician, Nurse, Office Clerk, Pawnbroker, Personal Assistant, Primary School Teacher, Private Tutor, Purchasing Agent, Railway Guard, Retail Dealer, Revenue Collector, Salesman, Sanitary Inspector/ Technician, Selling Agent, Stenographer, Steward, Subordinate Administrative and Executive Assistants and Officers in Government and non-Government offices and institutions, Supervisors, Surveyer, Teacher in Nursery/Kindergarten Schools, Teletypist, Trainer, Travelling Salesman, Typist, Vaccinator, Village 'Karnams', Village Patwari.

Other professional sportsmen, legal practitioners, medical/health technicians, teachers; and similar non-manual occupations not specified above but which do not correspond to or are similar to the occupations of high or low grade.

Non-manual low grade: Bearer, Checker, Conductor, Duftry, Hawker, Pedlar, Peon, Postman, Retail Shop Assistant, Starter, Storekeeper, Street Vendor, Ticket Seller, Time Keeper, Wholesale Shop Assistants.

Other staff in managerial/administrative/executive/clerical jobs; and similar non-manual occupations not specified above but which do not correspond to or are not similar to the occupations of high or middle grade.

Manual skilled: Annealer, Artificial Teeth-maker, Assembler, Baker, Barber, Basket maker, Beautician, Bee-keeper, Bender, Biri maker, Blacksmith, Bleacher, Blender (tobacco), Block maker, Blower, Blowroom worker, Boat maker, Boatman, Body-builder, Boiler maker, Book binder, Brick layer, Brick maker, Butcher, Cable joiner, Carder, Carpenter, Carpet maker, Cart builder, Coach builder, Cleaner, Coffee processing worker, Combatant forces in army/navy/air forces, Compositor, Confectioner, Construction equipment operator, Converter, Cooks (domestic and institutional including their assistants), Coppersmith, Copyholder, Crane-operator, Crusher, Cultivator, Curer (tobacco), Cutlery maker, Cutter, Dark room worker (press/printing), Decorator, Dhopa/Dhobi, Diemaker, Dramer, Driller, Driver (railway/tram/motor/motor cycle/steam and oil engine), Drycleaner, Dyer, Earth-moving equipment operator, Electrician, Electrical assembler, Electrical fitter, Electronic equipment operator, Electroplater, Embroiderer, Engraver, Erector, Etcher, Farm machine operator, Farm tractor operator, Fibre preparer, Finisher, Fire fighter and similar occupations, Fisherman, Fitter, Food canner, Food preserver, Forger, Furnaceman, Gardener, Ginner, Glazier, Goldsmith, Grader (tobacco), Grinder, *Gur* maker, Hair dresser, Hat maker, Hardener, Head-gear maker, Heat treater, Hoist operator, Honey Collector, Hot-dip plater, Husker, Hut-builder, Idol-maker, *Jarda* maker, Jeweller, Joiner, *Khandsari* sugar maker, Kilnman, Knitter, Lace-maker, Laskar, Laundryman, Liftman, Lifting equipment operator, Linesman, Machine operator, Machine-tool fitter, Maker of aerated water and similar occupations, Mason, Mechanic (metal machining/fitting/assembling and similar occupations), Melter, Metal cutting machine operator, Metal drawer, Metal rolling mill operator, Mica splitter, Miller, Mixer (cement/clay and other ceramics),

Moulder, Musicial instrument maker, Musical instrument tuner, Non-combatant forces in army/navy/airforce, Ore-treater, Oven-man, Paper product maker, Parcher (grain), Patternmaker, Photolithographer, Photolithooperator, Piecer, Pipe-fitter, Plasterer, Plumber, Potter, Pounder, Powerstation operator, Presser, Pressman, Printer, Producer of indigeneous liquor, Proofreader, Pulverizer, Quarry driller, Quarry shot firer, Radio mechanic, Rearer of animals/birds/insects, Repairman (metal machining/fitting/assembling and similar jobs), Rivetter, Sailor, Sareng, Swayer, Scouner, Seaman, Setter, Shipwright, Shoemachinist, Showmaker, Shotfierer, Signaller, Silversmith, Sizer, Smelter, Snuff-maker, Spinner, Stone carver, Stone cutter, Store dresser, Structural metal worker, Sweetmeat maker, Switchboard attendant, Tailor, Tea-processing worker, Telegraphist, Telegraph fitter, Telephone fitter, Telephone operator, Temperer, Tilemaker, Tinsmith, Thatcher, Toy maker, Turner, Type-setter, Umbrella maker, Upholsterer, Warper, Washerman, Watchmaker, Weaver, Welder, Well-digger, Well driller, Wheelwright, Wicker product maker (umbrella-stick/fishing rod/stick, etc.), Winder, Wine drawer, Wireless operator, Wireman, Wood worker machinist.
Skilled manual occupation of any other category not mentioned above but which do not correspond to or are not similar to the occupations of the semi-skilled level.

Manual semi-skilled: Ayah, Bearer, Bhisti, Barge Crew, Boat Crew, Boilerman, Butler (domestic and institutional), Cattle grazer, Chowkidar, Cleaner, Cobbler, Conch gatherer, Customs examiner/patrol and other allied jobs, Driver (animal drawn vehicles), *Duli*-bearer, Fireman, Fuel collector, Grasscutter, Harvester of forest products including lac, Herdsman, Hunter, Loco-fireman, Log-feller, Maid (domestic and institutional), Miner, Packer, *Palki*-bearer, pearl diver, Pointsman, Police and other operatives in allied jobs, Quarryman, Servant (domestic and institutional), Sharecropper, Shell gatherer, Ship Crew, Signalman, Sponge diver, Sweeper, Tanner, Tapper, Trapper, Waiter, Watchman, Waterman, Woodcutter, Wrapper.
All other occupations not specified above which are not totally unskilled, on the one hand, and cannot be definitely rated as skilled, on the other.

CHAPTER SEVEN

Appraisal

The design of a survey ensures the validity and anticipates the precision of the deductions to be made, and the inferences to be drawn, from the data to be collected. Ultimately, however, the reliability of any deduction or inference depends on the accuracy of the field data. Bias may creep into survey data mainly on three counts: (1) the failure, for various reasons, to accurately demarcate the areal units, (2) the informants' reaction to the survey, and (3) the investigators' way of verbal communication with the informants and interpretation of the answers from the latter.

The first can be regularly checked by field supervisors and researchers engaged in the survey, as was done for all the surveys taken into account for the present study. But the check may not resolve a limitation; only point it out. On the second and third counts, the supervisors can check gross errors, which were not found for any one of these surveys. The reliability of data on these two counts, therefore, could be ascertained indirectly, namely, from an examination of (a) the ability and willingness of the informants as evaluated by the investigators, and (b) the variations noticed in the sub-sample estimates from each survey by employing Mahalanobis's IPNS scheme. The two procedures were followed for all the surveys, with the exception that for the 1946–47 survey the investigators were not required to record their evaluation of the informants' ability and willingness.

In this chapter we shall appraise the reliability of survey data from the aforesaid three aspects, dealing mainly with the 1960–61 data on which our study is based. However, we shall note some details of the investigators' evaluation of the informants for the 1951 data because the National Sample Survey was launched in 1950 and so the 1951 surveys could have been the least rigorously conducted of all those considered for this study. And, after an examination of the three aspects of field-data, we shall describe how the sampling errors for the respective sets of data were calculated and discuss the precision of the data on that basis. In this way, we shall indicate the reliability and precision of our data for the conclusions drawn in Part 1 of this volume.

II

The design for the 1960–61 survey involved three distinct operations in the field: (1) demarcation of contiguous blocks in the cities and towns, (2) listing of households in the sampled blocks, and (3) interviewing the family and non-familial units constituting the sampled households. Each of these operations had implied possibilities to affect the reliability or precision of the data.

The first operation was undertaken by the research assistants for the towns of Siliguri, Adra and Contai. They were guided by K. Chattopadhyay and S. Bandyopadhyay in their initial attempt at Contai. The blocks in Darjeeling were demarcated by Bandyopadhyay himself, with the help of some officials of the local self-government and the field supervisor and investigators locally recruited. It was not necessary to undertake this task for Calcutta, Howrah and Berhampore because the Field Investigation Department of the Indian Statistical Institute, Calcutta, had already collected relevant data for these two cities and the town in connection with the previously mentioned Urban Frame Survey (UFS).

As for UFS, the research assistants and Bandyopadhyay demarcated blocks in the respective towns by eye-estimation. Any other method was ruled out in view of the excessively long time it would require. The method, however, has two serious limitations which deserve mention in the context of the present study.

1. The demarcation of blocks within an urban location is based on no other factor than the number of households they contain. In respect of the areas (not households) they cover, very large and very small blocks may, therefore, occur in the sample with equal probability. Hence, if this largeness or smallness of blocks (irrespective of their same number of constituent households) is due to such unascertained factors as have a bearing upon the present study, then the method adopted to stratify a location

into contiguous blocks (and the selection of some of them subsequently) may make the survey design less efficient and the field data, in consequence, less precise. But this limitation cannot be resolved until master samples are prepared for social surveys, which will take note of the already ascertained factors of variation in reference to the objectives of study and also keep room for taking other factors into account. Hardly anything, however, has been done so far in India in this respect although its urgency has been underlined [Mukherjee, 1961b]. We have to accept, therefore, any weakness in our data from this aspect.

2. Although the stipulation was to demarcate blocks of about 150 households each, mere eye-estimation could not conform to this stipulation in all cases. Since the eye-estimation of households takes as its cue the number of habitable structures in an 'area' with some allowance given from *a priori* knowledge to the nature of local habitation (for example, slum area, market place, etc.), the method gives only a rough approximation of the real situation. For the 1960–61 survey, the mean (± s.d.) of numbers of households per sampled block in the 'city' sector of West Bengal was found to be 125.6 (± 73.6); in the 'town' sector, 80.8 (± 32.4). Obviously, the only alternative is to give up eye-estimation altogether and make a thorough survey of the 'areas'; but this merely reaffirms the need for master samples for social surveys. However, blocks with too few households (or too many) were found to constitute only about one-fifth of the total number of selected blocks. This anomaly, therefore, need not affect the representative character of our data. In any case, the method of eye-estimation has been employed to obtain even the final information from sample surveys (not merely to determine the sample frame) and the attempt has proved to be reliable and useful [Mahalanobis, 1944].

Thus, in consideration of the resources at our disposal, the first of the three field operations could not have been accomplished better. The data for the other time-periods face the same problem.

III

The second of the three field operations (that is, listing all households in the sampled urban blocks and sampled villages) was undertaken by the field investigators who were duly trained and supervised on the spot by Bandyopadhyay and Chattopadhyay during their first attempt in Calcutta and Howrah. Bandyopadhyay supervised this operation in Darjeeling, executed by the trained field investigators and supervisor from the locality. Also, Bandyopadhyay and Chattopadhyay guided the field operations in the village Kaylapara; and B. Ray, who was thus trained in field operations, undertook the task for the village Dumriguri Chhat. Lastly, P. Chakrabarti, who was the only one left with us out of the six recruited at the beginning of this study, undertook the task for the village Algarah Bazar with the initial guidance from Chattopadhyay and continued assistance of the locally recruited investigators for the survey. All possible care was thus taken to list completely all the households in thesa mpled urban blocks and the sampled villages so as to ensure the accuracy of the sample frame.

We may note, incidentally, that the listing of households was a painstaking task and a time consuming process, especially in the urban areas. This may be appreciated from only two out of several difficulties faced by our investigators:

(1) In a slum or commercial area, a room may appear to be inhabited by one household defined in terms of coresidence and commensality but, actually, it may contain a number of households with one of the room-dwellers claiming to be the 'head'. Several such cases noticed in Calcutta and Howrah, particularly, called for the patience and ingenuity of the investigators to ascertain the exact number of households in one room.

(2) The structure of a dwelling in some areas may be such that one can easily miss some distinct portions of its habitation. For example, one of our investigators found in a block in the northern outskirts of Calcutta that while a dwelling faced a very narrow by-lane and was so numbered by Calcutta Corporation, it had another 'opening' to a still narrower lane which was virtually concealed from the outsiders' view. If one of such 'openings' were by-passed, the number of households to be listed would have been reduced appreciably.

We have described the above two out of many such instances in order to emphasize two points:

(1) Because no master sample of households is available for

surveys like the present one, the first and second operations take altogether an inordinately large share of the total time for field investigation although the third operation of interviewing the sampled households (that is, the family and non-familial units) is the crux of field investigation.

(2) If such a master-sample is prepared suitably stratified by the attributes relevant to social surveys and maintained up-to-date by a permanent field organization, an enquiry like the present one can be conducted at a higher order of precision.

As to the first point, we found during the field investigation that the demarcation of 205 blocks in the 5 sampled towns (Berhampore 85, Siliguri 40, Contai 34, Darjeeling 26, and Adra 20) took about 46 mandays. The listing of a total of 18,123 households (11,806 in 94 sampled blocks in Calcutta and Howrah, 3,420 in 46 sampled blocks in the 5 towns, and 2,897 in the 23 sampled villages) took 100 mandays. Whereas the third and the most important operation of interviewing the 4,119 family-units and 815 non-familial units (constituting the total of 4,672 households from which data could be collected) took about 268 mandays.* Thus, the time-requirements for the three operations in a town were: (1) 4–17 mandays for the demarcation of 20 to 85 blocks, (2) 3–4 mandays for the listing of households in the sampled 8 to 10 blocks, and (3) 8–10 mandays for the actual interview of the sampled households in the sampled towns. For a village, on an average, the listing of households took 1–2 mandays, and interviewing the households about 5 mandays.

Hence, if we had an up-to-date and properly characterized master sample at hand, our urban sample could have been nearly doubled at the given time and cost for the survey because we could have virtually done away with the first two field operations. We could also bring under examination a much larger rural sample than we did for the 1960–61 survey by drawing samples of households within the sampled villages. Furthermore, in the light of our previous discussion, we could then have evolved and operated a more efficient survey design for the West Bengal

*Table 6.1 in the previous chapter records that a total of 4,717 households were allocated to the field investigators. Of these, 21 were untraced at the time of canvassing the Schedules 1.0 and 1.1, and 24 refused to be interviewed.

society, as we have pointed out in respect of social surveys [Bandyopadhyay and Chattopadhyay, 1962, 1963; Mukherjee, 1961b]. Evidently, the same problem is involved with the data for other time-periods, which were collected by regularly employed staff of trained investigators working under proper supervision.

IV

The quality of data in reference to the third field operation of interviewing the units of observation (namely, the family and non-familial units constituting the selected households) depends, obviously, on two concomitant factors: (1) the sincerity, ability and diligence of the field investigators to elicit accurately what information are scheduled to be collected from the specified informants; and (2) the selection of the informants, and their ability and willingness, to furnish the required details. We shall first discuss the investigator-component of the precision and reliability of our data.

That the investigators worked conscientiously for the 1960–61 survey is indicated at once by the fact that they failed to collect data for only 21 households out of the total of 4,717 to be interviewed. These households referred to 4 villages where not a single member of these households was present when the investigators went there. The investigators could not prolong their stay in those villages without disturbing the field programme; also the consequent increase in the cost of field investigation forbade their revisits. However, since the 21 'non-contact' households accounted for only 0.4 per cent of the total number to be surveyed, it could hardly affect the precision of our 1960–61 data. In respect of the data collected for other time-periods, the situation was similar.

The ability of the investigators for the 1960–61 survey was assured, firstly, by their academic qualification; secondly, by the fact that while the Bengali investigators worked in the plains of West Bengal, local people undertook the task in the 'hill' area; thirdly, by the training all of them received under the guidance of the author and at the hands of Bandyopadhyay and Chattopadhyay; and, fourthly, by the supervision of their work. We have no reason, therefore, to doubt the reliability of the 1960–61 data from this aspect; and as regards the data for other time-periods, they were collected by a fully trained and regular staff of investigators whose ability for the task was assumed by their selection for this job and long experience. Even so, we may cite an instance to substantiate the ability of our investigators to shoulder the responsibility delegated to them. Out of all the interviewees specified for the 1960–61 survey, 114 were recorded by the investigators at the time of listing the households as unwilling to be interviewed, but 89 decided on the contrary at the time of actual interrogation and cooperated fully. This change in their attitude was effected by the investigators who could convince them that the purpose of the survey was not against their interest. However, since the remaining 25 (involving 24 households) accounted for only 0.5 per cent of the total number of sampled interviewees, we need not suspect the reliability of 1960–61 data due to 'non-response' error.

The diligence of the field-workers was substantiated by the few instances found in Schedules 1.0 and 1.1 (after they were returned to the headquarters) which required post-survey corrections or resurvey. It will be seen from the facsimile of the two schedules that the information they contain were so intricately structured for cross-reference as to require sustained and meticulous attention of the investigators. Otherwise some information or their coding would not be duly recorded, and that may even call for re-survey of the relevant units of observation. A few points in thus structuring the two schedules are enumerated below:

(1) Any individual labelled K_0, K_1, or K_2 in col. (5) of Block 9 must be re-entered in sub-blocks 10.0, 10.1, and 10.2, respectively.

(2) For every person labelled K_0 in Block 9, there must be codes in cols. (6) and (7); whereas for every K_1 and K_2 in the same block the code must be entered in col. (8).

(3) The item no. 9 in Block 3 (namely, the 'Ego's position in the unit') must tally with the entry in col. (4) of Block 12 and with those in col. (3) of sub-blocks 10.1 and 10.2.

(4) The entry of code 1 with respect to any person in col. (6) of sub-block 10.1 or 10.2 implies that his or her consort is coresidential and commensal with him or her.

Such inter-dependence of the items of information and their coding in the schedules were so diligently attended to by the investigators that only in 1 per cent cases errors were detected during scrutiny. Where necessary, the mistakes were rectified by further visits to the relevant units of observation; mostly, however, they could be corrected without such visits. For Darjeeling, 8 schedules contained duplicate information: they referred to the same 'heads' of the units of observation who were interviewed at their residence and again at their shops. We rejected the duplicate schedules from analysis, instead of replacing them, as we did not replace the village Lakshmihat in Murshidabad district when we found it uninhabited.

V

With reference to the informant-component of the third operation in the field, our selection rested upon the 'heads' of the respective family-units and, obviously, upon the respective persons returned in the field-schedules as non-familial units. This we had decided because (a) the 'head' of a family-unit (and each and every non-familial unit) will be the best choice as the meeting point of the complementary configurations of family structures in terms of forming coresident and commensal kingroups and holding the image of 'what is a family'; (b) he or she would be the easiest to identify, being customarily regarded to speak for the 'family'; and (c) several important items of information contained in the field-schedules were expected to be best obtained from him or her as the acknowledged authority in the unit. The assumptions, made on *a priori* grounds, were found to be true during the surveys. For instance, in 73 per cent cases the 'head' for the 1960–61 survey was the seniormost person in the family and also its principal or only earner; and in 14 and 12 per cent cases, respectively, he or she was the seniormost (but a subsidiary earner or dependent) and the principal or only earner (but not the seniormost) in the family.

The 'head' of a unit, therefore, was the best choice as informant for the 1960–61 survey, as it was found for the other surveys providing us with comparative data. The possibility could not be overlooked, however, that for various reasons this person may live elsewhere during the period of the survey. Hence, in order to collect information about such a unit without causing inordinate delay in field investigation or inflating its cost, the investigators were directed to approach that person who was officiating for the 'head' during his or her absence; and, in case this secondary 'head' was not a family member, the informant was to be the seniormost of all those present in the family (see Block 3 of Schedules 1.0 and 1.1).

The lattitude thus given to the field investigators could have seriously affected the reliability and precision of our data if it were used on a large scale. However, as in the case of the surveys providing us with comparative data, for the 1960–61 survey also this discretion was used sparingly. Only for 136, or less than 3 per cent of the total number of family and non-familial units surveyed, the informant was not the *primary* 'head' of the unit; and out of this small number, for 114 the informant was the secondary 'head', for 2 the seniormost person available in the unit who was not its 'head'—primary or secondary, and for 20 any other person. Moreover, in 117 cases out of the total of 136, the informant was related to the 'head' as son, consort, brother or mother; for an additional 16 cases as his or her kin or affine; and only in 3 cases as a member of the household but not of the unit of observation.

The decision we made regarding the selection of informants is thus seen to have been carried out during the field investigation in the best possible manner. Also, insofar as we can judge from external characteristics, the ability and attitude of the interviewees to furnish the information required were assured. Most of them were adults but not too old: 1 per cent below 21 years of age, 4 per cent above 60, and 95 per cent between 21 and 60. Also, according to the investigators' assessment of the interviewees' ability to answer the questions put to them, 55 per cent were rated to be 'excellent', 43 per cent 'fair', and 2 per cent 'tolerable'. Besides, the attitude of the interviewees was rated by the investigators as 'cooperative' in 86 per cent cases, 'indifferent' in 13.5 per cent cases, and 'unwilling' in only 0.5 per cent cases.

Although only a small number of all interviewees were rated as not cooperative, significant variations were noted among them. Sector-wise, the indifferent interviewees were the most frequent in the towns, unwilling interviewees in the villages, and cooperative interviewees in the cities. Ethnicity-wise, when the total of 9,800 households in the sampled blocks of Calcutta were listed and their 'heads' were asked to declare their willingness to be interviewed for Schedule 1.0, 99 per cent of the 'heads' of Bengali households were found to be willing as against 93 per cent of the 'heads' of non-Bengali households. Locality-wise, 98 and 97 per cent of the 'heads' of households residing in the residential and slum areas of Calcutta declared their willingness to cooperate with the 1960–61 survey as against 76 per cent of the 'heads' living in the commercial areas.

However, these variations in the attitude of the informants to the survey are mainly of academic interest because of the small number involved. Even so, to ensure the reliability of our data, we rejected those schedules from analysis which contained information from unwilling interviewees. It was not necessary to take this step regarding the indifferent interviewees since there is no reason to believe that the information obtained from them will not be reliable.

The informant-component of the data for the other time-periods was similar to the one for the 1960–61 survey. Since the details are available elsewhere [NSS, 1951, 1965], we do not propose to discuss them. However, while for all these surveys the reliability of data from this aspect is ensured, we wish to present the following information on the informants' willingness to be interviewed for the 1951 surveys (NSS Rounds 2 and 3) for the reason stated at the beginning of this chapter:

(1) Out of the 658 informants for the 1951 surveys, the investigators noted their attitude to the investigation as 'helpful' in 69 per cent cases, 'indifferent' in 7 per cent cases, and 'unwilling' in 24 per cent cases. The proportional differences between the 'helpful' and the 'indifferent or unwilling' informants could not be attributed to sampling fluctuations only.[2]

(2) 85 per cent of the Muslim and 77 per cent of the 'middle and low caste' Hindu informants were recorded as 'helpful' against 49 per cent of the 'high caste' Hindu informants. The proportional differences between the 'high caste' Hindu and the other two

[2]The sample design of the National Sample Survey being a two-stage one with the first stage units (villages) selected with probability proportional to their population or area and with replacement, all the estimated proportions referred here were derived as the ratio of unbiased estimates of the respective numerator and the denominator. The formulae for estimating the standard errors, etc., for the purpose of building up confidence intervals of such ratios were also modified accordingly.

categories are significant at the 1 per cent level, while that between the latter two categories is not significant even at the 20 per cent level. The differences in proportions of 'indifferent' informants among the three categories are in no case significant even at the 20 per cent level, indicating thereby that the attitude of helpfulness was dominant among the 'middle and low caste' Hindus and the Muslims while unwillingness was appreciably present among the 'high caste' Hindus.

(3) Correspondingly, 42 per cent of the big landholders and businessmen, and 37 per cent of the sharecroppers, were found unwilling to cooperate with the 1951 surveys as against 9 per cent of the wage-labourers and 6 per cent of the self-supporting peasants and craftsmen. Statistically significant difference was noticed among the two sets of percentage-values, but not within each set.

(4) 44 per cent of villagers living more than 10 miles away from the nearest railway or steamer stations were found to be unwilling to cooperate with the 1951 surveys, while those living increasingly nearer to these transport and communication centres were found to be less and less unwilling. The proportion was reduced to 1 per cent for the villagers living within 2 miles from the nearest railway or steamer stations. On the other hand, those living at a corresponding distance of 2 to 5 miles were found to be more 'indifferent' than 'unwilling'; as if, unwillingness gave way, first, to indifference and, then, to cooperation as the villagers were more and more exposed to the outerworld from the parochial existence.[3]

VI

Since the field operations were carried out at an optimum level of satisfaction, we expect our data to be sufficiently precise and reliable. Some measure of these two qualities can be obtained from the consistency of the investigator-wise estimates of the same item of information. We have considered for this purpose 4,

[3]I am indebted to my colleague Suraj Bandyopadhyay from whose unpublished paper I have collected the above data on the informants' attitude to the 1951 surveys.

5, or 6 investigators for the 1960–61 survey, at a time, and not always the same set of 6, for reasons explained in the last chapter and detailed in Table 6.1.

Two sets of investigator-wise sub-sample estimates have been prepared referring to their (a) subjective appreciation of field conditions, and (b) collection of objective data. In both cases, the efficiency of the survey design (and of the field operations relating to the identification of the units of sampling and observation) will be accounted for in regard to the precision of the estimates obtained for West Bengal or its different sectors. In addition, the first set of estimates will take into account any subjective variation among the investigators, and the second set will further account for variations among the informants.

The subjective appreciation of the investigators refers, firstly, to their appraisal of willingness of the informants to furnish information regarding the family and non-familial units in the city, town and village sectors of West Bengal. Table 7.1 shows that in this respect the data are very consistent; and similar consistency is noticed in Table 7.2 with respect to the investigators' appraisal of the willingness of the 'heads' of households in Calcutta to be interviewed for the data in Schedules 1.0 and 1.1.[4]

The second set of estimates refers to the relative incidence of different family structure categories in West Bengal. The proportional representations of these structures were estimated for each of the investigators who worked in Calcutta, Howrah, and four sampled towns. Similar estimates were also prepared for (1) the city, town and village sectors of West Bengal, (2) the arid plain and the riverine plain of the rural sector, and (3) the state as a whole. The results, in the above order, are given in Tables 7.3–7.14 by retaining the serial-wise identification of the investigators as noted in Table 6.1 of last chapter.[5] In these tables the

[4]All tables of this chapter are appended at the back.

[5]Since the sampling design was not self-weighted, the estimated proportional distributions of the family structure categories for respective investigators would be mutually comparable. The distributions were obtained as the ratio of the estimated total number of family or non-familial units belonging to a category to the estimated total number of units for West Bengal [Cochran, 1953: 248, 264]. The two estimates used as the numerator and the denominator of the ratio would, evidently, be unbiased estimates of their corresponding population values. The obtained ratios, therefore, may be

structures are denoted by numbers; their characteristics are as follows:
(1) non-familial unit: man; (2) non-familial unit: woman; (3) consorts only; (4) nuclear, other than as (3); (5) patrilineally-patrivirilocally joint; (6) non-patrilineally joint with male 'head'; (7) non-patrilineally joint with female 'head'; (8) non-patrilineally jont with the 'head' and his/her consort; (9) non-patrilineally joint with the 'head's' sub-unit as in (4); and (10) patrilineally and non-patrilineally joint.

Tables 7.3–7.14 not only register variations among the sub-sample estimates for the respective family structure categories but the order of these variations also seems to vary from table to table. It thus appears that the 1960–61 data are not so consistent as was expected. However, a test of the rank order difference among the sub-sample estimates given in each table indicates a very high order of concordance among them, as shown in Table 7.15.[6]

The high degree of concordance among the sub-sample estimates points to the fact that in spite of so many factors of variation, such as, stratum effect according to the design of the survey, individual village characteristics, subjective bias of the investigators, etc. (which are, again, confounded with one or

regarded as consistent estimates of the corresponding population values. Following the same assumptions and procedure, the proportional distributions for various segments of West Bengal were computed and compared. Also, in order to obtain the overall proportional distribution, the entire data were pooled together instead of computing the average of the values of the proportions obtained separately for each of the investigators. For, the latter one may yield a biased estimate of the population proportions [Rao, 1965: 154–55].

[6]Since the total sample was equally distributed at random among the investigators, the units surveyed by each of them would constitute a random sub-sample of the original total sample. Hence, if the variations in the proportional distributions between the sub-samples were to be accounted for as primarily due to chance causes, the revealed trend could be considered as internally consistent in the sense that it is attested independently by each of the sub-samples. Therefore, as the proportional distributions could be compared on the basis of a minimum number of assumptions about the universe, it was decided to serially rank the estimated proportions obtained with each sub-sample separately and to test whether the rank order differences among the sub-samples might have occurred by chance causes or not [Kendall, 1955: 94–106].

another sub-sample because of the amendments to the survey design during the field-work), their net effect proceeded in the same direction for all the sub-samples. This interpretation is also applicable to the analyses given in Tables 7.1 and 7.2, as it is in regard to the comparative data. Tables 7.16–7.20 have been prepared in this context to confirm that we should be justified in regarding all our data to be reliable for purposes of analyses in Part 1 of this volume.

VII

In spite of all the care taken to formulate and execute a survey design, and to collect data in the best possible manner, a major source of error may be in the nature of the sampling technique itself. The design might have been followed accurately, but this component of the total error may not be insignificant and thus seriously affect the precision of the data. This aspect of the precision of data is indicated by the standard errors of each estimate. Due to differences in sampling designs of the 1960–61 survey and the National Sample Surveys, the sampling errors were estimated differently. Due to the limitations stated earlier, it was not possible to compute standard errors of the estimates obtained from the 1946–47 survey. For this one, we have to rely only upon half-sample comparisons presented earlier.

For the National Sample Survey data, the estimates of a proportion is a ratio estimate, that is, the ratio of the unbiased estimates of the numerator and the denominator. For example, the proportion of joint families was estimated by the ratio of the estimate of the total number of joint families to the estimate of the total number of families in West Bengal. The problem of estimation, therefore, is to estimate the total number of families of a particular variety (type) on the basis of the sample of households. Accordingly, the estimate of the total number of families of a particular type in a stratum was obtained by counting the number of such families in each sample household, multiplying that number by the reciprocal of the probability of selection of the sample household, and then summing their products over all sample households in that stratum. The estimate of the state total is the sum of the estimates of the stratum totals calculated by taking all sub-samples together. The estimate of the sampling error was built up from the sub-sample-wise estimates. The details of the estimation procedure for each round of the NSS are described below.

1951 Survey Data (NSS Rounds 2 and 3)

ESTIMATE OF TOTALS

Let y_{sij} denote the number of families belonging to a specified category in the jth household of the ith village of sth stratum and let x_{sij} denote the total number of families in that household. The problem is to estimate Y, X and R where Y and X are the state (West Bengal) totals of the variables y and x, and $R=Y/X$. The unbiased estimates of Y and X based on any sub-sample are obtained as:

$$Y=\sum_{s=1}^{L} Y_s=\sum_{s=1}^{L} \frac{1}{n_s}\sum_{i=1}^{n_s} \frac{1}{P_{si}} M_{si} \frac{1}{m_{si}} \sum_{j=1}^{m_{si}} y_{sij} \quad (1)$$

$$X=\sum_{s=1}^{L} X_s=\sum_{s=1}^{L} \frac{1}{n_s}\sum_{i=1}^{n_s} \frac{1}{P_{si}} \cdot \frac{M_{si}}{m_{si}} \sum_{j=1}^{m_{si}} x_{sij} \quad (2)$$

where L = total number of strata in West Bengal

n_s = number of sample villages in the concerned sub-sample of sth stratum

P_{si} = probability of selecting the ith sample village in sth stratum

M_{si} = total number of households in ith village of sth stratum

m_{si} = number of sample households in ith village of sth stratum

y_{sij} = 0 if the particular type of family is non-existent in the jth household.

COMBINED ESTIMATE

Let Y_1 and Y_2 be the estimates of the state total Y obtained from sub-sample 1 and 2 respectively. Then the combined estimate based on the total sample is given by

$$Y_0=1/2\,(Y_1+Y_2) \quad (3)$$

Similarly, $$X_0=1/2\,(X_1+X_2) \quad (4)$$

The sub-sample-wise estimates of the ratio R are

$$R_1 = Y_1/X_1 \text{ and } R_2 = Y_2/X_2$$

The combined estimate of R is:

$$R_0 = Y_0/X_0 = (Y_1 + Y_2)/(X_1 + X_2) \quad (5)$$

ESTIMATES OF ERROR

Let Y_{si} be the estimate of sth stratum total based on the ith sub-sample ($s=1, 2, \ldots L$; $i=1, 2$). Then an unbiased estimator of the variance of Y_0 is given by

$$V(Y_0) = 1/4 \sum_{s=1}^{L} (Y_{s1} - Y_{s2})^2 \quad (6)$$

An estimate of the variance of R_0 is given by

$$V(R_0) = \frac{1}{4X_0^2} \sum_{s=1}^{L} [(Y_{s1} - Y_{s2})^2 + R_0^2 (X_{s1} - X_{s2})^2 - 2R_0 (Y_{s1} - Y_{s2})(X_{s1} - X_{s2})] \quad (7)$$

The estimates of relative standard errors (rse) or percentage errors of Y_0 and R_0 are respectively given by:

$$\text{rse} \quad (Y_0) = \frac{+\sqrt{V(Y_0)}}{Y_0} \times 100\% \quad (8)$$

$$\text{rse} \quad (R_0) = \frac{+\sqrt{V(R_0)}}{R_0} \times 100\% \quad (9)$$

1956 Survey Data (NSS Round 10)

RURAL SECTOR

The estimate of state total Y from any sub-sample is obtained as:

$$Y = \sum_{s=1}^{L} \frac{1}{n_s} \sum_{i=1}^{n_s} \frac{1}{P_{si}} \cdot \frac{M_{si}}{m_{si}} \sum_{j=1}^{m_{si}} y_{sij} \quad (10)$$

where the notations have their usual meaning.

COMBINED ESTIMATE

There were four sub-samples in the tenth round. Let Y_i be the estimate of state total from ith sub-sample ($i=1, 2, 3, 4$). Then the combined estimate is given by

$$Y_0 = 1/4\,(Y_1 + Y_2 + Y_3 + Y_4) \tag{11}$$

The combined estimate for R_0 is $R_0 = Y_0/X_0$ (12)

ESTIMATES OF ERROR

As before, let Y_{si} be the unbiased estimate of sth stratum total based on the ith sub-sample and let $Y_s = 1/4\ (Y_{s1} + Y_{s2} + Y_{s3} + Y_{s4})$. Then an unbiased estimate of the variance of Y_0 is given by

$$V(Y_0) = \frac{1}{12} \sum_{s=1}^{L} \sum_{i=1}^{4} (Y_{si} - Y_s)^2 \tag{13}$$

Also an estimate of the variance of R_0 is given by

$$V(R_0) = \frac{1}{12X_0^2} \sum_{s=1}^{L} \sum_{i=1}^{4} (Y_{si} - Y_s)^2 + R_0^2\,(X_{si} - X_s)^2 - 2R_0\,(Y_{si} - Y_s)(X_{si} - X_s)] \tag{14}$$

The formulae for relative standard errors are as given in (8) and (9).

URBAN SECTOR

Notations

s : subscript for stratum
t : subscript for sub-stratum (type of households) $t=1, 2$
i : ,, ,, block
j : ,, ,, household
N_s : total number of blocks in sth stratum
n_s : number of sample blocks in one sub-sample of sth stratum
M_{sit} : total number of households in tth sub-stratum of ith sample block of sth stratum
m_{sit} : number of sample households in tth sub-stratum of ith sample block of sth stratum.

Then the estimate of state total Y based on one-sample is given by

$$Y = \sum_{s=1}^{L} \frac{N_s}{n_s} \sum_{i=1}^{n_s} \left[\frac{M_{si1}}{m_{si1}} \sum_{ij}^{1} y_{si1j} + \frac{M_{si2}}{m_{si2}} \sum_{j}^{2} y_{si2j} \right]$$

y_{sitj} = value (no. of households of a given type) in the jth household of tth sub-stratum of ith village of sth stratum.

$\sum_{s=1}^{L}$ extends over all urban strata in the state

Σ^1 extends over m_{si1} type 1 sample households

Σ^2 extends over m_{si2} type 2 sample households

The combined estimates and the estimates of variance are obtained as for the rural sector.
That is,

$$Y_0=1/4\ (Y_1+Y_2+Y_3+Y_4),\ X_0=1/4\ (X_1+X_2+X_3+X_4)$$

$$R_1=Y_i/X_i,\ \ R_0=Y_0/X_0$$

where Y_i and X_i are the estimates based on the *i*th sub-sample.

1965–66 Survey Data (NSS Round 20)

The sample design was *self-weighting* in the sense that only one multiplier was required for estimating the state total from the rural sample and two multipliers from the urban sample.

RURAL SECTOR

An unbiased estimate of state total Y is obtained as

$$Y=M\sum_{s}\sum_{i}\sum_{j} y_{sij}$$

where M is the constant multiplier for all sample households selected.

URBAN SECTOR

In this case $$Y=\sum_{s=1}^{2} M_s \sum_{i}\sum_{j} y_{sij}$$

where M_1 and M_2 are the two constant multipliers from stratum 1 and stratum 2 respectively.

The combined estimates and the estimates of error are obtained by the formulae (11), (12), (13), and (14). The estimates of relative standard error are obtained by the formulae (8) and (9).

In the case of tenth and twentieth rounds, some of the estimates furnished in this volume relate to the whole state of West Bengal, rural and urban areas taken together. The estimate of the state total of a characteristic is simply the sum of the estimates for the rural and the urban areas of the state. The estimate of a ratio (for rural and urban areas taken together) is obtained as the ratio of the estimates of state totals (rural and urban areas taken together) of the numerator and the denominator. In short, the whole state is considered as comprising a number of strata some of which belong to rural areas and the rest relate to urban areas.

The estimates in all tables of this volume have been given by the individual sub-samples combined together. It is possible to build up fairly reliable estimates of standard errors of the combined estimates on the basis of the sub-sample-wise estimates for different strata. The relative standard errors of some estimates calculated by utilising the formulae mentioned above have also been given. It may be noted, however, that the estimates of errors are themselves subject to sampling error and too much reliance should not be attached to them. On *a priori* grounds, it is felt that the estimates for the twentieth round are more reliable than the estimates of earlier rounds because of the comparatively large sample size in the twentieth round.

For the 1960–61 survey the method of estimation was somewhat different. Before proceeding to give the various formulae for estimation we shall point out a few difficulties arising at the stage of estimation of errors for the 1960–61 survey.

It is well known (Hanurav, 1966: 175–204) that in finite sampling theory the variance of an unbiased estimator of the population total (or proportion) is unbiasedly estimable if and only if all the first and second order joint inclusion probabilities are strictly greater than zero. That is, the sampling design is such that there is at least one sample which contains any given unit and one sample containing any given point of units. In our survey, this condition is satisfied by the sampling design in the city sector since two blocks were selected from each stratum therein. Therefore, we have no problem regarding error-estimation for the city sector.

Unfortunately, due to limitations inherent in an *ad hoc* sample survey (as discussed in the previous chapter), which would have seriously inflated the cost-time components of the present study, only one town was selected per stratum in the town sector and one village per stratum in the village sector. Consequently, it is not possible to estimate the between-town variation within a stratum in the town sector and the between-village variation within a stratum in the rural sector unbiasedly. We pool the strata in these cases and use the well-known collapsed strata method for the estimation of error. The 1961 Census population is used as the auxiliary information for the 'collapsed strata' method. We may note that although there is another method for estimation of variance in stratified sampling with one unit per stratum [Rao, Hartley and Kiefer, 1969], we did not use it since it is not known whether it is superior to the 'collapsed strata' method. Moreover, since the 'collapsed strata' method overestimates the variance, we are always on the safe side in making inferences.

In the town sector, since the number of strata is small (namely 5), we pool the 5 strata together whereas in the rural sector we collapse the 24 strata into 8 groups of 3 each since no degree of freedom will be left for the estimates if we pair the strata into 12 groups. The formulae used thereafter are well known and can be seen in any standard book in sampling theory [Hansen, Hurwitz and Madow, 1960]. In order to facilitate a better understanding of the formulae, intuitively at least, we shall briefly describe their designs while maintaining mathematical rigour. We use the abbreviations SRSWOR, *fsu* and *ssu* to denote simple random sampling without replacement, first stage unit and second stage unit respectively.

CITTES

Let y_{hij} denote the number of families belonging to a specified class in the jth household in the ith block in stratum h and X_{hij} denote the total number of families in that household.

Let $Y = \Sigma\Sigma\Sigma Y_{hij}$ and $X = \Sigma\Sigma\Sigma X_{hij}$

The problem is to estimate Y and R=Y/X. Clearly Y denotes the total number of families belonging to a specified class and R denotes the proportion of families belonging to a specified class in the city sector. It is clear that the sampling design is a stratified two-stage sampling design, the *fsu*'s being blocks and the *ssu*'s being households.

Unbiased estimates for Y and X are given by

$$Y = \sum_{h=1}^{L} \frac{N_h}{n_h} \sum_{i=1}^{n_h} M_{hi}\,\bar{y}_{hi} = \sum_{h=1}^{L} Y_h \quad \text{and}$$

$$X=\sum_{h=1}^{L} \frac{N_h}{n_h} \sum_{i=1}^{n_h} M_{hi}\, \bar{x}_{hi}=\sum_{h=1}^{L} X_h \text{ where}$$

L =total number of strata (= 47 here)
N_h =total number of blocks in stratum h
n_h =number of sampled blocks from stratum h (= 2)
M_{hi} =total number of households in the ith block in stratum h
m_{hi} =number of households selected from the ith block in stratum h (=10 here)

and $\bar{y}_{hi}=\frac{1}{m_{hi}} \sum_{j=1}^{m_{hi}} y_{hij}$, and $\bar{x}_{hi}=\frac{1}{m_{hi}} \sum_{j=1}^{m_{hi}} x_{hij}$.

Now R is estimated by the ratio estimate Y/X. And,

$$V(R)=\frac{1}{X^2} \sum_{h=1}^{L} [V(Y_h)-2R \operatorname{Cov}(X_h, Y_h)+R^2 V(X_h)].$$

Estimate of V(R) is given by

$$\frac{1}{X^2} \sum_{h=1}^{L} [V(Y_h)-2R \operatorname{Cov}(X_h, Y_h)+R^2 V(X_h)]$$

where

$$V(Y_h)=N_h^2\left(\frac{1}{n_h}-\frac{1}{N_h}\right) s_{bhy}^2+\frac{N_h}{n_h} \sum_{i=1}^{n_h} M_{hi}^2\left(\frac{1}{m_{hi}}-\frac{1}{M_{hi}}\right) s_{whiy}^2$$

$$V(X_h)=N_h^2\left(\frac{1}{n_h}-\frac{1}{N_h}\right) s_{bhx}^2+\frac{N_h}{n_h} \sum_{i=1}^{n_h} M_{hi}^2\left(\frac{1}{m_{hi}}-\frac{1}{M_{hi}}\right) s_{whix}^2$$

$$\text{and} \operatorname{Cov}(X_h, Y_h)=N_h^2\left(\frac{1}{n_h}-\frac{1}{N_h}\right) s_{bhxy}+\frac{N_h}{n_h} \sum_{i=1}^{n_h} M_{hi}^2\left(\frac{1}{m_{hi}}-\frac{1}{M_{hi}}\right) s_{whixy}$$

where

$$s_{bhy}^2=\frac{1}{n_h-1}\left[\sum_{i=1}^{n_h} M_{hi}^2\, \bar{y}_{hi}^2-\frac{1}{n_h}\left(\sum_{i=1}^{n_h} M_{hi}\, \bar{y}_{hi}\right)^2\right]$$

$$s_{whiy}^2=\frac{1}{m_{hi}-1}\left[\sum_{j=1}^{m_{hi}} y_{hij}^2-m_{hi}\, \bar{y}_{hi}^2\right] \text{ with similar expressions}$$

for x, and

$$s_{bhxy}^2=\frac{1}{n_h-1}\left[\sum_{i=1}^{n_h} M_{hi}^2\, \bar{y}_{hi}\, \bar{x}_{hi}-\frac{1}{n_h}\left(\sum_{i=1}^{n_h} M_{hi}\, \bar{y}_{hi}\right)\left(\sum_{i=1}^{n_h} M_{hi}\, \bar{x}_{hi}\right)\right]$$

and $s_{whixy} = \frac{1}{m_{hi}-1}\left[\sum_{j=1}^{m_{hi}} y_{hij}\, x_{hij} - m_{hi}\, \bar{y}_{hi}\, \bar{x}_{hi}\right].$

TOWNS

Stratum I: Contai

Let y_{ij} denote the number of families in the jth household in the ith block belonging to a specified type and x_{ij} the total number of families in that household. Unbiased estimators of the total number of families of a specified type and the total number of families in stratum 1 are given by

$$Y_1 = \frac{N_1}{n_1} \sum_{i=1}^{n_1} \frac{M_i}{m_i} \sum_{j=1}^{m_i} y_{ij}$$

$$X_1 = \frac{N_1}{n_1} \sum_{i=1}^{n_1} \frac{M_i}{m_i} \sum_{j=1}^{m_i} x_{ij}$$

where $N_1=34$, $n_1=8$, $m_i=10$ for all i, M_i=number of households in the ith selected block.

Stratum II: Darjeeling

Let y_{ij} denote the number of families of a specified type in the jth household in the ith block and x_{ij} the number of families in that household. Estimates for stratum II are given by

$$Y_2 = \frac{N}{1} . \frac{N_2}{n_2} \sum_{i=1}^{n_2} \frac{M_i}{m_i} \sum_{j=1}^{m_i} y_{ij}$$

$$X_2 = \frac{N}{1} . \frac{N_2}{n_2} \sum_{i=1}^{n_2} \frac{M_i}{m_i} \left(\sum_{j=1}^{m_i} x_{ij}\right)$$

Here

N = 3=total number of towns in stratum II

N_2=26=total number of blocks

n_2 =10=number of blocks selected

M_i=total number of households in the ith selected block, $i=1, 2, \ldots, n_2$.

m_i=20=number of households selected from the ith block.

Stratum III: Siliguri

Design similar to that for stratum II. Estimates for stratum III are given by

$$Y_3=\frac{N}{1}\frac{N_3}{n_3}\sum_{i=1}^{n_3}\frac{M_i}{m_i}\sum_{j=1}^{m_i}y_{ij}$$

$$X_3=\frac{N}{1}\frac{N_3}{n_3}\sum_{i=1}^{n_3}\frac{M_i}{m_i}\sum_{j=1}^{m_i}x_{ij}$$

Here $N=3$

$N_3=40$

$n_3=8$=number of blocks

M_i=total number of households in the ith selected block, $i=1, 2, \ldots, n_3$.

$m_i=25$=number of households selected from the ith sampled block.

Stratum IV: Adra

Design similar to that in stratum II and III.

$$Y_4=\frac{N}{1}\cdot\frac{N_4}{n_4}\sum_{i=1}^{n_4}\frac{M_i}{m_i}\sum_{j=1}^{m_i}y_{ij}$$

$$X_4=\frac{N}{1}\cdot\frac{N_4}{n_4}\sum_{i=1}^{n_4}\frac{M_i}{m_i}\sum_{j=1}^{m_i}x_{ij}$$

where

$N=28$

$N_4=20$

$n_4=10$

M_i=total number of households in the ith selected block, $i=1, 2, \ldots, n_4$.

$m_i=20$=number of households selected from the ith sampled block.

Stratum V: Berhampore

Let y_{ijk}=number of families of a specified type in the kth household in the jth block in the ith segment.

$$Y_5=\frac{N}{1}\sum_{i=1}^{4}\frac{N_i}{n_i}\sum_{j=1}^{n_i}\frac{M_{ij}}{m_{ij}}\sum_{k=1}^{m_{ij}}y_{ijk}$$

$$X_5=\frac{N}{1}\sum_{i=1}^{4}\frac{N_i}{n_i}\sum_{j=1}^{n_i}\frac{M_{ij}}{m_{ij}}\sum_{k=1}^{m_{ij}}x_{ijk}$$

Here $N=85$

$$\frac{N_1}{n_1}=\frac{21}{3}=\frac{\text{Number of blocks in the first segment}}{\text{Number of blocks selected from it}}$$

$$\frac{N_2}{n_2}=\frac{20}{3},\quad \frac{N_3}{n_3}=\frac{13}{2},\quad \frac{N_4}{n_4}=\frac{31}{3}$$

M_{ij}=number of households in the jth block in the ith segment.
m_{ij}=number of sampled households from it=20 here.

ESTIMATES FOR THE TOWN SECTOR AS A WHOLE

Unbiased estimates for the total number of families of a specified type and total number of families for the town sector are given by

$$Y=Y_1+Y_2+Y_3+Y_4+Y_5$$

and

$$X=X_1+X_2+X_3+X_4+X_5,$$

The proportion of families of a specified type is then estimated by $R=Y/X$. R being a ratio of two random variables is not unbiased for $R=Y/X$. Since it is not possible to estimate V(Y) and V(R) unbiasedly (since only one town has been selected per stratum) and the number of strata is small (namely 5), we pool the 5 strata together and use the well-known collapsed strata method to give estimates of V(Y) and V(R), though biased. The 1961 census population is used as the auxiliary information, namely: (1) 1.83 per cent for the 3 towns in the hill area; (2) 3.31 per cent for the 3 towns in the sub-Himalayan forest belt; (3) 14.40 per cent for the 28 towns in the arid plain area; (4) 79.95 per cent for the 83 towns in the riverine plain area; and (5) 0.51 per cent for the single town in the coastal belt.

V(R) is estimated by

$$V(R)=\frac{1}{X^2}[V(Y)-2R\,\mathrm{Cov}\,(X, Y)+R^2V(X)]$$

where

$$V(Y)=\frac{5}{4}\sum_{i=1}^{5}\left(Y_i-\frac{A_i}{A}-Y\right)^2$$

$$V(X)=\frac{5}{4}\sum_{i=1}^{5}\left(X_i-\frac{A_i}{A}-X\right)^2$$

$$\mathrm{Cov}\,(X, Y)=\frac{5}{4}\sum_{i=1}^{5}\left(Y_i-\frac{A_i}{A}-Y\right)\left(X_i-\frac{A_i}{A}-X\right)$$

A_i=1961% population in the ith stratum.

It may be noted that V(Y) and V(R) are overestimates of V(Y) V(R) respectively.

VILLAGES

An unbiased estimate for the total number of nuclear families in the rural sector is given by $Y=\sum_{i=1}^{24} Y_i$ where Y_i is an unbiased estimate of the total number of nuclear families in the ith stratum and is given by $N_i Y_i$ where N_i is the number of villages in the ith stratum and Y_i is the number of nuclear families in the selected village from the ith stratum.

An unbiased estimate of X, the total number of families, is given by

$X=\sum_{i=1}^{24} X_i$ where X_i is an unbiased estimate of the total number of families in the ith stratum.

The proportion of nuclear families in the rural sector is estimated by R=Y/X. Obviously, R is not an unbiased estimator of R=Y/X. The approximate expressions for the bias and variance of R are given by

$$B(R)=E(R)-R=\frac{1}{X^2}[RV(X)-\text{Cov}(X, Y)]$$

and $$V(R)=\frac{1}{X^2}[V(Y)-2R\ \text{Cov}(X, Y)+R^2V(X)].$$

Since only one village has been selected per stratum it is not possible to estimate B(R) and V(R) unbiasedly. Some biased estimates can be obtained by using the method of collapsed strata. Since no degree of freedom will be left for the estimates if we pair the strata, it is decided to collapse the 24 strata into 8 groups of 3 each. As in the case of estimation of towns, here also 1961 Census population is used in collapsing the strata. Details are given in Table A.

An estimate of V(R) is given by

$$V(R)=\frac{1}{X^2}[V(Y)-2R\ \text{Cov}(X, Y)+R^2V(X)]$$

where $$V(Y)=\sum_{g=1}^{G}\frac{L_g}{L_g-1}\sum_{i=1}^{Lg}\left(Y_{gi}-\frac{A_{gi}}{A_g}Y_g\right)^2$$

TABLE A

Stratum	*Ecological Zone*	*District*	*1961 Population*	*Percentage to Total*	*Rank According to Population Size*
(1)	(2)	(3)	(4)	(5)	(6)
1	Hill area	Darjeeling	325626	1.234	5
2	Sub-Himalayan	Darjeeling	154377	0.585	2
3	Forest belt	Jalpaiguri	1235478	4.682	17
4	Arid plain	Bankura	1105388	4.189	13
5		Birbhum	1345389	5.099	19
6		Burdwan	707366	2.681	8
7		Hooghly	124512	0.472	1
8		Malda	277394	1.051	4
9		Midnapur	938556	3.557	10
10		Murshidabad	1145382	4.341	14
11		Purulia	1267538	4 804	18
12	Riverine	Bankura	436968	1.656	7
13		Burdwan	1814402	6.878	22
14		Cooch Behar	948360	3.594	11
15		Hooghly	1527623	5.790	21
16		Howrah	1213385	4.599	15
17		Malda	893744	3.387	9
18		Midnapur	2716961	10.298	23
19		Murshidabad	949164	3.597	12
20		Nadia	1397986	5.298	20
21		24-Parganas	4079808	15.463	24
22		West Dinajpur	1224828	4.642	16
23	Coastal	Midnapur	352052	1.334	6
24		24-Parganas	203150	0.769	3
		Total	26385437	100.000	

$$V(X)=\sum_{g=1}^{G} \frac{L_g}{L_g-1} \sum_{i=1}^{L_g} \left(X_{gi}-\frac{A_{gi}}{A_g} X_g\right)^2$$

$$\mathrm{Cov}\,(X, Y)=\sum_{g=1}^{G} \frac{L_g}{L_g-1} \sum_{i=1}^{L_g} \left(Y_{gi}-\frac{A_{gi}}{A_g} Y_g\right)\left(X_{gi}-\frac{A_{gi}}{A_g} X_g\right)$$

In our case, $G=8$, $L_g=3$, for $g = 1, 2, \ldots, 8$.

Y_{gi} is an unbiased estimator of Y_{gi} for the ith stratum in the gth group

X_{gi} is an unbiased estimator of X_{gi} for the ith stratum in the gth group

A_{gi} = %population of the *i*th stratum in the *g*th group

$$A_g = \sum_{i=1}^{Lg} A_{gi}$$

$$Y_g = \sum_{i=1}^{Lg} Y_{gi}$$

$$X_g = \sum_{i=1}^{Lg} X_{gi}$$

It may be noted that V(R) is an overestimate of V(R).

VIII

In Part 1 of this volume we have presented the standard errors along with the estimated mean values of the items of analysis. Since the relative precision of the analyzed items cannot be examined unless the standard errors are compared against the estimated mean values, we prepared Tables 7.21–7.27 to denote the coefficients of variation of the major items analyzed. As the obtained values of the coefficients of variation were found scattered over a long range from 1.0 per cent to 136.9 per cent, a summary of these values is given in Table 7.28. Now, since the coefficients of variation of an appreciable number of our estimates yield a large value, the order of precision of our data requires further scrutiny. We find, accordingly, from a rearrangement of all these values in Table 7.29 that most of the large coefficients occur in the case of analysis of the non-familial units, while they occur much less for the extended families and still less for the nuclear families.

For the nuclear and extended family-units, however, the values of the coefficients of variation tend to increase as one proceeds from the undifferentiated total field of West Bengal represented in Tables 7.21 and 7.22 to the increasingly differentiated sub-fields formed by considering the social structural characteristics in Tables 7.23–7.25, and finally to a joint consideration of two or more such characterisitcs in Tables 7.26 and 7.27. In contrast, the coefficients of variation for the non-familial units appear to be rather large irrespective of the nature of the field considered. Details are given in Table 7.30.

These features of our data suggest an intrinsic characteristic of the non-familial units as distinct from that of the nuclear and the extended family-units. The analysis in Part 1 of this volume has brought out that the non-familial units emerge in some specific societal categories rather than as a general secietal pattern; that is, the existence of the non-familial units depends upon a larger number of contingencies than the other coresident and commensal kingroups. Accordingly, a precise and comprehensive appreciation of the non-familial units requires either a larger sample or a more specific research design than the one on which the present study is based. However, since the issues involved are in the nature of the societal units themselves, we may proceed to interpret the situations arising out of a wide range of variations, interrelations, and trends of association among the classificatory and analytical categories even when the corresponding mean values are based on large or small samples of primary data.

This is the advantage of a properly designed and executed random sample survey which, within the limited resources in time, money and men, can give us such an extensive and representative coverage of information as is denied to the subjectively circumscribed census of one or a few purposively selected areas. At the same time, it can precisely indicate where the lacunae lie in the field of observation, how can they be removed, and what would be the possible gain from future undertakings in their respect. With reference to these two guiding principles, therefore, the scope and limitation of the deductions made in Part 1 of this volume, the inferences drawn therefrom, and the generalizations made thereafter, should be appraised.

TABLE 7.1*

Investigator-wise Sub-sample	*Percentage to Total of Cooperative Interviewees*		
	City	*Town*	*Rural*
(1)	(2)	(3)	(4)
1	87.21	83.41	80.66
2	91.50	91.72	80.05
3	89.38	86.52	81.27
4	90.24	88.52	85.04
5	92.74	92.46	86.38

*The value of Kendall's coefficient of concordance W, obtained from the above data after ranking them in an ascending order of the proportions within each sub-sample, was 0.84. The value of chi-square, calculated accordingly, was 8.4, with probability between 0.01 and 0.02 [Kendall, 1955: 94–106].

TABLE 7.2

Investigator-wise Sub-sample	*Percentage to Total 'Heads' of Households in Calcutta of Those Who were willing to be Interviewed for Schedule 1.0*				
	*Community**		*Area of Habitation†*		
	Bengali	*Non-Bengali*	*Commercial*	*Slum*	*Residential*
(1)	(2)	(3)	(4)	(5)	(6)
1	93.59	89.43	60.04	88.13	95.59
2	99.07	92.37	72.28	92.87	97.86
3	95.03	90.24	19.19	98.71	95.37
4	98.86	94.17	23.05	99.83	99.05
5	97.23	94.68	93.34	90.20	96.83
6	98 98	96 03	98.53	98.74	99.41

*The Kruskal-Wallis one-way analysis of variance by ranks, as applied to the above data after ranking them in an ascending order of the proportions within each sub-sample, gave a chi-square value of 5.0256 against 1 degree of freedom, with probability between 0.05 and 0.02 [Siegel, 1956: 184–94].

†The same course of analysis as noted for * gave a chi-square value of 11.1043 against 2 degrees of freedom, with probability between 0.01 and 0.001 [Siegel, 1956: 184–94].

Although not of any significance, it may be noted that the variations under col. (4) of the table are possibly due to sporadic representation of commercial areas by investigators.

TABLE 7.3

Categories of Family Structure	Investigator-wise Sub-sample Estimates for Calcutta						Total
	1	2	3	4	5	6	
(1)	(2)	(3)	(4)	(5)	(6)	(7)	(8)
1	25.90	32.66	26.63	36.22	30.83	28.52	30.40
2	5.03	1.58	1.00	1.58	1.39	3.90	2.47
3	3.49	6.13	2.74	6.15	1.43	3.71	3.80
4	24.30	23.73	34.78	31.43	37.26	27.62	30.24
5	23.89	15.86	18.34	10.19	24.34	24.54	19.97
6	0.12	0.00	0.58	0.00	0.00	0.55	0.10
7	1.20	1.71	1.11	0.00	0.00	0.00	0.60
8	0.90	0.00	2.88	1.43	0.79	0.00	0.93
9	6.06	6.52	4.89	5.92	1.49	6.20	4.88
10	9.11	11.81	7.05	7.08	2.47	4.96	6.61
Total	100.00	100.00	100.00	100.00	100.00	100.00	100.00
n	141	170	134	142	167	154	908

TABLE 7.4

Categories of Family Structure	Investigator-wise Sub-sample Estimates for Howrah						Total
	1	2	3	4	5	6	
(1)	(2)	(3)	(4)	(5)	(6)	(7)	(8)
1	34.24	40.82	20.64	22.14	28.78	36.29	28.44
2	4.58	2.32	2.09	5.90	1.15	5.16	3.54
3	0.00	2.56	10.99	6.47	8.70	3.04	6.30
4	27.19	24.47	21.24	47.29	42.11	45.89	37.69
5	27.52	17.29	32.14	16.86	9.62	8.20	17.13
6	0.00	0.00	0.00	0.00	0.00	0.00	0.00
7	0.00	0.00	0.00	0.00	0.00	0.00	0.00
8	0.00	0.00	1.00	0.00	0.00	0.00	0.20
9	6.47	0.00	7.93	0.00	3.07	0.94	3.01
10	0.00	12.54	3.97	1.34	6.57	0.48	3.69
Total	100.00	100.00	100.00	100.00	100.00	100.00	100.00
n	36	32	43	41	37	37	226

TABLE 7.5

Categories of Family Structure	Investigator-wise Sub-sample Estimates for Siliguri 1	2	3	4	Total
(1)	(2)	(3)	(4)	(5)	(6)
1	11.72	24.57	3.32	26.27	13.86
2	0.00	0.00	0.00	0.00	0.00
3	5.07	12.00	3.93	3.90	6.00
4	53.75	40.00	51.57	52.92	49.74
5	20.00	17.86	21.51	14.52	19.18
6	0.00	0.00	2.27	0.00	0.84
7	0.00	0.00	0.00	0.00	0.00
8	0.00	0.00	0.00	0.00	0.00
9	9.46	5.57	14.08	2.39	9.15
10	0.00	0.00	3.32	0.00	1.23
Total	100.00	100.00	100.00	100.00	100.00
n	50	50	50	51	201

TABLE 7.6

Categories of Family Structure	Investigator-wise Sub-sample Estimates for Adra 1	2	3	4	5	Total
(1)	(2)	(3)	(4)	(5)	(6)	(7)
1	14.64	34.21	17.33	5.00	6.70	15.71
2	0.00	1.97	0.00	0.00	0.00	0.42
3	27.32	11.18	10.00	13.01	11.15	15.03
4	47.68	42.14	43.32	66.02	67.42	52.77
5	10.36	10.50	27.01	13.98	12.94	15.01
6	0.00	0.00	0.00	0.00	0.00	0.00
7	0.00	0.00	0.00	0.00	0.00	0.00
8	0.00	0.00	0.00	0.00	0.00	0.00
9	0.00	0.00	2.34	1.99	1.79	1.06
10	0.00	0.00	0.00	0.00	0.00	0.00
Total	100.00	100.00	100.00	100.00	100.00	100.00
n	40	44	40	40	41	205

TABLE 7.7

Categories of Family Structure	Investigator-wise Sub-sample Estimates for Berhampore				Total
	1	2	3	4	
(1)	(2)	(3)	(4)	(5)	(6)
1	12.11	16.80	5.10	6.34	9.92
2	4.12	17.25	2.55	1.54	6.05
3	6.20	1.61	1.88	8.83	4.62
4	36.95	30.40	23.75	48.49	34.64
5	32.31	15.05	45.38	20.24	29.09
6	0.00	0.00	0.00	0.00	0.00
7	0.00	0.00	1.88	5.74	1.86
8	0 00	0.00	0.00	0.00	0.00
9	4.14	10.01	8.17	4.41	6.62
10	4.17	8.88	11.29	4.41	7.20
Total	100.00	100.00	100.00	100.00	100.00
n	54	60	51	51	216

TABLE 7.8

Categories of Family Structure	Investigator-wise Sub-sample Estimates for Contai				Total
	1	2	4	5	
(1)	(2)	(3)	(4)	(5)	(6)
1	25.38	37.20	41.78	51.75	38.82
2	8.67	7.20	5.89	0.00	5.30
3	8.67	10.00	4.11	0.00	5.53
4	43.97	27.17	34.11	36.19	36.15
5	13.31	10.00	14.11	9.34	11.64
6	0.00	0.00	0.00	0.00	0.00
7	0.00	0.00	0.00	0.00	0.00
8	0.00	0.00	0.00	0.00	0.00
9	0.00	2.81	0.00	2 72	1.37
10	0.00	5.62	0.00	0.00	1.19
Total	100.00	100.00	100.00	100.00	100.00
n	22	20	20	21	83

TABLE 7.9

Categories of Family Structure	Investigator-wise Sub-sample Estimates for the City Sector of West Bengal 1	2	3	4	5	6	Total
(1)	(2)	(3)	(4)	(5)	(6)	(7)	(8)
1	26.60	33.20	25.58	33.88	30.52	29.81	30.13
2	4.99	1.63	1.19	2.29	1.35	4.10	2.62
3	3.20	5.90	4.19	6.21	2.50	3.60	4.14
4	24.54	23.78	32.40	34.06	37.98	30.66	31.26
5	24.19	15.96	20.77	11.30	22.17	21.83	19 58
6	0.11	0.00	0.48	0.00	0.00	0.45	0.09
7	1.10	1.60	0.91	0.00	0.00	0.44	0.52
8	0.82	0.00	2.55	1.19	0.67	0.44	0.83
9	6.09	6.08	5.42	4.94	1.73	5.33	4.62
10	8.36	11.85	6.51	6.13	3.08	4.22	6.21
Total	100.00	100.00	100.00	100.00	100.00	100.00	100·00
n	177	202	177	183	204	191	1134

TABLE 7.10

Categories of Family Structure	Investigator-wise Sub-sample Estimates for the Town Sector of West Bengal (as Based on Samples from 4 Towns of Siliguri, Adra, Berhampore, and Contai) 1	2	3	4	5	Total
(1)	(2)	(3)	(4)	(5)	(6)	(7)
1	13.44	19.33	5.23	9.71	27.49	13.84
2	3.12	10.14	1.45	1.81	0.00	3.81
3	8.31	7.85	3.15	8.80	4.85	6.19
4	42.68	36.12	35.19	48.93	52.56	40.65
5	25.44	15.03	35.47	18.96	12.79	23.62
6	0.00	0.00	0.83	0.00	0.00	0.22
7	0.00	0.00	1.07	4.56	0.00	1.03
8	0.00	0.00	0.00	0.00	0.00	0.00
9	4.63	6.76	9.96	3.73	2.31	6.24
10	2.38	4.77	7.65	3.51	0.00	4.40
Total	100.00	100.00	100.00	100.00	100.00	100.00
n	166	174	141	111	113	705

TABLE 7.11

Categories of Family Structure	*Investigator-wise Sub-sample Estimates for the Rural Sector of West Bengal (as Based on 20 Sampled Villages in the Arid, Riverine Plain, Coastal and Sub-Himalayan Forest Belt Areas)*					*Total*
	1	2	3	4	5	
(1)	(2)	(3)	(4)	(5)	(6)	(7)
1	4.75	11.69	7.49	5.51	3.15	5.31
2	4.92	2.56	4.05	3.66	3.80	3.74
3	8.86	7.32	4.05	6.81	9.03	7.91
4	48.20	50.42	38.69	47.92	55.49	49.82
5	22.81	19.93	31.89	27.69	25.21	24.80
6	0.33	0.41	1.27	0.18	0.51	0.57
7	0.12	0.28	1.40	0.04	0.00	0.33
8	1.07	0.80	0.81	0.54	0.43	0.74
9	4.76	3.84	3.93	3.66	1.09	3.47
10	4.18	2.75	6.42	3.99	1.29	3.31
Total	100.00	100.00	100.00	100.00	100.00	100.00
n	471	329	439	439	516	2194

TABLE 7.12

Categories of Family Structure	*Investigator-wise Sub-sample Estimates for the Arid Plain and Sub-Himalayan Forest Belt (Excluding Dumriguri Chhat) Areas—(Rural)*					*Total*
	1	2	3	4	5	
(1)	(2)	(3)	(4)	(5)	(6)	(7)
1	0.00	20.00	3.50	2.75	2.56	1.98
2	0.00	0.00	5.15	1.37	4.27	3.51
3	0.00	20.00	5.20	8.49	7.69	8.51
4	66.67	40.00	39.50	56.94	55.73	53.71
5	33.33	20.00	33.49	26.29	25.90	25.45
6	0.00	0.00	0.95	0.00	0.43	0.60
7	0.00	0.00	0.00	0.17	0.00	0.13
8	0.00	0.00	1.90	0.00	0.00	0.51
9	0.00	0.00	3.30	1.37	1.71	3.00
10	0.00	0.00	7.01	2.62	1.71	2.60
Total	100.00	100.00	100.00	100.00	100.00	100.00
n	95	15	181	185	325	791

TABLE 7.13

Categories of Family Structure	Investigator-wise Sub-sample Estimates for the Riverine and Coastal (Excluding Kaylapara) Areas—(Rural)					Total
	1	2	3	4		
(1)	(2)	(3)	(4)	(5)	(6)	(7)
1	4.09	11.26	8.75	6.49	3.77	7.05
2	5.31	2.53	3.70	4.47	3.50	3.96
3	8.84	6.85	3.68	6.21	9.67	7.14
4	46.94	50.76	38.44	44.72	53.18	46.90
5	23.86	20.15	31.38	28.19	26.58	25.27
6	0.13	0.43	1.37	0.24	0.82	0.53
7	0.14	0.29	1.85	0.00	0.00	0.43
8	0.98	0.84	0.46	0.74	1.36	0.86
9	5.13	4.01	4.13	4.47	0.27	3.93
10	4.58	2.88	6.24	4.47	0.85	3.93
Total	100.00	100.00	100.00	100.00	100.00	100.00
n	376	324	258	254	191	1403

TABLE 7.14

Categories of Family Structure	Investigator-wise Sub-sample Estimates for West Bengal (Excluding Darjeeling Town and the Villages of Kaylapara, Dumriguri Chhat and Algarah Bazar)					Total
	1	2	3	4	5	
(1)	(2)	(3)	(4)	(5)	(6)	(7)
1	7.44	15.13	10.82	11.12	6.86	9.50
2	4.92	2.46	3.50	3.38	3.84	3.55
3	8.17	7.10	4.07	6.70	8.27	7.27
4	45.31	46.14	37.51	45.19	52.07	46.68
5	22.99	19.26	29.86	24.42	24.73	23.92
6	0.30	0.34	1.12	0.14	0.50	0.49
7	0.24	0.49	1.31	0.06	0.00	0.37
8	1.04	0.67	1.13	0.67	0.37	0.75
9	4.92	4.21	4.24	3.91	1.68	3.67
10	4.67	4.20	6.44	4.41	1.68	3.80
Total	100.00	100.00	100.00	100.00	100.00	100.00
n	814	705	757	733	820	3829

TABLE 7.15

Sub-sample Estimates in	*W= Coefficient of Concordance (d.f.=9)*	*Chi-square Value*	*Percentage Level of Significance*
(1)	(2)	(3)	(4)
Table 7.3	0.9332	50.3928	0.1
Table 7.4	0.8659	46.7586	0.1
Table 7.5	0.9315	33.5340	0.1
Table 7.6	0.9256	41.6520	0.1
Table 7.7	0.7971	28.6956	0.1
Table 7.8	0.8804	31.6944	0.1
Table 7.9	0.9495	51.0517	0.1
Table 7.10	0.8658	38.9623	0.1
Table 7.11	0.9128	41.0741	0.1
Table 7.12	0.8287	29.8332	0.1
Table 7.13	0.8587	30.9132	0.1
Table 7.14	0.9366	42.1458	0.1

TABLE 7.16

Categories of Family Structure	*Percentage to Total by half-Samples: 1946–47 (Rural only)*	
	A	B
(1)	(2)	(3)
1+2	16.05	15.81
3+4	43.26	44.32
5	26.38	26.75
6–10	14.31	13.12
Total	100.00 (2180)	100.00 (1936)

TABLE 7.17

Categories of Family Structure	*Estimated Percentage to Total by Sub-samples: April-June* 1951 *(Rural Only)*	
	1	2
(1)	(2)	(3)
1+2	20.50	13.26
3+4	38.80	46.60
5	25.87	22.45
6–10	14.83	17.69
Total	100.00	100.00
	(317)	(294)

TABLE 7.18

Categories of Family Structure	*Estimated Percentage to Total by Sub-samples: August-November* 1951 *(Rural only)*	
	1	2
(1)	(2)	(3)
1+2	22.38	15.75
3+4	34.97	45.89
5	32.16	25.34
6–10	10.49	13.02
Total	100.00	100.00
	(143)	(146)

TABLE 7.19

Categories of Family Structure	Estimated Percentage to Total by Batches of Investigators: 1955–56	
	1	2
(1)	(2)	(3)
	Urban	
1+2	34.23	34.67
3+4	32.44	33.15
5	20.09	18.79
6–10	13.24	13.39
Total	100.00 (891)	100.00 (926)
	Rural	
1+2	12.46	11.80
3+4	44.41	48.20
5	30.03	28.85
6–10	13.10	11.15
Total	100.00 (313)	100.00 (305)

TABLE 7.20

Categories of Family Structure	Estimated Percentage to Total by Batches of Investigators: 1965–66	
	1 & 3	2 & 4
(1)	(2)	(3)
1+2	22.19	24.08
3+4	42.90	45.42
5	24.94	21.26
6–10	9.97	9.24
Total	100.00 (7534)	100.00 (6816)

TABLE 7.21

West Bengal at Different Time-periods	*Sample Size*	*Coefficients of Variation in Each Family Structure Category*		
		Non-familial Unit	*Nuclear Family*	*Extended Family*
(1)	(2)	(3)	(4)	(5)
1951	900	18.0	12.7	7.1
1955–56	2435	9.1	5.8	8.1
1960–61	4934	14.4	6.7	6.9
1965–66	14350	4.0	1.4	2.1

TABLE 7.22

Different Regions of West Bengal	*Sample Size (1960–61)*	*Coefficients of Variation of Each Family Structure Category*		
		Non-familial Unit	*Nuclear Family*	*Extended Family*
(1)	(2)	(3)	(4)	(5)
Urban	2031	20.2	5.0	14.2
City	1134	13.6	9.1	14.0
Town	897	1.0	7.1	7.2
Rural	2903	18.1	6.0	6.5
Villages within 10 miles of a town	2087	23.4	7.9	8.6
Villages beyond 10 miles of a town	816	17.6	1.8	4.0
Villages under Hill and Sub-Himalayan forest belt	442	20.2	5.2	13.9
Villages under Arid plain area	838	4.9	2.7	5.1
Villages under Coastal and Riverine plain area	1623	8.8	4.8	5.7

TABLE 7.23

Age-Categories of the 'Heads' in West Bengal (in Years)	*Sample Size (1960–61)*	*Coefficients of Variation in Each Family Structure Category*		
		Non-familial Unit	*Nuclear Family*	*Extended Family*
(1)	(2)	(3)	(4)	(5)
Up to 19	29	54.4	36.3	46.9
20–24	177	18.1	11.6	25.9
25–29	466	25.6	13.2	19.2
30–34	751	22.3	7.0	12.0
35–39	824	21.7	5.0	7.0
40–44	1062	28.0	5.4	12.1
45–49	583	23.7	4.5	8.0
50-54	458	18.5	7.7	9.7
55-59	240	41.4	8.6	6.6
60–64	173	24.1	22.8	21.6
65–69	84	32.8	15.5	5.7
70+	87	65.5	29.7	7.0

TABLE 7.24

Social Characteristics in West Bengal	Sample Size (1960–61)	Coefficients of Variation in Each Family Structure Category		
		Non-familial Unit	Nuclear Family	Extended Family
(1)	(2)	(3)	(4)	(5)
1. Hindu 'high' castes	1052	13.8	7.3	8.7
2. HIndu others	2877	14.2	4.4	5.8
3. Muslim 'high' groups	230	16.0	2.6	14.0
4. Muslim others	439	23.5	7.8	13.6
5. Others	336	33.2	6.3	16.4
6. Scheduled castes	928	25.4	5.5	10.9
7. Scheduled tribes	274	45.2	6.5	14.5
8. Others	3732	13.8	8.6	9.6
9. Mother tongue: Bengali	3541	16.9	7.8	7.2
10. Mother tongue : Others	1393	16.0	7.9	15.8
11. Displaced from Pakistan	163	37.7	11.9	12.1
12. Not displaced from Pakistan	4771	15.3	6.7	6.6
13. Belongs to West Bengal	4103	15.5	6.7	6.4
14. Belongs to any other State in India	831	18.6	16.2	22.3
15. Ancestral home: Not left or left<1 year	3036	19.8	7.8	6.8
16. Ancestral home: Left>1 year	1898	9.6	6.8	9.8

TABLE 7.25

Educational, Economic and Property Characteristics in West Bengal		Sample size (1960–61)	*Coefficients of Variation in Each Family Structure Category* Non-familial Unit	Nuclear Family	Extended Family
(1)		(2)	(3)	(4)	(5)
1. Literacy	Illiterate	1971	18.4	6.3	6.5
2.	Literate	2963	18.3	6.2	5.4
3. Occupation	Non-manual high and middle, manual skilled	2696	14.3	6.2	6.0
4.	Non-manual low and manual semi- and unskilled	2097	21.5	6.2	6.6
5.	None	141	10.0	13.8	23.0
6. Employment status	Employer and own-account worker	2102	27.7	6.6	7.6
7.	Employee	2691	15.7	7.1	8.5
8.	None	141	10.0	13.8	23.0
9. Industry	Agriculture	2225	22.4	5.9	7.0
10.	Handicrafts, Trade and Commerce and others	1484	23.1	5.5	12.4
11.	Manufacture and Service	1100	14.5	6.6	15.3
12.	Dependent on others	125	11.6	16.4	22.8
13. Property	Possesses some	1986	21.7	5.7	5.3
14.	None	2948	13.6	7.7	10.8
15. Residence	Owned	2847	136.9	6.0	8.8
16.	Rented or provided by others	2087	13.0	10.6	13.0
17. Familial obligation	None	3171	21.6	7.8	5.4
18.	Exists and is shared — Singly	1583	23.7	4.6	6.2
19.	Exists and is shared — Jointly	180	56.3	30.7	9.2

TABLE 7.26

Sl. No.	*Combination of Social Characteristics in West Bengal as Serially Numbered in Tables 7.24 and 7.25*					*Sample size (1960–61)*	*Coefficients of Variation in Each Family Structure Category*		
	7.24		7.25				*Non-familial Unit*	*Nuclear Family*	*Extended Family*
(1)	(2)		(3)			(4)	(5)	(6)	(7)
1	2,4	9	3	6	2	481	29.0	8.6	6.8
2	1,3,5	"	3	"	"	137	93.9	6.5	9.0
3	1–2	"	3–4	6–7	1–2	570	23.4	5.5	12.0
4	3–5	"	"	"	"	267	20.1	9.0	25.9
5	1–5	"	4	7	1	770	22.9	5.2	10.0
6	"	10	3–4	6–7	2	1177	28.7	6.6	10.8
7	"	11	3	"	"	587	20.5	10.0	12.1
8	"	10–11	3–4	"	1–2	534	17.5	9.1	17.2
9	"	12	5	8	1–2	125	11.6	16.4	22.8
10	"	11	3–4	6–7	1	286	9.1	15.3	32.1

TABLE 7.27

Age Categories of the 'Head' from Table 7.23	*Categories of Combination from Table 7.26*	*Sample Size (1960–61)*	*Coefficients of Variation in each Family Structure Category*		
			Non-familial Unit	*Nuclear Family*	*Extended Family*
(1)	(2)	(3)	(4)	(5)	(6)
Up to 29 years	1	42	18.9	15.5	26.3
	2–8	572	19.8	11.9	18.4
	9–10	58	31.2	47.3	34.0
30–44 years	1	208	103.6	8.9	9.7
	2–8	2185	21.1	6.1	8.8
	9–10	244	7.7	25.4	37.9
45–54 years	1	138	93.2	11.0	7.3
	2–8	850	22.8	6.4	11.9
	9–10	53	31.3	22.9	42.8
55 years or above	1	93	86.8	31.2	5.2
	2–8	435	29.9	6.8	6.1
	9–10	56	31.2	34.4	19.7

TABLE 7.28

Range of Coefficients of Variation (in Percentage)	*Total Frequency*
(1)	(2)
Less than 10.0	112
10.0—20.0	69
20.1+	65
Total	246

TABLE 7.29

Range of Coefficients of Variation (in Percentage)	*Frequency by Family Types*		
	Non-familial Unit	*Nuclear Family*	*Extended Family*
(1)	(2)	(3)	(4)
Less than 10.0	10	58	44
10.0–20.0	30	15	24
20.1+	42	9	14
Total	82	82	82

TABLE 7.30

Range of Coefficients of Variation (in Percentages)	*West Bengal (Tables 7.21 and 7.22)*			*Characteristics Considered*					
				Singly (Tables 7.23—7.25)			*Jointly (Tables 7.26 and 7.27)*		
	Non-familial Unit	*Nuclear Family*	*Extended Family*	*Non-familial Unit*	*Nuclear Family*	*Extended Family*	*Non-familial Unit*	*Nuclear Family*	*Extended Family*
(1)	(2)	(3)	(4)	(5)	(6)	(7)	(8)	(9)	(10)
Less than 10.0	5	12	10	3	34	26	2	12	8
10.0–20.0	5	1	3	21	9	14	4	5	7
20.1+	3	—	—	23	4	7	16	5	7
Total	13	13	13	47	47	47	22	22	22

References

BANDYOPADHYAY, S., CHATTOPADHYAY, K., MUKHERJEE, R.
1963 : 'A Note on the use of Societal Factors for Stratification in Social Surveys', *Bulletin of the Cultural Research Institute*, Calcutta, II (2), pp. 41–47.

CENSUS OF INDIA
1951 : *District Handbook for West Bengal*, Delhi, Government of India.
1953 : *Census of India 1951, Vol. VI, Part I(A), West Bengal, Sikkim and Chandernagore—Report*, Delhi, Government of India.
1954 : *Census of India 1951, Vol. VI, Part III, Calcutta City*, Delhi, Government of India.

CHATTERJEE, S.P. (ed.)
1957 : *National Atlas of India*, Calcutta, Dehradun, The National Atlas Organization.

CHATTOPADHYAY, K., BANDYOPADHYAY, S.
1962 : 'Notes on a Method of Studying Rural Society', *Man in India*, 42 (3), pp. 206–16.

COCHRAN, C.H.
1953 : *Sampling Techniques*, New York, John Wiley.

DESAI, I.P.
1964 : *Some Aspects of Family in Mahuva*, Bombay, Asia Publishing House.

ENGELS, F.
1948 : *The Origin of the Family, Private Property and the State*, Moscow, Foreign Languages Publishing House.

EPSTEIN, T.S.
1962 : *Economic Development and Social Change in South India*, Bombay, Oxford University Press.

FISHER, R.A., YATES, F.
1957 : *Statistical Tables for Biological, Agricultural and Medical Research*, London, Oliver and Boyd.

FORTES, M.
1949 : *The Web of Kinship Among the Tallensi*, London, Oxford University Press.

GAIT, E.A.
1901 : *Census of India, 1901, VI,* New Delhi, Government of India.

GOODE, W.J.
1963 : *World Revolution and Family Patterns,* London, Collier-Macmillan.

GOI [GOVERNMENT OF INDIA]
1961 : *Census of India, 1961, Age Tables,* New Delhi, Government of India.

HANSEN, M.H., HURWITZ, W.N., MADOW, W.G.
1960 : *Sample Survey Methods and Theory, Vol. I* (*Methods and Applications*), New York, John Wiley.

HANURAV, T.V.
1966 : 'Some Aspects of Unified Sampling Theory', *Sankhya* (The Indian Journal of Statistics), Series A, Vol. 28, Parts 2 & 3, pp. 175–204.

HOMANS, G.C.
1950 : *The Human Group,* New York, Harcourt, Brace & Co.

ISI [INDIAN STATISTICAL INSTITUTE]
1951 : *Final Report of Enquiry into the Conditions of Agricultural Labourers in West Bengal, 1946–47,* Calcutta, West Bengal Government Press.
1952 : *Final Report on Rural Indebtedness Enquiry* (*1946–47*) *West Bengal,* Calcutta, West Bengal Government Press.

KENDALL, M.G.
1955 : *Rank Correlation Methods,* London, Charles Griffin.

LERNER, D.
1963 : 'Toward a Communication Theory of Modernization', pp. 327–50 in Pye, L.W. (ed.), *Communications and Political Development,* Princeton, N.J., Princeton University Press.

LINTON, R.
1952 : 'Cultural and Personality Factor Effecting Economic Growth', pp. 73–88 in Hoselitz, B.F. (ed.), *The Progress of Underdeveloped Areas,* Chicago, Chicago University Press.

MAHALANOBIS, P.C.
1944 : 'On Large Scale Sample Surveys', *Philosophical Transactions of the Royal Society of London,* Series B, No. 584, Vol. 231, pp. 329–451.
1961 : *Experiments in the Statistical Sampling in the Indian*

Statistical Institute, Calcutta, Statistical Publishing Society.

MAJUMDAR–SASTRI, S.

1924 : *Cunningham's Ancient Geography of India*, Calcutta, Chuckervertty, Chatterjee & Co.

MALINOWSKI, B.

1944 : *A Scientific Theory of Culture and Other Essays*, North Carolina, North Carolina University Press.

MARX, K.

1942 : *The German Ideology*, London, Lawrence & Wishart.

MARX-ENGELS-LENIN INSTITUTE OF THE CENTRAL COMMITTEE OF THE COMMUNIST PARTY OF THE SOVIET UNION (BOLSHEVIKS)

1948 : 'Preface', pp. 5-9 in Engels, F., *The Origin of the Family, Private Property and the State*, Moscow, Foreign Languages Publishing House.

MENDE, T.

1959 : 'Southeast Asia and Japan', *Bulletin of the International House of Japan*, Winter, No. 3.

MORRISON, W.A.

1959 : 'Family Types in Badlapur: An Analysis of a Changing Institution in Maharashtrian Village', *Sociological Bulletin*, Bombay, 8 (2), pp. 45–67.

MUKHERJEE, R.

1957 : *The Dynamics of a Rural Society*, Berlin, Akademie Verlag; Bombay, Popular Prakashan.

1961a : 'Caste and Economic Structure in West Bengal in Present Times', pp. 157–67 in Saksena, R.N. (ed.), *Sociology, Social Research and Social Problems in India*, Bombay, Asia Publishing House.

1961b : 'A Note on Village as Unit or Variable for Studies of Rural Society', *Eastern Anthropologist*, 14 (1), pp. 3–29.

1962 : 'On Classification of Family Structures: Dimension-Kinship Composition', pp. 352–98 in Madan, T.N. and Sarana, G. (eds.), *Indian Anthropology*, Bombay, Asia Publishing House.

1965 : *The Sociologist and Social Change in India Today*, New Delhi, Prentice-Hall.

1968 : 'Some Observations on the Diachronic and Synchronic Aspects of Social Change', *Social Science Information*, Paris, 7 (1), pp. 31–55.

1971a: *Six Villages of Bengal*, Bombay, Popular Prakashan.
1971b: 'Family in India: A Perspective', *Perspective* (Supplement to the *Indian Journal of Public Administration*), New Delhi, 17 (4), pp. 41–107.
1972 : 'Concepts and Methods for the Secondary Analysis of Variations in Family Structure', *Current Anthropology*, Chicago, 13 (3 & 4), pp. 417–43.
1976 : *Family and Planning in India*, New Delhi, Orient Longman.

MUKHERJEE, R., BANDYOPADHYAY, S.
1964 : 'Social Research and Mahalanobis's D^2', pp. 259–82 in Rao, C.R. (ed.), *Contributions to Statistics*, Calcutta, Statistical Publishing Society; Oxford, Pergamon Press.

MURDOCK, G.P.
1949 : *Social Structure*, New York, Macmillan.

MURDOCK, G.P., FORD, C.S., HUDSON, A.E., KENNEDY, R., SIMMONS, L.W., WHITING, J.W.M.
1950 : *Outline of Cultural Materials*, Vol. I, New Haven, Human Relations Area-Files.

NSS [NATIONAL SAMPLE SURVEY]
1951 : *Instructions to Investigators (and Other Field Workers): Indian (Multipurpose) National Sample Survey 1951–52*, Calcutta, Indian Statistical Institute (mimeo.).
1953 : *Tables with Notes on the Second Round (April–June 1951)*, New Delhi, Department of Economic Affairs (Ministry of Finance).
1954 : *Tables with Notes on the Third Round (August–November 1951)*, New Delhi, Department of Economic Affairs (Ministry of Finance).
1960 : *Tables with Notes on Employment and Unemployment, Tenth Round (December 1955–May 1956)*, New Delhi, The Cabinet Secretariat.
1965 : *Instructions to Field Workers, Vol. I (Design, Concepts, Definitions and Procedures), Twentieth Round (July 1965–June 1966)*, Calcutta, Indian Statistical Institute.
1970 : *Tables with Notes on Couple Fertility (Report 154, Seventeenth Round)*, Nasik, Government of India Press.

OGBURN, W.F., NIMKOFF, M.F.
1953 : *A Handbook of Sociology*, London, Routledge & Kegan Paul.

OLDENBERG, H.
1897 : 'Zur Geschichte des indischen Kastenwesens', *Zeitschrift der Deutschen Morgen Ländischen Gesellschaft,* Vol. 51, pp. 267–90.

PARSONS, T.
1954 : *Essays in Sociological Theory*, Illinois, Free Press.

PARSONS, T., BALES, R.F.
1956 : *Family: Socialization and Interaction Process*, London, Routledge & Kegan Paul.

RADCLIFFE-BROWN, A.R.
1950 : 'Introduction', pp. 1–85 in Radcliffe-Brown, A.R., Forde, D. (eds.), *African System of Kinship and Marriage*, Oxford, Oxford University Press.
1959 : *Structure and Function in Primitive Society*, London, Cohen and West.

RAO, C.R.
1965 : *Linear Statistical Inference and Its Applications*, London, John Wiley.

RAO, J.N.K., HARTLEY, H.O., KIEFER, G.
1969 : *Variance Estimation with One Unit per Stratum*, Calcutta, Indian Statistical Institute, Technical Report No. Math/Stat/6/69.

RAY, N.
1949 : *Bangaleer Itihas* (in Bengali), Calcutta, Book Emporium.

SERVICE, E.R.
1960 : 'Kinship Terminology and Evolution', *American Anthropologist*, 62 (5), pp. 747–63.

SIEGEL, S.
1956 : *Non-parametric Statistics for the Behavioral Sciences.* New York-Toronto-London, McGraw-Hill.